Profiles in Small Business

Profiles in Small Business

A competitive strategy approach

Gavin C. Reid, Lowell R. Jacobsen
and Margo E. Anderson

London and New York

HD
2341
.R3537
1993

First published 1993
by Routledge
11 New Fetter Lane, London EC4P 4EE

Simultaneously published in the USA and Canada
by Routledge
29 West 35th Street, New York, NY 10001

© 1993 Gavin C. Reid, Lowell R. Jacobsen and Margo E. Anderson

Typeset in Plantin by Solidus (Bristol) Ltd
Printed and bound in Great Britain by
T.J. Press (Padstow) Ltd, Padstow, Cornwall

British Library Cataloguing in Publication Data
A catalogue record for this book is available from the British Library

Library of Congress Cataloging in Publication Data
Reid, Gavin C.
    Profiles in small business : a competitive strategy approach /
Gavin C. Reid, Lowell R. Jacobsen and Margo E. Anderson.
        p.   cm.
Includes bibliographical references and index.
ISBN 0-415-09828-9
    1. Small business.   I. Jacobsen, Lowell R.   II. Anderson, Margo
E., 1969-   . III. Title.
HD2341.R3537   1993   93-23855
658.02′2—dc20   CIP

ISBN 0-415-09828-9 (hbk)

To Charlotte and to Maureen

If Enterprise is afoot, wealth accumulates. . . .
If Enterprise is asleep, wealth decays

John Maynard Keynes,
A Treatise on Money (1930)

Contents

List of figures and tables

FIGURE

TABLES

Preface

Blackboard economics. The firm and the market appear by name but they lack any substance ... there is little doubt that a great deal more empirical work is needed

R.H. Coase, *American Economic Review* 82 (1992)

This book is intended to serve both as a stand-alone work, and as a complementary volume to *Small Business Enterprise: An Economic Analysis* by Gavin C. Reid (Routledge 1993). It should be made clear that it is an entirely self-contained work considered from the former standpoint, and that it is a far less technical work in orientation, considered from the latter standpoint. Even the briefest perusal will reveal this book for what it is: an applied work, replete with illustrations from small business enterprises (SBEs as we call them), expressed in largely non-technical terms, using the vehicle of competitive strategy analysis, suitably modified for the small firms' case. Above all, we hope to have avoided the 'blackboard' (or come to that, 'whiteboard') economics that are mentioned in Coase's strictures. Whilst our firms and markets lack names for reasons of confidentiality, it is our hope that they do not lack substance.

Though the book is free of mathematics, statistics and econometrics, we have tried to avoid putting in its place sloppy thinking. The data that lie behind our 'Profiles' were gathered by rigorous fieldwork methods using carefully devised instruments. Michael Porter's competitive strategy approach, which we have tailored to the small firms' case, while non-technical, is based on the rigorous research literature generated by industrial economists. The broad division of the book is into *evidence* (where the Profiles are laid out) and *analysis* (where the competitive strategy approach is deployed). Whilst our goal has been to avoid sloppy thinking, this does not mean making the study of small firms dull, so we have tried to enliven it by reference to small business reality, including the argot of the owner-manager. We hope the presentation adopted will inform, instruct and inspire: inform, by displaying the characteristics of small business enterprises in a revealing way; instruct, by showing how analytical devices from the competitive strategy approach can give coherence and form to this evidence; and inspire, by encouraging others – students, practitioners, academics and consultants alike – to construct and analyse their own profiles according to the methods we demonstrate.

We believe that profiles constructed in this way have a useful role to play as a kind of structured self-analysis of oneself as an owner-manager of a small business enterprise. Not only should our work help such a reader to understand how to undertake a competitive strategy analysis him or herself, it should also facilitate a prescriptive approach. That is to say, it should inspire (e.g. by imitation and modification of the strategies described) ideas as to how competitive strategy analysis can lead to implementable strategies in practical situations, which have the power to translate into competitive advantage in the marketplace.

Sponsors of the work that lies behind these Profiles include the Nuffield Foundation, the Scottish Economic Society and the Leverhulme Trust, whose support we warmly acknowledge. The volume took its present form during an intense period of work in the autumn of 1992, when all three of us were working daily within the newly founded Centre for Research into Industry, Enterprise Finance and the Firm (CRIEFF), Department of Economics, University of St Andrews. L.R. Jacobsen wishes to acknowledge, with thanks, the leave granted from William Jewell College which permitted him to engage in this collaboration. The useful assistance of Julia Smith (also of CRIEFF) in the final stages of preparation of the manuscript is gratefully acknowledged. The help of a vast number of individuals, too many to mention individually, in both the academic and business communities, in providing data and discussing ideas, is also acknowledged from the bottoms of our hearts. Needless to say, any errors of omission or commission that the work may yet contain are entirely the authors' collective responsibility. Finally, we express thanks to our families, for the loyalty and support that allowed us to carry this work through to completion.

Gavin C. Reid
Lowell R. Jacobsen
Margo E. Anderson

Part I
Introduction

1 The small business enterprise

1.1 INTRODUCTION

The structure of this book is twofold. On the one hand, it presents what we call 'Profiles' of a set of modern small business enterprises (SBEs). These provide detailed pictures of each SBE, constructed within an analytical framework that draws on both industrial economics and business strategy. On the other hand, it engages in comparative analysis of these SBEs. Thus it reaches conclusions about the effectiveness with which certain business strategies are translated into competitive advantage in the marketplace.

The book draws on the same body of evidence that has been treated with some statistical and econometric thoroughness in Reid's *Small Business Enterprise* (1993). Its style, approach and indeed content are, however, quite different from that companion volume. Here, our concern has been to ensure accessibility of treatment. Thus readers from diverse backgrounds in economics, accounting, finance and business should be able to follow the arguments of the following chapters.[1] The intention is still to present arguments with clarity and tolerable rigour, but without recourse to that arsenal of technical equipment which is increasingly making economic arguments impenetrable to the non-specialist. We believe that would be unfortunate, because small firms play an important role in the economy. Yet their behaviour, and (on an even more mundane level) their character, are poorly understood.

An important reason for being interested in small firms (i.e. SBEs) is that they are so numerous. Recent figures by Daly and McCann (1992) show that at the end of 1989 there were about 3 million small firms in the United Kingdom. It is estimated that over 95 per cent of all UK businesses employ fewer than twenty people. Despite their small size, their sheer volume is important for employment, a point first articulated clearly in a US context by Birch (1979, 1981). In the United Kingdom, small firms account for 35 per cent of total employment outside of local and central government. Between 1979 and 1989, the period of most relevance to the Profiles presented here, the number of businesses rose by two-thirds, the vast majority being small. To achieve this nationwide, about 500 additional firms were being created every day.[2] We hope that this book will help to advance the general understanding of how this process works, and may perhaps contribute to enhancing the quality and durability of this abundance of new small firms' activity.

The plan of the rest of this chapter is as follows. Firstly, we argue in favour of the profit maximization hypothesis, which will be presumed to be applicable to the SBE throughout this book. Secondly, we explain the field-work methods by which we were able to gather a large body of data from interviews with owner-managers of SBEs. Thirdly, we look at key features of the Profiles sample, in relation to the parent sample, and provide a characterization of the typical SBE. Fourthly, we look at models of markets, choosing three 'off the shelf' as being of particular utility to our analysis of the Profiles sample of SBEs. Fifthly, we expound the competitive-forces/competitive-advantage framework associated with the writings of Michael Porter (1980, 1985, 1990).These preliminaries accomplished, we turn to the main substance of the book. In Part II seventeen Profiles of SBEs are presented, classified according to the degree of market concentration in which they function. A consistent framework is used for each Profile, drawing on mainstream industrial economics, and also the business strategy approach, as modified to the small firms case. In Part III, a comparative analysis of the SBEs is undertaken within a framework of 'extended rivalry' that goes well beyond the conventional analysis of intra-industry rivalry. Competitive and defensive strategies are considered, and a novel extension is undertaken to financial considerations of competitive advantage. The book concludes by arguing that its subject matter presents a case for a more grounded approach to industrial analysis, which always keeps real business conduct in the foreground. But all this is to delay, by anticipation, the work to be done. We turn, therefore, to substantive analysis.

1.2 THE PROFIT-MAXIMIZING SBE

The way in which economists, both in business and management, look at firms, especially small firms, is in terms of a model. Standards vary as to what may be accorded this term. Some might find a model which views firms as bundles of contractual relations too woolly in conception. Others might find dangerously overprecise in conception those formulations of the firm which run in terms of a smooth, well-behaved profit function which is to be maximized. Our view is that the appropriateness of the model depends on the purpose at hand and the subject discipline of the analyst. It does not seem unreasonable to us, for example, to regard a set of accounts (financial, managerial, etc.) as constituting a model of the firm. It is a precise, consistent, revealing framework, with significant predictive content. It involves abstraction and simplification, which is also characteristic of a model. However, it is unlikely that economists would admit that a set of accounts is an appropriate model.

The criticism advanced by economists would perhaps be that the set of accounts lacks behavioural content or, what often amounts to the same thing, some optimization hypothesis. The central maximization hypothesis which economists choose when they model the firm is, of course, profit maximization, which carries with it the corollary hypothesis of cost minimization. The advantage of this central hypothesis is that it can be turned to many uses and, despite its simplicity, has implications with surprisingly powerful predictive content. We shall not engage in explicit model building, and narrow statistical testing of models so derived, in this book. That has been the concern of Reid (1993) in the companion volume. However, we shall use the categories of economic models, very often by appeal to classes of models – for example, oligopoly, as competition amongst few firms in significant interdependence, and monopolistic competition as free competition amongst many firms with brand monopolies. In both these cases, profit-maximizing conduct is assumed: the economist's central behavioural hypothesis is being asserted. In using these classes of models, appeal will be made to general properties that they may display, like excess capacity, a kinked demand curve, and so on. The implications of this approach for models of markets will be explored further in section 1.5 of this chapter, but our concern here is with models of the firm, rather than the market, and the appropriateness of the profit maximization hypothesis.

In the extensive fieldwork that the authors engaged in to gather the evidence for this book, it became apparent that of all the competing hypotheses to which one could appeal in modelling the individual SBE, the profit maximization one was the most robust. It has both descriptive and prescriptive content. The typical SBE usually looks as if its owner-manager is trying to maximize profit, and if he is not quite succeeding, it is his avowed aim to maximize profit. This, of course, does not mean that profitability is high. Indeed, it typically is not, as SBEs frequently function in highly competitive market environments. Precisely because of the sharpness of competition, and therefore the fierceness of the SBE's struggle for survival, profit maximization becomes more than an economist's hypothesis: it acquires both descriptive and prescriptive connotations. Managerial economists take profit maximization as a prescription (Reekie, Allen and Crook 1991), and certainly small business counsellors will motivate their clients in this way.

It is no criticism of the profit maximization hypothesis to say that problems arise in taking account of risk, variations in abilities of entrepreneurs, and features of the internal structure of the firm like monitoring and coordination mechanisms.[3] In an earlier volume by two of the authors, Reid and Jacobsen (1988, ch. 2), a fairly detailed account of the small business enterprise is presented, and it is shown how these complexities may be incorporated within the profit maximization hypothesis. For example, for the internally monitored firm, the marginal product is not set equal to price but to price plus the implicit cost of monitoring: a small adjustment to the standard theorem.

We say all this in praise of profit maximization by way of making our job of using models simpler and thus more accessible. But there is more to it than mere convenience, because the competitive strategy approach we introduce in section 1.6 and use extensively in Part III, has as an unwritten but important tenet, that firms maximize profits. Indeed, the rigorous industrial organization literature on which this analytical approach is erected, invariably is founded on the profit maximization hypothesis.

Finally, it should be said that the SBE is particularly suited, of all firm types, to the profit maximization hypothesis. It is notably free of the 'agency costs' which dog larger enterprises. There is no divorce of ownership from control, with managers or directors pursuing unprofitable personal goals at the stockholders' expense. The manager typically *is* the owner. For all the SBEs in our sample there is no external equity. The owner-manager is typically hiring in informationally efficient local labour markets where reputations are accurately established, so problems of adverse selection (e.g. a slow worker trying to mimic a fast worker at the hiring interview) are mitigated. Once personnel are in the firm, problems of moral hazard (e.g. of relaxing effort once one has got the job) are attenuated because monitoring of effort is almost continuous and virtually costless.[4] Within the SBE, because it is so small, problems associated with hierarchy, like information degradation between hierarchical levels, control loss, and incomplete compliance, do not arise.[5] Certainly there are specific problems of SBEs of which small firm counsellors are aware, exposure to risk being the most obvious, but few of them militate against the presumption of profit maximization. In conclusion, therefore, it will be taken as a working hypothesis throughout the rest of this book.

1.3 FIELDWORK

A distinctive feature of the analysis contained in the Profiles in this book is that all the data used were gathered by fieldwork methods.[6] We went out and talked to owner-managers, gathering data as we went. These are primary source data, and they were gathered with a specific analytical purpose in mind (e.g. investigating how competitive advantage is achieved). As a result, many of the questions one would wish to ask about small business enterprises (SBEs) can actually be answered directly, without having to use unsatisfactory proxy variables or similar devices for bridging the gulf of ignorance. This puts within our purview simple matters of fact like capacity utilization, expectational phenomena like forecasts of the trajectory for the debt–equity ratio over three years, and strategic considerations like the formulation and implementation of a policy of market pre-emption. A wide range of data types, both qualitative and quantitative, are provided by the fieldworker, and they have advantages over most alternative data sources so far as accuracy, completeness and relevance are concerned. They are, however, expensive types of data to gather, and in an era of tight budgetary constraints on research grants, severe financial limits are imposed on the extent to which fieldwork is pursued. One therefore gathers data in this way with great care, adhering to a rigorous methodology, and fully exploring the potential of the data from a research standpoint.

The starting-point for fieldwork is typically unstructured, simply because one usually starts from the standpoint of relative ignorance. In the case of the fieldwork on which this book is based the unstructured fieldwork was of two types: networking and participant observation. Networking involved using personal contacts, referrals, reference books, trade literature, and so on, to access 'the field'. The relevant field here is the collection of markets in which small business enterprises are active. We talked to academic special-ists on small businesses, on entrepreneurship, on business strategy, and so on; to directors of quangos of various sorts (enterprise trusts, development corporations, etc.) concerned with enterprise stimulation; to entrepreneurs and businessmen experienced in setting up and running businesses of various sizes and types; to accountants and financial specialists of various sorts who provide services to owner-managers of small firms; and to members of chambers of commerce and small business clubs. From these multifarious contacts, 'high communicators' were identified (i.e. those who had access to particularly rich information sources) who were pivotal points in an informal network of communication which enmeshes the small business world. The director of Scottish Business in the Community (SBC) provides one such example. By this stage we were already beginning to get a good feel for what the field looked like, and for general characteristics of 'sites' within the field, that is, SBEs.

Of equal status with networking as an aspect of our unstructured field-work, was participant observation. One of the authors became a participant observer in the first enterprise trust to be established in Scotland.[7] During a period of eight months he was regularly involved with the internal function-ing of this institution, and for a period of two months was fully involved on a daily basis. He became familiar with the project involvements of 157 clients, and had full knowledge of thirty-nine completed projects (a 'project' being a proposal taken to the enterprise trust for advice on a client basis). Completion meant that the project had resulted in a new small business being set up. New business starts were tracked with follow-up involvements by the enterprise trust. Client involvement typically required looking at the assistance required, the business plan, premises, marketing, funding and possibly employment created. This part of the unstructured fieldwork gave us considerable insight into SBEs and helped us to clarify the questions we wished to ask. It had an important bearing on the type of instrumentation chosen.[8]

Through these two forms of unstructured fieldwork (namely, networking and participant observation) we were able, firstly, to get access to sites (i.e. SBEs) in the field, for the purposes of gathering data by interviews, this being a benefit from networking, and secondly, to put in place ideas for interview procedures (i.e. 'instrumentation'), this being a benefit from participant observation. We ended up investigating seventy-three sites in the field in our main study, after a phase of pilot work. We used three different instruments: an administered questionnaire and a semi-structured interview in the first phase of fieldwork proper, and a reinterview questionnaire in the second phase three years later, using the same sites (if available). Thus the data offer variety both in a cross-site and in a longitudinal sense.

The technical details of the instruments are of little interest here, and the Appendix to this book provides a summary of the main points they covered. Briefly, the administered questionnaire covered employment, products, markets, pricing, costs and financial structure; the semi-structured interview, which was inspired by Michael Porter's writings,[9] covered competitive forces, competitive strategy and defensive strategy; and the reinterview questionnaire covered matters like survival rates, skills gaps, company structure, scale economies and the enterprise culture. Participant observation influenced the choice of designs of the first two instruments. They appealed to the mainstream literature of industrial economics in the first case (administered questionnaire) and to the business strategy literature in the second case (semi-structured interview). What we were aiming for was what is sometimes called a crossover analysis that brings closer together different methodologies (broadly, economics and management) with the intention of each enriching the other. Our feelings as authors who have worked with both methodologies is that the consequences in this case have been clearly synergistic: the value of the integrated approach exceeds the sum of the values of the unidisciplinary approaches. The design of the reinterview questionnaire itself drew on our (by then) extensive fieldwork experience, as well as models of small firm growth and survival.[10] A key insight which was used in the latter case was simply that non-negative profit (defined net of exit costs) was a prerequisite to small firm survival over a period as long as three years.[11]

These instruments were all used in personal face-to-face interviews with owner-managers, typically at their place of work. Data were hand recorded on schedules, and these were later entered into a computer database. A full audit has since then been carried out on the data, and we have considerable confidence in their reliability and accuracy.[12]

1.4 THE SAMPLE

The parent sample of this set of SBEs for which we have constructed and compared profiles consists of seventy-three small firms in Scotland from which data were gathered by fieldwork methods, as described above. Three different questionnaire, or interview, instruments were used, within a time-frame of three years in the 1980s, to gather sufficient data to construct and analyse profiles, as in the present volume, as well as to engage in more technical econometric and statistical analysis, as in the companion volume *Small Business Enterprise* by Reid (1993).

For this parent sample, average employment was nine (counting part-timers as a half),[13] average market share was 8 per cent in the principal market, average age was 41 months, average sales (excluding VAT) were £85,000 (at 1985 prices), and average assets were £76,000 (at 1985 prices). The average number of product groups (e.g. hats, gloves, making two) was six and of products (e.g. bowlers, boaters; mittens, golf gloves, making four) was fifty. For this sample, the modal description of the degree of product differentiation was 'similar' to rivals (32 per cent), with 'different' coming close (23 per cent), few (11 per cent) saying 'the same' and a significant minority (34 per cent) not knowing, or not being able to judge. Put another way, 55 per cent of owner-managers laid a categorical claim to product differentiation for their main product-line.

Regarding form of organization of the SBE, 50 per cent were private companies, 20 per cent were partnerships and 30 per cent were sole pro-prietorships. There was generally a close and positive association between employment (and sales) and 'form of firm'.[14] For example, one-man businesses employ three persons on average, but partnerships five and private companies thirteen (again, on average). Similarly, average sales for a sole proprietorship were £20,000, for a partnership £100,000, and for a private company £225,000 (all at 1985 prices).

Any sub-sample should inherit similar characteristics to the parent sample, but clearly sampling variation can be considerable, particularly where small numbers are involved. Table 1.1 displays some of the most important variables for the sample of seventeen Profiles. Mean values are given at the foot of the table. There are notable similarities in terms of employment, degree of product differentiation and market share. However, the Profiles firms are younger (two years compared to three-and-a-half) and have a much higher average sales–asset ratio (3.1 compared to 1.1). Argu-ably there is a tendency for young, immature SBEs to 'over-trade', and this looks possible for the Profiles sample. Sectoral composition is similar between the two samples, with the services–manufacturing proportions being 34 per cent/66 per cent for the Profiles sample and 37 per cent/63 per cent for the parent sample. The distribution of the Profiles sample of SBEs across industrial sectors is given in Table 1.2.

Deliberately excluded from the parent sample were agriculture, fishing, energy and the extractive industries. This takes out of consideration many sectors with the lowest standard industrial classification (SIC) numbers. The mix of manufacturing versus service-sector SBEs, with the former pre-dominant, reflects the caseloads of enterprise trusts and development corporations, suggesting service-sector entrepreneurship is more likely to occur without formal recourse to institutional advice.

It is useful, before proceeding to the more detailed analysis in Parts II and III of the book, to consider the general characteristics of SBEs in the Profiles sample, over a wide range of attributes. Table 1.3 examines variables from all the major categories of the administered questionnaire

Table 1.1 Age, size, market share and products for seventeen Profiles

SBE	Age (months)	SIC code	Market share (%)	Main product	Degree of product differentiation	Employ-ment	Sales[+] (£000s)	Assets[+] (£000s)
A	16	96	<1	Blind cleaning	3	2	18	16
B	32	49	15	Security printers blankets	2	11	600	105
C	17	43	<1	Knitwear manufacturer	3	5	22	7
D	6	35	<1	Auto repairs	2	2	n.a.	9
E	9	61	<1	Industrial cleaning	2	6	150	30
F	40	41	2	Food manufacturers	2	47	650	130
G	15	97	2	Holiday tours	2	0	7	15
H	5	64	>50	Cosmetics retailing	3	8	245	65
I	17	34	<1	Computer software	2/3	15	250	100
J	125	34	<1	Cassette tapes	1	4	200	100
K	12	34	<1	Electronic instruments	2	5	25	20
L	13	61	40	Wine distribution	2	1	72	27
M	9	97	n.a.	Aerobatic aircraft	3	1	0	35
N	15	43	2	Bulk bag manufacturers	2	27	200	50
O	22	46	2	Fencing manufacturing	2	3	96	50
P	29	47	15	Printing lamination	1	5	240	180
Q	7	49	25	Theatrical props	1	4	35	7

Notes:

Mean values: Age, 23 months; Market share, 9%; Employment, 9; Sales, £176,000; Assets, £56,000.

Degree of product differentiation: 1 = identical; 2 = similar; 3 = different; 0 = don't know. (Mode = 2.)

*Only full-time employees counted. Details are given in the Profiles.

[+]Sales and assets are at 1985 prices; where a range was given, the mid-point is reported; n.a., not available.

Table 1.2 Distribution of Profiles sample by industry

SIC no.	Classification	Profiles sample
Manufacturing		
34	Electrical and electronic engineering	3
35	Manufacture of motor vehicles and parts	1
41/2	Food, drink and tobacco manufacturing	1
43	Textile industry	2
46	Timber and wooden furniture industries	1
47	Manufacture of paper and paper products: printing and publishing	1
49	Other manufacturing industries	2
Services		
61	Wholesale distribution	2
64	Retail distribution	1
96	Other services provided to the general public	1
97	Recreational services and other cultural services	2

(which we have summarized in the Appendix). That is to say, it covers general characteristics, employment, products, pricing, costs, sales, competition and finance. We can use the data in this table to draw a general picture of the SBE. This will be a kind of composite of the various SBEs that make up the sample. Details of the individual Profiles will come later, in Part II: what we seek for the moment is a kind of statistical overview.

The typical SBE has a narrow product range (2–5) and operates in a regional market. It has a few major competitors (about three) and substantially more minor competitors (about twenty). It produces a mildly differentiated product, and has to keep an eye on rivals' price when it is making its own pricing decision. When the chips are down it is prepared to hold down its price to beat rival competitors for orders. It suffers a moderate degree of excess capacity (about one-third) and enjoys falling unit variable costs in the short run.

As befits a firm producing a differentiated product, the SBE engages in independent (as opposed to generic) advertising of its wares. It is thereby assisted in establishing a small market share in its principal market, of about 10 per cent by sales. It finds that competition is generally strong (e.g. by customer service) but may be weak in some respects (e.g. by price).

Typically the SBE starts up by using only personal finance. It encounters cash-flow difficulties and has to take on new debt after inception. It desires as low a gearing (i.e. debt–equity) ratio as possible: preferably zero. From a quantitative standpoint, it employs nine workers, has an age of two years, assets of £56,000 and enjoys an annual sales turnover of £176,000 (both at 1985 prices). Like any average or model view, the one presented in the paragraphs above ignores the richness of variation of individual cases;

Table 1.3 Main characteristics of firms A to Q

Firm	A	B	C	D	E	F	G
Attribute							
Employment	2	11	5	2	6	47	0
Sales	£18k	£600k	£22k	N.A.	£150k	£650k	£7k
Product group	3	3	3	3	3	3	3
Main market	reg.	int.	int.	reg.	reg.	reg.	Scot.
Market share	<1%	15%	<1%	<1%	<1%	2%	2%
Major competitors	3	3	20	3	20	8	3
Minor competitors	3	0	>50	>50	>50	>50	20
Product differentiation	diff.	sim.	diff.	sim.	sim.	sim.	sim.
Rivals' pricing	No	Yes	Yes	Yes	Yes	No	No
Beating rivals	Yes	Yes	Yes	Yes	Yes	Yes	No
Capacity utilization	<50%	65%	55%	∞	∞	∞	∞
Cost structure	b	b	b	a	b	b	b
Advertising form	Indep.	Indep.	None	Indep.	Indep.	None	Indep.
Competition	S/W	S/W	S/W	S/W	S/W	S/W	S/W
Personal finance	Yes	Yes	Yes	Yes	Yes	No	No
Cash-flow problems	Yes	Yes	Yes	No	Yes	Yes	Yes
Assets	£16k	£105k	£7k	£9k	£30k	£130k	£15k
Gearing	0	0.5	3.5	0	1	4	3
New debt	Yes	No	Yes	No	Yes	Yes	Yes
Age (yrs)	1	3	1	1	1	3	1

Firms:

A Blind cleaning	G Holiday tours	M Aerobatic aircraft
B Security printers blankets	H Cosmetics retailing	N Bulk bag manufacturer
C Knitwear manufacturer	I Computer software	O Fencing manufacturer
D Auto repairs	J Cassette tapes	P Printing lamination
E Industrial cleaning	K Electronic instruments	Q Theatrical props
F Food manufacturer	L Wine distribution	

H	I	J	K	L	M	N	O	P	Q
8	15	4	5	1	1	27	3	5	4
£245k	£250k	£200k	£25k	£72k	£0k	£200k	£96k	£240k	£35k
>50	3	1	3	3	1	1	1	3	8
reg.	int.	UK	Scot.	reg.	int.	UK	Scot.	Scot.	Scot.
>50%	<1%	<1%	<1%	40%	N.A.	2%	2%	15%	25%
0	20	3	8	8	N.A.	3	3	3	15
8	>50	0	20	8	3	3	8	3	3
diff.	sim./ diff.	ident.	sim.	sim.	diff.	sim.	sim.	ident.	ident.
No	Yes	Yes	Yes	Yes	No	Yes	Yes	No	No
No	No	Yes	Yes	No	Yes	Yes	No	Yes	No
∞	∞	95%	75%	<50%	<50%	<50%	85%	65%	55%
d	d	b	b	d	b	b	b	a	e
G/I	Indep.	Indep.	Indep.	Indep.	Indep.	Indep.	Indep.	G/I	G/I
W	S/W	S	S/W	S	W/S	S	S/W	S/W	W/S
Yes	Yes	Yes	Yes	Yes	No	No	No	Yes	Yes
No	Yes	Yes	No	No	Yes	No	Yes	Yes	Yes
£65k	£100k	£100k	£20k	£27k	£35k	£50k	£50k	£180k	£7k
0	0	0	0	0	2.5	0	10	0	2.5
No	No	No	Yes	Yes	No	Yes	Yes	Yes	Yes
1	1	10	1	1	1	1	2	2	1

Notes:

Employment: number of full-time employees.

Rivals' pricing: are your rivals' pricing decisions crucial to your own?

Beating rivals: do you hold down price to beat competitors?

Personal finance: was your business started using only personal finance?

Competition: S = strong, W = weak.

Advertising: Indep. = independent, G/I = generic and independent.

Cost structure: a = ╱ , b = ╱ , d = ⌐╯, e = ╲ .

Main market: reg. = regional, int. = international, Scot. = Scotland.

Product differentiation: diff. = different, sim. = similar, ident. = identical.

Gearing: at financial inception.

but we shall come to that shortly. In the meantime, our general picture is complete, and constitutes a handy reference point.

1.5 MARKET MODELS

It will be a familiar fact to most readers that market structures may be discussed in terms of models. These are not descriptions of markets but, rather, stylizations. Certainly they can be related to real market types, but the correspondence is rarely exact. Nevertheless, they provide a good organizing principle for examining markets, and as well as improving our powers to explain and understand market behaviour, they can also, under certain well-defined conditions, provide us with predictions about market outcomes (in terms, for example, of market shares or price-cost margins). Usually there is no unique way of applying a model to a market circumstance. Different models may be applied to the same markets with different ends in mind. What we wish to offer here is not a unique characterization of appropriate market models, but one which we have personally found useful, after much experimentation with alternatives.

The crucial organizing principle we will use is the degree of market concentration. It has the great advantages of transparency and ease of measurement. In its most simple form, market concentration is measured by the proportion of output (employment, sales, etc., will also do) accounted for by a certain number (e.g. two, three or four) of the largest firms operating in a market or industry. Suppose, for example, we had data on the proportions of total market sales accounted for by the three largest firms active in the market, and these were 20 per cent, 10 per cent and 5 per cent respectively. Then the three-firm concentration ratio would be 35 per cent, and we would clearly have a medium-concentration market, in that a moderate part of the activity therein was accounted for by the three largest firms.[15] Of course, there could be many more firms (say, thirty) active in the market accounting, in sum, for the remaining 65 per cent of market sales, but these firms are clearly small by the criterion of the market in which they operate, with on average a market share of 2 per cent. We might well find one of our SBEs being a minor player in this 65 per cent of the market, and indeed we will on occasion explicitly model this situation. In this case, SBEs located in this market segment are said to be 'in the fringe' or 'fringe competitors'. The other firms, the three largest are 'dominant firms' and might be regarded as 'calling the shots' for the market as a whole (e.g. they might act together as price leaders, expecting, or indeed requiring under threat of reprisal, the fringe firms to act as price followers). In the above we have a situation of medium market concentration, to which we have applied the model of a dominant firm (or group of firms) with a competitive fringe.[16] Especially in Chapters 5 and 6, we have found this market model to be a useful organizing principle in real market situations.

Two other market structures we have found to be valuable are monopolistic competition and conjectural oligopoly. The former finds its main application in market situations in which firms are small in relation to the market as a whole, goods are branded, or distinguished (i.e. differentiated) in some other way (e.g. by location), and firms find it relatively easy to set up afresh, or indeed to quit, in the market.[17] Suppose, for example, there were thirty or more firms active in a market, all with similar market shares (around, say, 3 per cent), and all having a coterie of loyal customers who would tolerate some measure of price-setting power by their favoured suppliers. Then this market might be modelled as monopolistically competitive, and one might expect predictions of the model (e.g. the existence of excess capacity, and of low profitability, in the typical firm) to be confirmed by actual small firms' market experience.

Thirdly, we come to conjectural oligopoly,[18] in which a few firms have significant and exhaustive shares of the market, all are significantly interdependent, and barriers to entry keep rivals out, and profitability high. Suppose, for example, there were just three players in the market, with market shares of 45 per cent, 30 per cent and 25 per cent, respectively. Interdependence might be a feature of their pricing decisions (e.g. Firm X will only cut price if Firm Z cuts price first) and a relatively high level of profitability might be sustained by barriers erected against new entrants like patent protection, scale economies and strong advertising-induced customer loyalty.

Some very practically minded industrial economists have argued that when we depart from the abstract realms of pure theory (where many exotic models of markets flourish) there are only two useful models: perfect competition and monopoly. The first is relevant to the case of homogeneous goods, many very small competitors, no profits, no frictions impeding setting-up in (or quitting) the market, and no excess capacity. Whilst this model is useful for making simple predictions at the aggregate market level (e.g. if demand rises, in the short run price will rise, profits will be made and new entrants will be attracted into the market), it strains credulity too much to apply it to any of the firms we have analysed which operate in low-concentration markets. Branding, some price-setting capability, excess capacity and a low (but strictly positive) profitability are so much the stuff of these SBEs that they cannot be ignored. One accepts the requirement of descriptive concordance with reality, along with the corresponding implication that the theory does not have such very sharp teeth (but enough to predict, for example, that if any one of quantity, quality or advertising becomes more expensive, less of it will be forthcoming). Further, modern variants of the older Chamberlin–Robinson constructions of monopolistic competition (e.g. 'address models' capturing the notion of spatially localized competition where space can be thought of in terms of characteristics rather than geographical coordinates) offer greater scope for this market model, compared to perfect competition.[19]

At the other extreme from perfectly competitive analysis is monopoly analysis, a market form which is also commended for wider application by those robust-minded industrial economists who require only two market models. Of course, the monopolist is an exclusive producer in a market and enjoys effectively infinite barriers to entry, very often founded on physical (e.g. natural resource) or legal (e.g. patent or franchise) circumstances. This right to exclusive production allows the monopolist to pursue gain without the restraint of competition. Because this leads to price elevation and output restriction, compared to the competitive alternative, such enterprises often attract the eye of the regulatory authority and may be subject to restraint in terms of pricing policy (e.g. marginal or average cost pricing), rate of return, or profitability (e.g. break-even or profit-ceiling requirements). None of our small business enterprises enjoyed exclusive production, and none was the subject of direct regulatory constraint. Such monopoly power as was enjoyed was typically limited by some form of competition. Whilst most firms followed the maxim 'if you can't be big, absolutely, at least aim to be big in your market segment, relatively' few even approached exclusive production, even with patent protection. The most helpful way of using monopoly analysis for our sample is to think in terms of brand monopoly, which again takes us back to monopolistic competition.

To summarize, many market models have potential use in our empirical analysis, and there is no unique way of modelling particular market outcomes. We have considered, but generally rejected, straightforward models of perfect competition and pure monopoly for all the market situations in which our SBEs found themselves. As alternatives, we have used what are best described as three *classes* of models, for each type really relates to a family of models, in terms of discussion in the modern literature of industrial organization. These classes of model are: *monopolistic competition*, which we have applied to low-concentration markets; *dominant firm with a competitive fringe*, which we have applied to medium-concentration markets, finding our SBEs generally located in the fringe; and *conjectural oligopoly*, which we have applied to high-concentration markets, in which firms are small in absolute size, but nevertheless are in significant strategic interaction, given their relatively large size in relation to a given market segment.

1.6 THE COMPETITIVE FORCES FRAMEWORK

Porter's five forces of competition consist of existing rivals, potential entrants, substitute products, suppliers, and buyers (i.e. customers).[20] These forces are displayed in the Figure 1.1 (Porter 1980: 4).[21] Potential entrants, substitute products, suppliers and buyers all created a kind of 'extended rivalry' which goes beyond the more obvious immediate rivalry of intra-industry competition. We shall occasionally use the shorthand of 'extended rivals'.

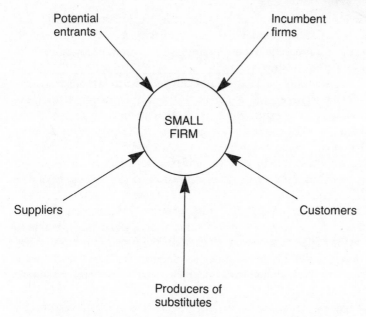

Figure 1.1 The five forces of competition on the small firm

Existing rivals

A priori existing rivals (i.e. other incumbent firms) are the most obvious and compelling competitive force that the owner-manager of the SBE might consider. The intensity of such competition is largely based on the extent of mutual dependence amongst firms in the industry. This is reflected in the positioning and repositioning of firms within the industry. Such tactics as the introduction of new products, price adjustment and marketing ploys are commonly used by SBEs to cope with the pressure of competition. They serve to reconfigure the competitive alignment of firms. Of course, the number of rivals and the extent of their differences, particularly in terms of size and capabilities, largely accounts for the type and intensity of competition. If an industry, for example, is dominated by one or a few firms, this dominant group or cartel can dictate, and even in a sense *define*, the nature of rivalrous behaviour (e.g. price leadership). Competition might even be orchestrated or manipulated by the dominant group of firms with industry stability being their primary objective rather than profitability, innovativeness or efficiency. Rivals, particularly of the nascent and small variety, who challenge such a status quo, risk retaliation which may be crippling in the short run and indeed may drive them out of the market altogether in the long run.

In addition to differences in size and capabilities, existing rivals may vary in terms of product lines, strategies, goals, personalities, and so on. The greater the diversity of firms in an industry, the greater the difficulty that rivals have in ascertaining the nature of competition. As a result, competitive behaviour is less predictable, and therefore its consequences potentially more disruptive if poorly anticipated.

The extent of growth in market demand can very much influence rivalry. Within an industry experiencing a general expansion in demand, the harmonious mutual growth of rival firms is possible without outbreaks of fierce inter-firm competition. By contrast, a stagnant or declining market demand will naturally intensify competition amongst existing rivals, because the only way in which a firm's growth can be achieved is through an increased market share, which in these circumstances must be at the expense of one or more rivals.

Another consideration which will be important to existing rivals is the magnitude of their fixed costs relative to value added. If a firm is unable to create much value added from inputs purchased, the pressure to fully utilize capacity is intensified. Large volume production in turn leads to a downward pressure on product prices which, *ceteris paribus*, heightens rivalry.

A related capacity consideration is that type of intermittent overcapacity which is attributable to seasonal factors and the 'lumpy' nature of added fixed inputs. Firms caught with excess capacity in this way are likely to resort to expanding output and cutting price, thereby possibly antagonizing rivals and engendering a rivalrous or retaliatory response, rather than a cooperative response.

Exit barriers can also influence the degree of rivalry. Firm-specific assets, an emotional attachment on the part of the owner-manager(s), and government restrictions are examples of forces which tend to keep firms actively competing in the industry, although strict profitability criteria might suggest they should abandon the industry. The greater the severity of exit barriers, the greater the tendency of such rivals to resort to interference tactics to maintain their industry presence. Such tactics are deployed directly at the expense of their rivals.

Potential entrants

The prospects of new rivals within an industry are directly related to, and determined by, barriers to entry and the reaction of existing rivals as anticipated by the potential entrants. The principal barriers to entry are often cited as being: scale economies, product differentiation, capital requirements and government policy. Porter's treatment also features switching costs, access to distribution channels, and cost disadvantages independent of scale.

Switching costs are one-time costs incurred by customers in switching their purchasing from one firm to a rival firm. Such costs can include the psychic cost of breaking a personal trading relationship. In general, the higher the switching costs in an industry, the more difficult it is for the merely potential entrant to become an actual extant rival.

Access to distribution channels is often a significant entry barrier in that existing rivals typically have secure, if not exclusive, relationships with the channels. Consequently, potential entrants must either convince existing channels to distribute their product(s) along with those of their rivals or else develop an entirely new channel. The more costly is either of the two approaches, the more intransigent is the barrier to entry.

Cost disadvantages independent of scale refer to absolute cost disadvantages that potential entrants may be subject to, which are firm-specific and not related to either size or scale. Examples of independent cost advantages possessed by incumbent firms include proprietary knowledge (including technology and experience), favourable geographic location, government assistance and an advantageous access to inputs (e.g. raw materials). Such absolute cost advantages enjoyed by incumbent firms must be confronted by any prospective industry entrant.

Substitutes

Within this extended-rivalry framework, substitutes are products from other industries which may serve the same need or function as that of the industry's product. Essentially, the greater the relative value/price of the substitute(s), the less profitable is the industry under consideration. In the face of such a threat to profitability, the key to a successful strategy is to identify possible substitutes before they come on stream commercially and have a direct impact on the industry. Substitutes which have their origins in highly profitable industries are particularly threatening to incumbent firms in the industry because their very profitability suggests that the resources exist to make an impact rapidly. To create the appropriate defence against this is rarely an easy undertaking, especially when one considers that a concerted action on the part of *all* firms in an industry is usually required in order to mount an effective response to incursions from well-financed substitutes. Moreover, it is quite difficult to gauge how quickly and significantly buyers will switch to substitutes, which makes it hard for incumbent firms to judge the timing, variety and magnitude of an appropriate defensive strategy.

Buyers

Another facet of rivalry within this extended framework arises from the actions of buyers or customers. A group of buyers exerts competitive pressure on a small firm by bargaining over dimensions like price, quality and service, as well as by playing off this firm against competitors. There are factors to be considered in gauging the extent of this leverage by buyers. For example, if there were a relatively large numbers of similar small firms in an industry (i.e. low supplier concentration) on the supply side, but a few large buyers and more small buyers (i.e. high buyer concentration) on the demand side, the buyers would be in a favourable bargaining position *vis-à-vis* the sellers. Also, if the products the buyers purchased entailed costs which were a relatively small proportion of their overall costs, buyers would be relatively less price sensitive and generally a less keen influence as a competitive force. Further, if the products were fairly homogeneous, even to the extent of approximating to a standard commodity (e.g. coal), buyers would be very likely to command more power than in the case of a heterogeneous good, especially as far as price were concerned. As a result, small firms are highly motivated to seek rapidly to differentiate their product from rivals, even if only by simple measures like the enhancement of after-sales service. These examples, though not exhaustive, serve to illustrate how buyers can act as a meaningful competitive force, thus extending further the notion of rivalry.

Suppliers

The third and final competitive force to be reviewed in this framework of extended rivalry is that of suppliers. Suppliers exert pressure on firms through manipulating price, quality, delivery and follow-up service of purchased inputs. Delaying delivery, for example, can impede production which in turn can jeopardize a firm's entire operations. Conditions which determine the strength of suppliers as a competitive force mirror those of buyers. The greater is the concentration of suppliers of factors of production compared to the concentration of firms within the industry the greater is the leverage that suppliers can impose. This particularly holds true when an industry is highly fragmented and contains many atomistic-sized firms. Another consideration is that whilst buyers can threaten backward integration, so too can suppliers threaten forward integration. Such a threat becomes credible when suppliers have the capacity to surmount entry barriers and have recognized attractive profitable opportunities in the industry. Furthermore, the importance of an input to the industry helps to delineate the influence of the supplier of that input. If the input, for example, represents a small cost in relation to the individual firm's overall costs, the firm may well be less sensitive to the supplier's price. Indeed, there are many other conditions which account for the extent to which it is possible for suppliers to wield competitive influence.

1.7 THE COMPETITIVE ADVANTAGE FRAMEWORK

Competitive advantage, or above-average performance, is basically achieved by successfully addressing the five competitive forces. Porter contends that firms essentially look to hold competitive advantage in terms simply of either low cost or differentiation, despite their rich mixture of relative strengths and weaknesses. These types of competitive advantage, matched with a firm's capabilities or activities in seeking above-average performance, bring about three generic competitive strategies. These strategies are overall cost leadership, differentiation and focus.

Overall cost leadership requires a firm to develop vigorously an optimally efficient scale of operations and to control tightly the firm's costs in all activities. Sources of cost advantage include scale economies, experience, limited overhead, and so on. Being the low-cost leader effects above-average returns even with the existence of pronounced competitive forces. If a firm is truly the low-cost producer, it will *ipso facto* still enjoy profitability even when rivals no longer do so in the aftermath of price-cutting wars. Given that the impact of substitutes is evaluated according to their relative value added/price, existing rivals will be adversely affected before the low-cost leader. Thus, buyers are limited to exerting their bargaining leverage over the second most productive rival. Finally, the low-cost leader will obviously be the most flexible in dealing with effects like suppliers increasing input prices. Furthermore, a low-cost leader's product is quite standardized, if not commodity-like, and therefore amenable to mass production techniques. Of course, such leadership often carries with it the ability to command a substantial market share.

Firms which follow the generic differentiation strategy seek to exploit firm-specific assets by producing goods or services which are almost unique compared to those offered by rivals. Of course, differentiation is not limited in its dimension to the physical nature of the product. Other significant dimensions of differentiation include distribution channels, marketing efforts, after sales service, and so on. Essentially, a firm looks to establish itself as unique within its industry. Firms that achieve and sustain effective differentiation of their products enjoy competitive advantage to an extent which is measured by the gap between the premium price charged and the additional costs incurred to effect the differentiation. Sustaining competitive advantage does require such firms to keep a vigilant watch over those costs which do not contribute to differentiation. Otherwise, its competitive advantage will be eroded, if not eliminated, by a subordinate cost position. Effective differentiation is generally resistant to the forces of competition. Potential and existing rivals must overcome the uniqueness of the product and try to erode customer loyalty. Customers are less likely to switch because of a perceived lack of similar alternatives. The bargaining leverage of suppliers on the factor market side is mitigated by the premium prices associated with differentiation on the product market side. The firm commanding greater customer loyalty is more impervious to the threat of substitutes than other firms within the industry. Advanced or extreme product differentiation often translated into exclusivity in terms of potential customers. It is therefore typically not associated with market share. Naturally, firms looking to position themselves uniquely within the market must expect a particularly small share of it.

A focus strategy requires a firm to concentrate on a particular market segment – which may be dictated by, for example, the buyer, the product, or the location – rather than the overall market. The strategy is predicated on the notion that a firm that devotes its entire energies to a niche or target can better achieve competitive advantage than those rivals which broadly compete across the market. Serving a limited target may entail strategies of differentiation, low cost or both. However, if the way in which a chosen market niche is being provided for loses its distinctiveness *vis-à-vis* other segments, then broadly competitive firms may seize the opportunity to dominate it. Low-volume production and small market shares are observed by firms adopting a focus strategy, precisely because the market segment to target is so precisely delineated.

Firms which effectively fail to make strategic choices which have a significant leverage on competitive advantage may experience the phenomenon which Porter calls 'stuck in the middle'. Typically, these firms have not properly assessed their industries' competitive forces and thereby misdiagnose their relative strengths and weaknesses. Moreover, they are likely to underperform in comparison to their rivals and will only be profitable if their market is growing. Firms which are prone to being 'stuck in the middle' may also succumb to weak competition and erroneously attempt to be 'all things to all people' (i.e. to satisfy the entire market). Firms which have hitherto satisfied a particular target, may become restless with inaction and become tempted to apply their focus strategy on other market targets. If the temptation proves irresistible, the strategy may be compromised, resulting again in a 'stuck in the middle' dilemma.

The 'value chain' is the intra-firm tool used by Porter to analyse systematically the sources of competitive advantage by disaggregating a firm's activities. In particular, isolating its activities permits a better understanding of both a firm's cost behaviour and its potential sources of differentiation. Creating value for customers is the essence of achieving competitive advantage. Value may be in the form of prices set lower than those of a firm's competitors for the same benefits, or of differentiated products that create benefits that more than offset the premium prices at which they sell. Differences in competitors' value chains are the sources of competitive advantage.

Value activities are divided into two general categories, primary and secondary activities. Primary activities are grouped into five specific categories: (1) inbound logistics, (2) operations, (3) outbound logistics, (4) marketing and sales, and (5) service. Inbound logistics are those activities concerned with receiving, storing and disseminating inputs of the product. Operations are responsible for converting inputs into finished products. Outbound logistics are those activities associated with collecting, storing and distributing the product to customers. Marketing and sales concern those activities connected with providing the means by which customers buy the product and are persuaded to do so. Finally, service involves those activities that enhance or maintain the value of the product.

Secondary, or support activities, support the primary activities and each other. These activities include procurement, technology development, human-resource management and the development of the firm's infrastructure. 'Procurement' refers to the purchase of inputs not directly associated with the product. They may be purchased anywhere in a firm's value chain. Technology development activities are concerned generally with the improvement of the product. Human-resource management involves the hiring, training and motivation of personnel. Finally, 'firm infrastructure' refers to those activities (such as the accounting and legal activities) that might be considered as overheads.

Some or all of the primary and support activities may apply to a particular firm, depending on the complexity of the firm and its industry. Nevertheless, all of a firm's activities are assigned a place within the value chain with regard to their economic impact on cost, and potential benefit to differentiation. In other words, the categorizing of activities is in accordance with their contribution to a firm's competitive advantage. This systematic and integrative approach to value-chain analysis allows all possible sources of competitive advantage to be revealed.

In determining the cost behaviour of activities, Porter employs the concept of 'cost-drivers'. To fully appreciate the relative cost position of a firm, costs must be identified according to their particular assigned activities within the firm's value chain. This approach is contrary to the traditional accounting systems, which tend to categorize costs according to type (e.g. labour) without regard to the activity affected. Consequently, significant strategic insight is not forthcoming. Examples of the ten cost-drivers Porter cites include scale economies, learning and location.

Relevant and important developments of the Porter framework include scenarios and defensive strategy. Industry scenarios are a relevant part of defensive strategy for those SBEs subject to great uncertainty and/or highly dynamic industry structures. As Porter correctly observes, strategies are often constructed on the belief that the future will very much reflect the past (i.e. they display adaptive expectations). Managers' forecasts of the future may be fraught with personal biases. As a corrective, Porter argues the case for constructing various scenarios aimed at capturing the form of possible future industry structures. Each scenario will be composed of certain, unalterable structural variables and will differ according to the way in which values are assigned to particular uncertain structural variables. The effect is to embrace uncertainty and to garner a more enlightened view of possible competitor behaviour. In so doing, the development of effective competitive strategy becomes more viable.

1.8 CONCLUSION

The groundwork for the two broad categories of analysis has now been accomplished. We have to hand the profit maximization hypothesis, three classes of market models, an extended-rivalry analysis and an account of how competitive strategy can lead to competitive advantage. Fieldwork has meanwhile supplied the evidence, so data and analysis must now be brought together.

Part II
Case profiles

2 Low market concentration

2.1 INTRODUCTION

Here we present for the reader the first set of Profiles. They relate to SBEs which operate in low market concentration environments. The SBEs chosen are indicated in Table 2.1.

These SBEs are all subject to mild product differentiation and capacity-utilization levels of around 50 per cent. In some cases – for example, Firm E (industrial cleaning) and Firm G (holiday tours) – it was reported that there was no limit to capacity and that therefore capacity utilization could not be computed. It would probably be more accurate to say that such SBEs tended to work close to current capacity and had not experienced difficulty in extending capacity in the past. In these cases a full order book was thought to denote an absence of capacity limitation, which is clearly an inaccurate interpretation. More to the point would be whether the SBE was still experiencing falling unit costs at its chosen output level, which was typically the case. Indeed, it was the case for Firms E and G. Market shares were typically small (< 1 per cent) and there were low entry and exit barriers. Firm L (wine retail distribution) and Firm G (theatrical props manu-facturer) reported market shares of around one-third, which is probably exaggerated for any sensible definition of the market for their main product-lines.

We have chosen to view these SBEs as essentially monopolistically competitive in a market models sense.[1] This is an important decision from the viewpoint of the comparative analysis of Part III. Obviously the features of these SBEs mentioned above, and perhaps even more those given in Table 1.3 above, support this decision. But to clinch the argument one has

Table 2.1 SBEs profiled in low-concentration markets

A	Blind cleaning	G	Holiday tours
C	Knitwear manufacturer	L	Wine retail distribution
D	Automotive repairs	Q	Theatrical props manufacturer
E	Industrial cleaning		

to look at the detailed within-site analysis of these SBEs, as contained in the seven Profiles that follow.[2] In reading these Profiles, readers should be sensitive to the fact that they may be interpreted as providing the basis for grounding new theories of the small firm in business reality. Monopolistic competition is not a unique model, but a class of models, and much new work remains to be done in advancing the theory of this particular class of model.

The framework used for constructing these Profiles is consistent and uses the instrumentation given in the Appendix. Broadly speaking, it draws on the literature of industrial economics, business strategy and business growth. A possible reader's approach to this material would be to select those Profiles that relate to personal experience or interest, to get a sense of what SBEs within a certain category of market concentration look like, and then to move on rapidly to the analysis contained in Chapters 5, 6 and 7, working back as required to the Profiles for further illustration and illumination of the analytics.

2.2 PROFILE A: WINDOW-BLIND CLEANING AND REPAIRING

Firm A's main product was the service of cleaning and repairing window-blinds (e.g. venetian blinds). It had been operating for one year at the time of the administered questionnaire of 1985 and there were two full-time workers. The business was a sole proprietorship and had an annual sales turnover (excluding VAT) of £18,000 (approx.) at 1985 prices. It had a narrow product group range (≤ 5) and few products in total (≤ 10). The principal market for its product was regarded as the region, and its market share within this was very small (< 1 per cent). The owner-manager could distinguish between major and minor competitors, and estimated there were no more than five of each. The industry structure was fairly stable. Backward integration (firms doing their own blind cleaning) and forward integration (suppliers of blinds becoming cleaners and servicers of blinds) were uncommon, but had been contemplated, particularly in the former case. This firm had only one supplier of venetian blinds and one supplier of cleaning solvents, but the owner-manager felt no bargaining leverage being exerted on him because suppliers were numerous and switching costs were low.

It was thought that customers were not highly informed, but needed information about technical features of the product. They would be guided by such advice. In general, customers would not be able to distinguish between this firm's products and those of rivals on technical grounds alone. Their attitudes would be influenced by price, brand, design, advertising intensity, packaging and service. Customers were not highly concentrated, though there was some dependence on a few high-volume customers, which included a large hospital and a university. The general public were thought to be poor customers: 'You can't bank on the general public, they're too fickle'. It was clear that even though customers were not well informed, they were willing to shop around. In terms of self-appraised or perceived degree of product differentiation, the owner-manager thought the principal product was 'different' from that of rivals (as distinct from identical, similar or non-comparable). A particular claim the owner-manager made was that he used an expensive ultrasound machine (market value of £7,000 at 1985 prices) for cleaning window blinds. Manual methods could be used, but were not so efficient or effective. The special know-how required to use the equipment, which included a learning effect, was felt to bestow a competitive advantage on Firm A, and combined with the relatively high capital costs for the equipment, created a barrier to entry. The only competitor using this ultrasound process as well was in a large town in another region of the country, which was regarded as outside this firm's principal market. Delivery costs were a significant component of total costs (£3 a trip at 1985 prices), hence the perception of the market in geographical terms.

Pricing was influenced by the volume of services which the owner-manager expected to sell. Price was set as a flexible percentage mark-up on variable (i.e. prime, or direct) cost per unit of output. The aim of pricing was to achieve a certain profit target. There was a reluctance to deviate from this aim. The owner-manager insisted, 'I wouldn't try to buy work'. The pricing policy of competitors was not thought to be crucial to that of this SBE's pricing, though the owner-manager claimed that price would be held down to beat competitors. This was particularly true when competing for the trade of some large volume customers like hospitals, colleges or factories, who were relatively price sensitive. However, the owner-manager did not believe in pursuing a very low price strategy to deter entry, a device which had been used against him when he was starting up in business. He felt it was an unethical form of competition. He did aim to minimize cost and felt that to the extent he did deter entry it would be by competitive pricing.

If a boom in demand were to occur, which could not be met by the firm's current capabilities, the first reaction would be to increase overtime or shift-work, the second would be to increase capacity (probably by increasing personnel in this case) and the third would be to lengthen order books. Given the tight competitive situation, the rather obvious third-ranked strategy would not be invoked for fear of losing the goodwill of customers. In a recession, the owner-manager thought he would first increase sales effort and then reduce stockholding. As the principal product was a non-storable service, the efficacy of the latter strategy was limited and confined to cleaning agents, spare parts and some complete window-blinds for direct sales. Sales effort, therefore, was particularly emphasized as a method for stimulating demand. This was particularly directed at 'channels', these being the personnel who were empowered to conclude contracts within client institutions. The owner-manager felt that a lack of established trade connections with such channels could be a significant barrier to entry.

One line of customer persuasion emphasized the relative disadvantage of manual methods over ultrasound. The owner-manager argued that rivals' processes 'don't do what my process does'. Another line emphasized the advantages of greater hygiene after cleaning. He would try to establish contact with health and safety or hygiene officers to make this point, and would refer to the ease with which he could solve their problem, saying, 'Give that job to me and I will take it off your hands'. On the hygiene angle he felt that 'customers need to be educated' and did not think this was easy to achieve by advertising (e.g. in newspapers). The owner-manager felt he would be phlegmatic in the face of a fall in demand for the main product-group and would take no action. At the time of the semi-structured inter-view in 1985 the industry was contracting and competitive pressure was increasing. The owner-manager had seen several rivals go out of business in the previous year. Exit costs were low, particularly if business premises were leased and little capital equipment was used (e.g. no ultrasound). There was some entry by cleaning firms in adjacent market segments. They had targeted what they perceived as low entry cost service industries as alterna-tives to their own rapidly declining trades. Despite the competitive pressure, the owner-manager did not sympathize with the notion of defensive strategy. He thought it had undertones of unethical competition. For example, in terms of retaliation, he felt he would be willing to match, or better, his rivals' guarantees, but thought that if this were done covertly, it would be unethical. He would not consciously create barriers to entry, but admitted he would not, for example, help inform a new entrant of market intelligence. Three years after the initial approach, one felt that events had not gone too favourably for this SBE. The owner-manager was unwilling to give a further interview, though the firm was still in business.

Costs were not split up into fixed and variable costs, and marginal cost was not calculated. A capacity output was recognized, and the owner-manager felt he normally operated at less than 50 per cent of capacity. Unit and marginal costs were thought to fall continuously with output though scale economies were not thought to be substantial. The owner-manager thought of himself as following a focus strategy with an emphasis on cost reduction, rather than product differentiation. Labour was regarded as the main cost-driver, with transport costs also being important, and given the technological choice of ultrasound equipment it was felt that there were few opportunities for reconfiguring the value chain. The owner-manager perceived his firm as a low-cost operation, which aimed to achieve an operational cost minimum. In pursuing this cost-focus strategy the owner-manager was unsympathetic to notions of responding to attacks on his strategy. On one level he felt that it was very hard in any case to discover potential moves. On another level he felt that if the value chain were not susceptible to reconfiguration, and cost was being tightly controlled, this was the best passive deterrent. As he put it, 'My own competitiveness will deter them'.

The owner-manager of this SBE did not use market research of any kind, nor the forecasts of outside bodies like trade associations. Demand was thought to be inelastic in response to small (5 per cent) and large (10 per cent) variations of price about the established price, assuming normal business conditions and no responses from rivals. The owner-manager did not believe a price reduction by him would bring forth a price reduction by his strongest competitors, irrespective of whether business conditions were normal, buoyant or depressed, and the same was felt to be true of price increases. Consistent with this, the owner-manager thought that he had a certain amount of 'elbow room' in pricing within which a price change would not bring about a reaction by competitors. This elbow room was estimated to be 10–15 per cent about current price. In Reid (1981, ch. 4) a number of theoretical arguments are examined for conjectured demand curves with relatively inelastic segments about the prevailing average price. They may best be understood as deriving from switching costs which customers must bear in changing suppliers. In the semi-structured interview the owner-manager did confess that switching costs of some customers were low, which suggests that a certain measure of customer ignorance encouraged lack of price responsiveness, though quality of service might also have played a role here. The owner-manager reported that changes in costs and changes in demand were the main reasons for altering selling price. A non-uniform price tariff was adopted with different prices being charged for large and small traders. Price rebates were offered in the form of bulk discounting. Large institutional customers in the public sector were perceived to be relatively more price sensitive than other purchasers and seemed to put tight controls on costs. The owner-manager said, 'On big orders the odd penny per square foot is significant'. The sorts of institutions he had in mind were hospitals or universities, which might make very big orders of several hundred window blinds at once, but would expect to pay only a very low price (e.g. a few pounds) per blind. These institutions were very tightly cash-constrained over the period concerned, as a consequence of budgetary stringency for most large public-sector institutions. The account given might well have been different for institutions like commercial factories in large industrial estates. There was no such thing as a controlled price (e.g. set by government or trade association) or a recommended price for this service. No collective industry action was ever taken. The owner-manager did not agree with forming coalitions and would not contemplate blocking tactics against rivals. Advertising was undertaken, promoting the firm's service over that of its rivals. Newspaper advertising had been tried, but was found to be ineffective. The owner-manager was prepared to increase advertising in slump conditions but not to reduce it in boom conditions. Competition was perceived to be generally strong, but weak in some aspects.

At the time of starting the business, the most important sources of advice were the local enterprise trust and the Scottish Development Agency,[3] in that order. The approximate size of the business at inception was £16,000 in terms of the book value of total assets at 1985 prices, and had not grown by the time of interview. The owner-manager had not experienced any difficulty in obtaining financial support to sustain his business, though he had initially started with only personal finance. Generally, the latter is a negative indicator of small firm survival, for selection theories of small firm finance suggest that the lower rated projects fail to attract external funding.[4] On the other hand, whilst the initial gearing ratio had been zero, it had risen to one-third in the course of the first year, and a capacity to raise debt finance is indicative of the perceived worth of a project in the eyes of the lender, which is reinforced by the existence of an equity stake by the owner-manager.[5] The owner-manager expected his equity gearing ratio to fall, then rise, then stay the same over each year of a three-year period subsequent to the interview. He thought it would fall in the first and third years due to ploughed-back profits, but rise in the second year due to increased debt. This pattern would make sense in terms of a business plan which involved 'pulses' of expansion, partly funded by debt finance. In fact, the firm had experienced cash-flow difficulties, which had been the reason for increasing borrowing. This had arisen primarily because of delinquent debtors, and secondarily from overinvestment. To the extent that there are good and bad reasons for acquiring debt, these are good reasons (as compared, for example, to an unexpected slump in demand), because behind the debt are potential assets. The soundness of this gearing ratio policy was emphasized by the owner-manager's expectation of growth in his business over the forseeable future. However, lacking a further interview, though the firm was still in business three years later, it was impossible to confirm whether the owner-manager's optimistic expectations had been realized.

2.3 PROFILE C: KNITWEAR MANUFACTURER

Firm C had been in existence since November 1983. In 1985 it employed five out-workers, one part-time worker, but no trainees. That year its sales turnover was thought to be £22,000 at nominal prices. In 1988, Firm C was still in business. It had not grown in terms of personnel by the time of re-interview in 1988. The owner-manager expressed the view that, since 1985, he had experienced a shortage of skilled labour. Difficulties had arisen, firstly, in recruiting out-workers, who often had to be enticed away from Firm C's competitors. Secondly, it was not easy to judge competitor's relative skill advantage–disadvantage ratio, which made it difficult to focus precisely on recruitment requirements. The result of this skill shortage had been to retard the growth of the business over the period 1985–8. In terms of legal form, the firm was a two-person partnership. One partner was an economic history graduate of a large and prestigious university and the other was an art school graduate in fashion design. The economic historian said he got the idea of using out-workers from his knowledge of economic history before the Industrial Revolution.

The main product group in terms of sale value generated was high quality, 'designer' cardigans. The striking designs were a product of the skills of the art school graduate. This SBE produced from two to five product groups and a total of between twenty-one and forty products. On a one-off basis work would be done exactly to customer specification (i.e. on a bespoke basis), but as this was thought likely to damage Firm C's design reputation, the partners generally called the shots in determining products and product ranges. The partner interviewed regarded his SBE's principal market as that of the international economy. Many sales went overseas, especially to the United States, where large department stores, especially in New York, were important customers. In terms of this international market the market share for Firm C's main product group, cardigans, was small at under 1 per cent. By 1988 there had been a change in competitiveness in the industry's main market. This had been due to an innovation undertaken by one of Firm C's largest rivals. The output of Firm C's main product line had also changed, substantially. Between 1985 and 1988 the output of the main product line had increased 100 per cent without incurring additional unit variable cost. On the other hand, the output mix had not altered over this three-year period, which is unusual in markets subject to innovation and buffeted by the vagaries of fashion.

Much of the fabrication of products was done by out-workers, and the partners were trying to do more design work within the workshop unit, with semi-skilled labour undertaken by the out-workers. The partners of the firm could distinguish between major and minor competitors, and estimated that there were between eleven and thirty major competitors and more than fifty minor competitors. There were many rivals, but competitors were not diverse. Thus industrial concentration was low. The firm sold its products in highly fashion-conscious markets. Given the great attention to individual garment designs, the product was thought to be highly differentiated. Firm C's catalogue, which had been subsidized by a grant, attempted to enhance the perceived product differentiation, by emphasizing the uniqueness of designs. The designs themselves were motivated by a feel for street fashion. An example of the source of uniqueness in design was the current use of geometrical patterns. This was inspired by the paintings of Pablo Picasso. There was an awareness of the trade-off between product differentiation and cost reduction, but design considerations came first, as this rather than price had the main leverage over customers' willingness to buy.

In terms of the ability of customers to make informed judgements on the products, two groups of customers were distinguished. The first group was thought to be expert and those within it could determine by their own judgements the technical quality of the product. These customers were themselves typically also knitters or designers. The second group was fairly expert about the product concerned and those within it could draw on their personal experience as well as technical information, available in specialist magazines and trade journals, in evaluating the quality of the product. Generally customer concentration was low, though it was thought to be higher for many of Firm C's rivals. Typically low concentration reduces customers' bargaining power. However, there were some big customers, with whom the partner thought there was no opportunity for haggling. It was thought worthwhile to retain big customers because they reduced transactions costs, and their big orders helped to boost confidence. This SBE had recently lost a big order which had reduced confidence and made planning harder. Forward integration was a real possibility: rivals had successfully tried it.

Suppliers of expensive yarns (especially cashmere) were highly concentrated. For wool, supplies were drawn from five mills and for cashmere from only two mills. In the latter case the suppliers tended to dictate the quality and the colour available. There was thought to be higher supplier concentration than customer concentration. There was a tendency therefore for bargaining pressure to come from the supplier side. This was strengthened by the precise technical standards which supplies had to meet. Department stores, who were the principal customers, were aware of such considerations and were sensitive to what the trade called 'the handle' of the garment (i.e. the way it feels to the hand). This would tend to increase the dependence of the SBE on suppliers. There were technical substitutes available, like acrylic, but they were not cheap and also not what the customer would wish as a material for a designer product.

The pricing of a new product would be determined independently of the amount to be sold. Price within the firm's main product group was determined by a flexible mark-up on variable cost, and the general aim was to set the price at the highest level the market could bear. However, a constraint on this was the pricing policy of competitors, which was considered crucial to Firm C's own pricing policy. The partner interviewed said that he did hold down Firm C's price to beat those of existing competitors. Further, an entry-deterring price might be set against potential entrants.[6]

The first action undertaken when a boom in demand could not be met from stocks would be to increase capacity, which could include the recruitment of more personnel. The second action would be to lengthen the firm's order books. Faced with a recession Firm C would take four courses of action which could be ranked in order taken, as follows. Firstly, sales effort would be increased, followed by cutting price. Then capacity would be reduced, possibly including the laying-off of personnel. Finally, an attempt would be made to improve productivity or efficiency, though this was not a dimension that was thought to be particularly susceptible to fine control in the case of Firm C. If the demand fell for a particular product within the main product group, the first course of action would be to switch to a new product, which in this SBE's case would probably involve its developing new designs. The second would be to increase sales effort, the third would be to cut price and the last would be to introduce short-time working.

Costs were split up into fixed and variable costs, and these cost divisions were thought to be useful in the running of the firm. Materials, out-work and the personal labour of the partners were thought to be Firm C's main cost-drivers. It was thought that some of these cost-drivers were hard to control. For example, raw materials costs (e.g. wool, cashmere) were effectively given. That is, raw materials were purchased in perfectly competitive markets. It was not known what rivals paid their own out-workers, because they were as cagey about revealing wages costs to rivals as was Firm C. It was thought that cost cutting here would be risky. The partners had considered a less controversial method of reconfiguring the value chain by buying new equipment.

When output of a product was increased the additional cost to the firm was calculated. The partner interviewed thought his firm did have such a thing as a 'capacity output'. It was thought that the firm normally operated at between 51 per cent and 60 per cent of its maximum possible output. The partner accepted that he was experiencing slight overcapacity. The pattern of the firm's cost variation with output was thought to be captured approximately by the statement that total cost did not increase as fast as the amount supplied (i.e. the cost of supplying each extra unit fell as more units were supplied). Once variations in plant were permitted it was felt that although in principle returns to scale should be constant, in practice they were probably decreasing, due to managerial diseconomies.[7] In principle, barriers to entry were low, as it was easy to start a similar business from home, and capital costs were low. Out-workers, who currently worked from their own homes to given designs, were one source of potential entrants. They knew of channels on the supply side but not on the distribution side. They might initially enter into the informal economy and therefore gain experience. However, they lacked design ability and flair, which constituted a major barrier to entry. Such entrants would have a low learning curve. By contrast, art school graduates were a greater threat, with steep learning curves. However, they lacked experience, not just on the business side, but in certain technical aspects of production, like garment finishing. The need for such potential entrants to learn the ropes of production, and their lack of experience, would put them at a cost disadvantage compared to established firms.

The partner interviewed said that he preferred to see his SBE using an offensive rather than defensive strategy. He would not attempt to block channel access, and shared the general feeling in the industry that 'good competitors' should be encouraged. Thus he saw the industry as a fraternity, even though competition was keen. Retaliation was thought to be costly and time-consuming, and likely to be frowned upon by the fraternity. Similarly, blocking likely attacks was thought to drain resources unnecessarily. For example, profit targets would not be reduced to this end. It was thought that the best defence was to look invulnerable: 'At the end of the day you need the stamina to keep going – like a marathon runner'. The use of false information, for example, to manage the assumptions of competitors, was frowned upon. It was said that 'deterrence was all verbal', but the implication here was that only accurate information would be used (e.g. to turn a customer in favour of your product and put him off another). A particular problem arose when a design had been pirated. A deterrent to this would be a verbal protest at a trade fair. The fraternity would disapprove of pirating. In the limit, litigation might be pursued as a deterrent. It was thought that 'Monitoring of trade shows helps you identify serious rivals, and also signals commitment to the industry'. A new entrant might be dissuaded by being made aware of the difficulties of the trade.

This firm did not use systematic market research methods of any kind. The partners would have wished to know more about customer types and locations but felt the acquisition of this information could be costly or impossible. They claimed that, in an informal way, 'You are gathering as much intelligence as possible'. This occurred through trade connections, especially the circuit of trade fairs. Unfortunately, some potentially useful technical conferences were too expensive to attend. Knowledge of college courses which might turn out potential design rivals was spread by word of mouth at trade fairs. This relative ignorance of market segments made the partners reluctant to follow a focus strategy either of the low-cost or product differentiation sort. A focus strategy was felt to be risky in the fashion business, though it was more or less forced on this SBE by its scale in relation to industry. In practice, something like a differentiation focus was adopted because a cost leadership strategy would be to the detriment of quality and design.

On the assumption that competitors did not react and that business conditions were normal, it could not be estimated what Firm C's sales reaction would be to a 5 per cent or 10 per cent price cut or increase. Switching costs of customers were thought to be high in some cases, which would tend to make demand more price inelastic. However, these costs were thought to be largely psychological, which would make their estimation difficult, and therefore their effects on price uncertain. Some customers were by reputation very price sensitive even though they were large, had operations which were highly profitable, and incurred costs in purchasing Firm C's goods which were small in relation to their overall costs. The partner said, 'Some simply push on price as a matter of principle', but it was possible that this conduct is explained by a desire on the part of the customer to give a strong demonstration effect to *all* suppliers. What might be forgiven of one supplier, because of their negligible effect on profitability, could not be forgiven for all suppliers as the summed effects of the erosion of cost control could be significant. A reputation for tight cost control is therefore worth cultivating. This type of customer tends to motivate the SBE to keep prices down by promising higher turnover. There was a slight threat of backward integration (e.g. designs could be pirated), but in practice this was uncommon.

It was thought that a reduction in the SBE's price would not provoke their strongest competitors to reduce their prices in any business conditions, normal, boom or recession. If Firm C increased its price in normal business conditions, and in recession, again it was thought that their competitors would not follow their actions. However, it was believed that when the economy was buoyant, competitors too would raise their price. Consistent with this it was believed that Firm C had a certain amount of 'elbow room' in pricing, implying that a price change would not bring about a reaction from its competitors.[8] However, the partner did not know how large this elbow-room might be, possibly partly because switching costs of customers were difficult to estimate. Reasons for altering the selling price included the start of a new business year (or new collection), cost changes and shifts in demand. Firm C practised price discrimination between different customers, but no price rebates were offered. There were no controlled or recommended prices for this SBE's products. Firm C did not advertise and competition in its main market was described as generally strong but weak in some aspects. Especially in the Scottish market, competition was thought to be intense. The general competitiveness of the whole market was attributed to the fashion consciousness of its customers. Because the product was fashion wear there was, in a sense, no substitute product. Technical substitutes existed for the raw materials (e.g. acrylic for wool), but they were no cheaper and were less well regarded by customers. That is, the value/price was perceived to be lower for products made with acrylic than those made with wool. Customers were thought to value quality and design, and would not readily purchase substitutes.

Advice was sought at the time of starting the firm. The Scottish Development Agency, currently Scottish Enterprise, was thought to be the most important contact for advice, followed by the local enterprise trust, and finally by the SBE's accountant. The approximate size of the SBE at inception was £1,500 in terms of total assets net of depreciation (book value at 1983 prices). In 1985 (at 1985 prices) it was estimated to be £7,000. Net profit in 1985 was £2,000 representing a profitability on assets of 29 per cent. The firm was initially launched using personal finance only, though it was thought that no difficulty would have been encountered in obtaining financial support at this time had it been wanted. This proved to be the case, and at financial inception as distinct from launch, the gearing ratio figure was 3.5, which had proven to be its highest level. The lowest level had been zero, and the level at the time of interview in 1985 was 0.3. The gearing ratio was expected to rise over the next year, due to the expectation of an increase in ploughed-back profits and an increase in debt. In the event, the gearing ratio actually fell in 1986 and then rose again in 1987. The firm had experienced cash-flow difficulties, mainly caused by overinvestment, but excerbated by delinquent debtors and sagging sales. External finance had been sought since inception of the business both to fund a move to larger premises and to overcome cash-flow problems.

The partner interviewed had expectations of growth in his business over the foreseeable future. He anticipated a 5–10 per cent growth rate per annum, from which he hoped his firm's sales would get a proportionate share. In fact, these expectations were not entirely fulfilled and in 1988 the partner interviewed admitted it had been 'a difficult year for the firms with a slow movement of sales in shops'. Nevertheless, he said that he did sense the emergence of an 'enterprise culture' in Scotland.

2.4 PROFILE D: AUTOMOTIVE BODY-PANEL REPAIRS

This SBE had been started in October 1984 with assets of £5,000 in book value at nominal prices. By the time of interview in April 1985 its assets were estimated to be £9,000 at nominal prices, though this was possibly an overestimate. It was a business partnership and specialized in body-work repairs for a range of motor vehicles. A particular specialization was high-quality panel work for a leading Volvo dealer in the locality. In 1985 there were two persons working full-time for the partnership, no part-timers and no trainees. This SBE had between two and five product groups (including panel beating, insurance estimates, spraying and chassis welding) and between one and ten products.

The partner interviewed in 1985 thought that his principal market was the region and estimated his SBEs market share was small (< 1 per cent). No turnover figures were available at the time of initial interview. Three years later, in June 1988, turnover was £40,000 and the premises had been doubled in size. In 1985 the partners had not expected growth in the industry, though they had expected to increase their market penetration. The same partnership still ran the firm in 1988, again with two employees. Assets in 1988 were estimated at £6,000, which actually represented a real reduction of 41 per cent from the 1985 figure. However, the assets at financial inception are probably a better guide, and imply a small real asset growth since starting (< 10 per cent growth). Actually, in 1988 the 1985 assets were estimated to have been £3,000, reinforcing the view that earlier estimated asset figures are to be taken with a pinch of salt.

The partner interviewed could distinguish between major and minor competitors and estimated there were between one and five major competitors and more than fifty minor competitors. The partner did not distinguish between 'good' and 'bad' competitors. He felt his firm was committed to the industry and was willing and able to defend its competitive niche. Entry and exit barriers were thought to be rising. Industrial concentration was generally low on the product market side, with one exception. One large customer provided almost 50 per cent of the trade. Switching costs were thought to be low for small buyers, but significant for this one large customer because of the specialized nature of the vehicle work required. Over the three years 1985–8 there had been no perceived change in competitiveness brought about by innovation. An eye was kept on developments in the industry, but

nothing threatening was anticipated at the general level. The partner interviewed saw no relevant new technology being around the corner. He said
confidently, 'Robots can't do smashed vehicles'. The partners were contemplating introducing a bake shop (for quality paintwork achieved at high
temperatures) as an extended facility, but this service was seen as being in a
different market niche. The main service provided (automotive body-panel
repairs) was perceived to be similar to that of rivals (i.e. not strongly differentiated). Differentiation was by effort and by quality. For example, after
doing a coachwork repair, the partners ensured the vehicle was returned to
the customer fully cleaned, inside and out.

In the search for quality, Firm D's owners favoured using only genuine
replacement parts from suppliers for their coachwork, as customers placed
so much emphasis on the 'finish' of a vehicle. Well-established customers
might get this top-quality product, but at a lower rate than usual, in order
to lock them in to future contracts by effectively raising their switching
costs. Customers purchasing this service were thought to be modestly
informed about the nature of the service, on a scale running from expert to
ignorant. If they were not technically minded, they might have in mind a
few technical aspects that the service should embody. If they were informed
about technical features of the service (e.g. options on the quality of replacement panels, or on paintwork) they would be guided by these in making a
decision to purchase. Typically, most small customers were not well
informed, though a few were. The main customer, a Volvo dealer, was very
well informed. In turn, buyers of the dealers' products, whilst not technically well informed, were fastidious about the final product.

In terms of competitive strategy a differentiation, rather than cost, focus
strategy was adopted. No attempt was made to pursue a cost leadership
focus strategy, despite its superficial attractiveness. There were too many
rivals trying to keep costs low, and following this strategy would ultimately
be self-defeating. An attempt was made to discover particular customer likes
and dislikes. The differentiation focus strategy had been narrowed down to
Volvo coachwork repairs for their main customer. This market niche had
been invaded by driving out the incumbent small firm through offering a
better-quality service at a more reasonable price. Customer dissatisfaction
was taken very seriously, and the partners were aware that, if neglected, it
could lead to challengers for their market. Customers were viewed as
channels, and these were cultivated. A loss of channels was thought likely to
encourage attacks on Firm D's market niche. Contrariwise, the partner
thought that blocking rivals' channels might be contemplated as an aspect
of defensive strategy, though he claimed not to be much concerned with
such actions. Strategic stakes were thought to be high. In general, the firm's
good work was thought to set an example in the trade, but this signalling of
quality and commitment was not high profile: 'We keep ourselves to
ourselves, and let our work speak for us'. It was known that customers
valued the quality of the job above all. Factors which were thought to

improve customers' perception of quality included the good appearance of
the premises and a clear and honest explanation of what coachwork would
be required. The partner said that colour matching was a particularly
praised aspect of Firm D's work and had established a reputation for quality
which he aimed to keep.

If a new service were brought onto the market, its price would be set
without regard to potential sales volume. The pricing policy adopted was to
set price at a mark-up on unit variable cost, with the mark-up being set to
achieve a certain desired gross profit, and typically a willingness to vary this
mark-up to increase gross profit. The pricing policy of competitors was
thought to be crucial to this SBE's own pricing, and the partner interviewed
expressed a willingness to hold down price to beat existing competitors. The
partner of Firm D interviewed said he would also contemplate price cutting
to deter a potential entrant. This would be one dimension of matching
guarantees, a strategy which met with approval. Should a boom in demand
for the main service occur which could not be met by existing capacity, the
first reaction would be to increase shiftwork or overtime, followed by a
lengthening of the order book, a price increase, engaging subcontractors,
and finally by increasing capacity. This last course of action had been taken
over the three years of operation 1985–8. Physical floor space of the workshop was doubled, but not plant and equipment or personnel. In a recession,
the first action taken would be to cut price; followed by an increase in sales
effort. As distinct from a general recession, if demand fell for a specific
service, the first reaction would be to seek a new service, followed by
attempts to increase quality and finally, to increase sales effort. In fact, over
the period 1985–8 the output mix (i.e. the proportion one output bore to
another) had not changed substantially nor had the volume of services
supplied, suggesting no slump in demand for any specific service.

Costs were split up into fixed and variable and this was thought to be a
useful distinction in running the SBE. The ratio of fixed costs to value
added was thought to be stable. An eye was kept on costs to keep them
down. Discounts were sought on paints and panels, and these were related to
the regularity and frequency of custom. In contemplating an increased
output, an incremental cost calculation would be made. When first interviewed, the partner said that he did not recognize his firm as having a
capacity or maximum possible output. By this we think he meant that there
were no circumstances under which he would turn away orders at that point
in time, on the grounds of inadequate capacity. Some months after the
initial interview this had had the consequence that though the firm had
been working at full capacity for many weeks, a reluctance to turn away
orders had resulted in a six-week waiting list. At this point an attempt was
made to extend capacity. The partner said a conscious aim was to extend the
scale of operations. It was thought that increased turnover would enhance
efficiency. By 1988 the premises had been doubled, presumably to be able to
guarantee fulfilling pledges to take on any orders, although the output of the

service typically remained at the earlier 1985 level. Installing reserve capacity in this way would increase the flexibility of the firm and give it a better competitive edge. The partners had consciously tried to manage other firms' assumptions whilst undertaking expansion to these ends.[9] Regarding the form of the cost curve, the partner interviewed thought that total cost increased in line with the amount supplied of the service (i.e. for each extra unit supplied, cost rose by the same extra amount). This corresponds to a linear total cost curve with positive fixed costs and constant marginal cost. The partner agreed that a break-even analysis could identify that scale of output beyond which the service would inevitably be profitable.

Within Scotland, there was high supplier concentration for materials like paints, parts and panels. Suppliers were more concentrated than customers. However, Firm D was not thought to be at a bargaining disadvantage *vis-à-vis* suppliers because substitutes were available from England, albeit after a time lag. Switching costs of suppliers were thought to be low. None had attempted forward integration: suppliers lacked the skill, knowledge and experience to switch readily to the coachwork trade.

Capital requirements were thought to constitute a significant barrier to entry. This was heightened by new trade regulations. These concerned regulations on equipment which had to be satisfied if a firm was to be validated as a coachworks, and also safety regulations. Compliance costs were significant and hence such regulations constituted a barrier to entry. Capital costs had been incurred to enlarge potential capacity, but the partner interviewed was also aware that this outlay had defensive advantages. A lack of channels would deter potential entrants. Location and customer access were potential sources of competitve advantage.

Informal market research methods were used to get an idea of future developments in the market. If it looked as though Firm D's main market niche were being attacked, the partners would seek more work through dealers, advertising and trade contacts. Generally, the partners felt unthreatened, but they were aware that it was important to maintain good relations with channels on both the supply and customer sides. It was not thought likely that any threat would be met by litigation.

For a small (5 per cent) increase or decrease in the price of the main service, given no reponse by rivals and normal business conditions, demand was thought to be totally price inelastic. For a larger (10 per cent) increase or decrease in price, under the same conditions, demand was thought to be *relatively* price inelastic, though not totally inelastic. The partner interviewed thought that if he reduced price, his strongest competitor would do the same in normal, boom or recession business conditions. If he increased price, he thought this price would be followed by strong competitors in a boom (i.e. a sellers' market) but not in normal or recession conditions. Consonant with the view that demand was price inelastic for local price variations, a certain elbow-room in pricing was recognized, within which changing Firm D's price evoked no reaction from rivals. This elbow room was estimated to be 4–6 per cent. It was thought that the high value added generated, relative to costs, lowered the price sensitivity of customers, and this was most especially so of their main customer, a large Volvo dealer, who did not seem very price sensitive. The main motivation of this customer, and some of the smaller customers as well, was 'to get a good job done, even if it was a bit more pricey'. Such customers were prepared to pay for quality. Firm D was proud to be a Volvo Club recommended dealer. It was found that Club customers favoured them as channels for business. A few small dealers, possibly on low profit margins, haggled a lot on price. It was felt that their custom was often 'not worth the trouble'.

Reasons for changing price included the commencement of a new tax year or new business year (i.e. a new season of production) and adjustments to new costs. Price discrimination was practised, with prices being set at different levels for different customers, and also for large and small purchases by customers. The nature of Firm D's main service (body-panel repairs on cars, vans, etc.) would preclude resale.[10] Price rebates were offered, and took the form of bulk discounting. Further, valuable customers might get special discounts to encourage repeat purchases. No services were provided at controlled or recommended prices. Some advertising was undertaken, and it was rivalrous in form (i.e. it aimed to promote Firm D's services over those of its rivals). Advertising would be increased to stimulate demand in slack business conditions, and reduced if demand were buoyant. Competition was perceived to be strong, but weak in some aspects (e.g. strong competition by quality, and strong inter-firm rivalry, but weak competition by price).

At the inception of this SBE the partners had sought advice on starting the business. Most important was the local Enterprise Trust, followed by the bank manager, family and friends, and the accountant. No difficulty had been experienced in obtaining financial support for starting the business. In fact, only personal finance had been used in setting up the business. It was launched purely on personal finance, without any debt (i.e. gearing ratio of zero) and had a gearing ratio of zero at the time of interview in 1985. The highest gearing ratio had been unity (i.e. debt matched exactly by equity) and the lowest had been zero. In 1985, it was thought that the gearing ratio would stay the same for two years and then rise in the third year through an increase in borrowing. Over the first two years of this three-year time horizon, it was planned to increase the owners' injections of equity. With zero debt this would of course leave the gearing ratio at zero. In practice, this is roughly what was done, according to the interview reponse of partners three years later, in 1988. Gearing was said to have fallen for two years (presumably because such little debt as had been acquired, had been just as quickly repaid) and then to have risen in the third (presumably to help fund the doubling of the size of the business premises). No special financial schemes (e.g. investment grants, reduced rentals on premises) had been necessary, helpful or applicable when this SBE was starting up. The partners had not experienced cash-flow difficulties in running the firm. At the time of initial interview in 1985, when gearing was zero, no debt had been acquired since the starting of the business.

In 1985 the partner interviewed anticipated growth in his business over the forseeable future, which here was interpreted as a three-year time horizon (1985–8). In practice, business was quite steady over the three-year time period between interview and reinterview. The product mix was unchanged, as were the scale of operation and the workforce. Some extra labour was bought in on occasion, but no difficulty had been experienced in getting people of the requisite skill. The main changes were that the business premises had been doubled in size, and concomitantly the gearing ratio had risen to one and a half. Based on asset figures at inception given in 1985 and net profit figures for the same year given in 1988, net profitability of this firm was 40–60 per cent. If asset figures given at interview in 1985 are used, this range falls to 22–33 per cent. When asked retrospectively for a direct estimate of net profitability in 1985 at the time of the 1988 interview, the partner put the figure at 83 per cent. However, at that point he was estimating his 1985 assets to have been just £3,000, which would give a profitability range of 66–100 per cent, were his net profit figures accurate. It seems likely the 83 per cent figure for net profitability involved an element of exaggeration, and possibly the unconscious neglect of partners' renumerations. The partner felt he would not reduce the firm's profit targets to deter potential entrants, again suggesting high estimate, as it seems unlikely that any conceivable entry barrier would prevent an erosion by entry of such high profitability, should it exist.

The partner interviewed in 1988 thought that he had sensed the emergence of an enterprise culture in Scotland. He referred to the greater coverage given to new businesses on the television. He also felt that more advice had become available to those setting up their own firms, and singled out his local enterprise trust as being 'very supportive and helpful'. The partner went on to say that he gained satisfaction from 'being his own boss'. He referred to the way in which personal growth could go hand in hand with business growth. However, he felt the pressure of greater responsibility because 'it's not just a case of collecting a wage packet at the end of a week, like it is in employment'.

2.5 PROFILE E: SUPPLIER OF INDUSTRIAL CLEANING CHEMICALS AND EQUIPMENT

Firm E had been in existence since July 1984. It was an industrial cleaning business which employed six full-time workers. The owner-manager was a graduate in economics and accounting from a large and prestigious university. He ran a number of firms (of which Firm E was just one), from the same office and warehouse facility. In this way, risk was diversified over several business ventures.[11] The owner-manager saw himself as being 'in business' *per se*, and not wedded to Firm E's activities. In this sense, his strategic stakes were not high. However, if he exited, he thought he would remain in the same broad area of the industry.

Firm E had grown substantially in terms of personnel. By the time of reinterview in August 1988, Firm E employed ten full-time workers and seventy part-time workers, having diversified into the provision of cleaning services. This had been a natural and profitable form of forward integration. The owner-manager said the firm had not experienced a shortage of any type of skilled labour since 1985. In terms of legal form the business was a private company. In 1985 the approximate size of Firm E's sales turnover (excluding VAT) was £150,000 and it had a net profit of £18,000, both at 1985 prices. When interviewed in 1988, the sales turnover (excluding VAT) had risen to approximately £400,000 at 1988 prices, representing a real (inflation adjusted) growth rate of 160 per cent in terms of sales. It was thought that market penetration had been achieved by product differentiation in terms of service. Firm E had between two and five product groups, the main product group (in terms of sales value) being cleaning chemicals. The firm sold between forty-one and sixty products. The owner-manager said that it would be easy to have a much wider range of products, but thought this would work against his focus strategy, which was directed at relevant market segments, with a great emphasis on marketing.[12] Rivals were also very attuned to the market and its segmentation.

One of the main suppliers of the necessary materials for Firm E's main product-line had, according to the owner-manager, 'given us a good deal', which partly explained the limitation on product range. Looked at another way, this 'good deal' imposed switching costs on Firm E. There was low supplier concentration, though Firm E only dealt with three suppliers. Negotiations with suppliers, as well as determining volume, price, delivery, and so on, also dealt with minor ways of differentiating the product (e.g. by the colour and odour of liquid soap). Forward integration by suppliers was rare because of the highly specialized nature of the next stage of production and service.

The owner-manager interviewed considered Scotland to be Firm E's principal market. He estimated that his market share for the main product-group, cleaning chemicals, was less than 1 per cent. A distinction was made between major and minor competitors, and it was estimated that there were between eleven and thirty major competitors and over fifty minor competitors. It was thought that barriers to entry were high but barriers to exit were low. The owner-manager did not think he had any control over entry barriers. They largely arose from significant capital requirements, though channels were essential and took time to cultivate: 'Experience and contacts count'.

Firm E's products were considered to be 'similar' to those of its competitors (i.e. there was mild product differentiation). Product differentiation tended to be by service, rather than by product characteristics, though there was some differentiation by packaging. Packaging was being used to create a brand image. An aspect of the service Firm E provided, of which the owner-manager was proud, was a turn-around time on most orders of two to three days. The owner-manager was contemplating the possibility of 'mimicking' at very low cost a powerful cleaning agent currently used only in the United States and not yet marketed in the United Kingdom. This was used in dishwashing machines, and the owner-manager thought that intensive users of many such machines (e.g. hospitals, caterers, restaurants) would provide good, high-volume business. Firm E's customers were not technically minded, though they did have in mind a few technical features the product ought to possess. Customers generally could not distinguish between technical characteristics of Firm E's products and those of its rivals. Therefore price, brand and service could all determine the customer's attitude to buying. There was a significant degree of customer concentration. The owner-manager said, '20 per cent of our customers give us 80 per cent of our business'. The switching costs of customers was low, and it was thought to be difficult to raise them. Contract cleaners supplied by firms like his had in the past backward integrated, though suppliers of hospital services had not, to his knowledge. Firm E itself had not been affected by backward integration. It had ultimately grown through forward integration into contract cleaning. Customers were aware of substitutes, which sharpened price competition. To prevent customer substitution the owner-manager put an important emphasis on salesmanship and promotion for his products.

If a new product were brought onto the market its price would be determined without regard to potential sales volume. Current new product development was very modest, involving the further differentiation of soap products, in a costless way, by introducing them in new colours and odours. In the longer term there was interest in commissioning a chemist to prepare a new compound. Price was usually determined as a flexible mark-up on variable cost, with the mark-up being set to achieve a certain desired gross profit. The aim was to set this price at the highest level the market could bear. The pricing policy of Firm E's competitors was considered to be crucial to that of its own pricing and as a result the owner-managers were willing to hold down prices to beat their rivals. The owner-manager interviewed said there was deliberately 'a bit of fat in our margins' which made price cutting a feasible retaliatory defensive strategy if threatened by a challenger. It was thought that other forms of retaliation might be used, but the owner-manager could not (or would not) be more specific. Certainly, challengers were taken seriously, though they were not entirely unwelcome, as, it was said, 'They sharpen up competition'. To the extent that margins were cut, this was regarded as more of an attempt to lower the inducement for attack.

If a boom in demand were to occur that could not be met from stocks, Firm E's response would be to increase capacity. This could include the recruitment of more personnel. The owner-manager thought that the lines of action taken in a recession would be, firstly, to increase sales effort; secondly, to try to improve productivity or efficiency; thirdly, to reduce stockholding; and fourthly, to reduce capacity (including the laying-off of personnel). If demand were to fall for a particular product rather than because of a general recession, then the first line of action would be to increase sales effort, followed by a switch to a new product.

Costs were split up into fixed and variable costs and these divisions were found to be useful in the running of the firm. The owner-manager did calculate the marginal cost involved in increasing output. He initially claimed not to recognize an output which could be regarded as *the* 'capacity'. However, in the very short run, a limit to capacity was perhaps recognized, as the owner-manager claimed never to have overcapacity, saying, 'We try to keep things tight'. What seems to have been suggested is that, as growth was rapid, no capacity limits to growth were perceived, but at any given instant of time the firm was delivering all it could with its existing capacity. When interviewed in 1988, the output of Firm E's main product line had increased substantially (by approximately 100 per cent) since 1985. The corresponding percentage increase in the firm's unit variable cost was just 10 per cent over a period in which prices had risen by 13 per cent. With regard to the shape of the firm's short-run cost curve, it was thought that the extra cost of supplying each additional unit fell as more was supplied. The owner-manager claimed to act consciously to identify and control principal cost-drivers. Next to wages, fuel was the major cost-driver. An attempt had been made to reconfigure the value chain by going over from petrol to diesel fuel for the fleet of delivery trucks which Firm E leased. There was an awareness of not always using the optimal delivery routes, in a least-cost sense. However, if a delivery were urgent, and necessary to acquire or consolidate custom (i.e. to cultivate consumer loyalty), then priority would be put on rapid delivery, to the detriment of the goal of minimizing fuel costs by the optimal routing of trucks. As well as these scale economies at the distribution end, there were also thought to be pecuniary economies, arising, for example, from negotiating favourable terms of bulk discounting.

Market research was undertaken by Firm E, particularly to identify strategically relevant market segments. The results of this research were used to determine (1) the price sensitivity of customers; (2) the extent of the market; (3) the interest of buyers in the SBE's products; (4) the reactions to rivals; (5) and the likely future developments in the market. The owner-manager did go to trade shows and saw this as partly an aspect of public relations, but also as a means of cultivating customers. It was not thought to be an aspect of defensive strategy. For a small (5 per cent) price change, up or down, given no response by rivals and in normal business conditions, demand was thought to be totally inelastic. For a larger (10 per cent) price increase or decrease, demand was thought to be relatively inelastic, though not totally inelastic. The owner-manager thought that if his firm were to reduce its price that his strongest competitors would not follow suit in any business conditions be they normal, depressed or buoyant. The same was thought to be true if Firm E were to raise its prices. Consistent with the view that demand could be inelastic was the belief that there was a certain amount of elbow room in pricing. It was estimated that this elbow room could in some cases be more than 15 per cent. However, some customers were known to be sharply price sensitive. This had been especially true of hospitals, which were major customers. The recent experience of the owner-manager was that whilst traditionally the most price sensitive of all customers, hospitals' price sensitivity had been falling, and a greater emphasis had been put on quality.

Events that might lead to an alteration in Firm E's selling price were said to be when cost changes occurred, when demand shifted substantially and when demand changed. Price discrimination was practised by the firm, with different prices being set for different market segments. Also different prices were set for certain types of customers and for small and large traders. Price rebates were offered and bulk discounting was also practised. There were no such things as either controlled or recommended prices. Firm E did advertise and it took the form of individual advertising (i.e. advertising aimed at promoting the firm's product over that of its rivals). Advertising was being increased irrespective of the level of business demand.

The owner-manager described the competition in his market as being generally strong, but weak in some aspects. For example, there was often an absence of price competition, but there was strong quality competition, especially by service, and intense inter-firm rivalry. It was accepted that the market was very competitive, but this did not seem to imply a willingness to use defensive strategies. For example, no attempt was made to manage rivals' assumptions as a defence, though the distribution system could be used informally in this way. It was said, 'One simply has to compete and survive'. In achieving this competitiveness, the emphasis was put on service and marketing.

At inception, advice was sought from suppliers first of all, followed by the bank manager, an accountant, the Scottish Development Agency and finally the local government authority. The approximate size of the business in terms of total assets (book value) at inception was £10,000 at 1984 prices. At the time of interview, 1985, the approximate size in terms of total assets (book value) was £30,000. The owner-manager found the only obstacle in obtaining financial support was the lack of personal financial injections. Firm E was set up with only personal finance. The equity gearing ratio figure at the start-up of the business stood at one. The gearing ratio at the time of interview in 1985 was a half, and this had also proved to be the lowest gearing figure. The highest gearing ratio figure had been 2.0. The owner-manager expected the gearing ratio to stay the same over the next three years due to an increase in ploughed-back profits and a parallel increase in debt over this period. By 1988, the gearing ratio had actually risen to 2.8. Although this figure was higher than had previously been expected the owner-manager was not concerned with the higher exposure to risk since his firm's growth had been quite rapid. In terms of total assets (book value, net of depreciation) Firm E's current size in 1988 was £54,557 at nominal prices implying a real annual growth of assets of 27 per cent. The owner-manager was actually more concerned with current liquidity restraints than exposure to risk. For example, servicing the interest on the firm's overdraft was thought to be more important than the absolute magnitude of the gearing ratio. Firm E had experienced cash-flow difficulties and these were due, most of all, to delinquent debtors, followed by, in decending order of importance, an inadequate credit policy with suppliers, overinvestment, an insufficient overdraft facility, an inadequate credit policy with suppliers and, finally, delinquent suppliers. External debt finance had been used since the inception of the business to purchase plant or equipment, to increase stock or inventory, to hire new employees and to deal with the cash-flow problems encountered.

The owner-manager expected to see growth in his business over the forseeable future. Three years earlier he had forcast an annual growth rate for the industry of 5–10 per cent per annum, but had added, 'We would hope to grow faster'. This ambition had been fully realized. In 1988 he reflected that rather than the emergence of a true enterprise culture in Scotland, only the perceptions of an 'enterprise culture' had been altered, the implication being that acting on perceptions had not yet occurred. He said, 'The basic situation is unchanged since 1985'. He added, 'If the Enterprise Allowance Scheme has helped even a few people it has been worthwhile despite its misuse by some'.

2.6 PROFILE G: HOLIDAY TOURS

Firm G had been in operation since January 1984. In 1985 it employed only two part-time workers. By the time of reinterview in 1988, Firm G had grown substantially, both in terms of personnel and sales turnover. Personnel had been increased to six full-time workers and one part-time worker. The sales turnover figure (excluding VAT) had increased significantly from £7,000 in 1985 to £500,000 in 1988, representing a real increase of over 6,000 per cent. In 1988 Firm G's profits in 1985 were reported as £5,000 (net of taxes and directors' remunerations). Net profitability was reported to have been 33⅓ per cent, which was consistent with reported assets and profits.

The owner-manager claimed that between 1985 and 1988 he had experienced a shortage of skilled labour. Difficulties that had arisen in trying to fill this skill gap, were, in decreasing order of importance, paying premium rates for scarce skills, identifying the skills required, releasing personnel for training and, finally, assessing competitors' relative skill advantages or disadvantages. This shortage of skilled labour had resulted in an impediment to Firm G's growth. There had been no change in competiveness in Firm G's principal market between 1985 and 1988 caused by innovation.

In terms of legal status, Firm G was a one-man business. It sold services which could be classified into between two to five product groups. In total, there were between one to ten products. Firm G's main product group was a particular type of holiday tour, and Scotland was regarded as the principal market for this product group. The number of new small firms active in this market kept increasing, because the market itself had displayed great potential growth. The infrastructure was already in place, and Scotland had much to offer, which the tourist could enjoy and the tour operator could exploit. Good hotels, excellent car hire facilities, and especially sporting opportunities (e.g. golf, skiing) were particularly mentioned as important dimensions of a quality tour package. The output mix changed substantially between 1985 and 1988. In terms of the value of sales attributable to the main product-lines as declared in 1985, value had declined by 90 per cent as reported in 1988. It was believed that Firm G's market share for tours in its principal market in 1985 was between 1 per cent and 5 per cent. The owner-manager could distinguish between major and minor competitors and he thought that his business had between one and five major and between eleven and thirty minor competitors. The tour industry was made up, predominantly, of many small firms, because fixed costs were low and specialization was high. There was as much differentiation or specialization as there were kinds of holiday. Firm G's main product was considered to be 'similar' to that of its competitors, in terms of product differentiation. Whilst differentiation was low, it was also extensive, in the sense that its forms were almost unlimited because tours were very much tailored to the needs and wants of the individual customers. In this sense, the service supplied had a 'bespoke' character. Location was thought to be important, in that one had to trade in a city to be successful. This aspect of location was more important than, for example, whether one traded from home or from an office.

The customers of Firm G were not thought to be technically minded, though they did have in mind some features that the service they purchased should have. Typically customers, who were characterized as 'upmarket individuals and companies', had little knowledge of the operations of tour agencies. They were more familiar with travel agents, who acted as brokers for particular trips. What Firm G did was to package various other trips offered by travel agents, along with other facilities like hotels, car hire and sporting activities, to provide a complete tour service. Customers lacked the channels and knowledge for doing this and would have found backward integration difficult. The switching costs of customers were low, given the mild product differentiation and extreme market fragmentation. However, given any significant involvement with the customer (e.g. in sketching out possible holiday arrangements) switching costs would tend to be higher, until, once the holiday arrangements were completed, the customer almost invariably followed through and purchased. The main attribute of the service which customers valued was its convenience, though they were also motivated to purchase by the lower total holiday expenses which the skilful tour operator could achieve. Costs of tours to the customer were often a small proportion of total holiday costs. Thus, whilst they would nominally seek the lowest-cost arrangement, they were not very price sensitive. Demonstrating that the firm could save the customer money was part of the sales pitch, as was the time saving involved, and the enhancement of the customer's holiday, in terms of variety, quality, and so on.

The typical customer was from the United States. Americans were described as 'wanting culture with a capital K'. They usually were poorly informed and were governed in their choices by general considerations like, 'staying in the "right" hotel, seeing the countryside, and visiting woolen mills'. The form of product differentiation that kept customers loyal was being very involved with them and fulfilling their wants through quality service.

Pricing of products was influenced by the volume which Firm G expected to deliver. Price was based on a flexible percentage mark-up on variable cost per unit. The owner-manager did not consider that his competitors' pricing policies were crucial to his own pricing and he said that he would not hold down Firm G's price to beat that of his competitors. If a boom in demand were to occur that could not be met from stocks it was thought that, firstly, Firm G would engage subcontractors and, secondly, would try to increase capacity (which could include the recruitment of more personnel). Faced with a recession the owner-manager thought that he would, firstly, cut price, followed by an increase in sales effort. If demand were to fall for a specific product within the main product group then it was thought that the initial action would be to switch to a new product, followed by an increase in sales effort for the specific product.

Firm G's costs were split up into fixed and variable costs. Fixed costs were low in relation to the value added, which would tend to be a stimulus to competition. These cost divisions were thought to be useful in the running of the business. Marginal cost was calculated, and it was thought to fall steadily as additional units of the service were supplied. As evidence of dynamic scale economies in the face of a marked decline in the volume sold of the main product over the three years from 1985 (down from 95 per cent by value of output to 5 per cent), unit variable cost rose for this product by 20 per cent. In the first interview in 1985 the owner-manager claimed not to recognize a capacity output. A subsequent interview in 1985 revealed that a capacity output could, in principle, be recognized, but this was invisible to the customer, as subcontracting was frequently used to deliver services beyond the firm's normal capacity. Given the seasonal nature of the tour business, with high demand in summer and low demand in winter, Firm G experienced intermittent 'off season' excess capacity. There was low supplier concentration, and Firm G's switching costs in changing suppliers were perceived to be very low by the owner-manager. Indeed, the rationale for Firm G's business revolved around this capacity to obtain suppliers' services at least cost. However, the whole supply network needed constant maintenance. Provided channels were established, and kept open by communication, even if deals were not always struck, a new deal could always potentially be concluded by a short telephone call. Hotels, for example, were usually eager to maintain contact with Firm G. They often had unanticipated excess capacity, and welcomed filling this on a one-off basis. For other closely networked suppliers as well, like car rental firms, and travel agents, it was felt to be mutually beneficial to keep channels open and busy.

Because channel access had to be so assiduously cultivated by incumbent firms in order to be successful in their brokerage function of creating tour packages, lack of these channels constituted a major barrier to entry for potential entrants. As the owner-manager put it, 'Knowing the right hotels, car rental firms and travel agencies is essential'. It was thought that incumbent firms could even survive with relatively inferior service, 'provided they had the contacts'. This provides a good example of a significant barrier to entry being an impediment to economic efficiency. Experience in the trade was important for channel access, and also in designing a good advertising campaign. It was possible that channels could be ruined (e.g. by slowness in honouring debts or by being overly punctilious with details after contracts had been concluded), so an investment on channels was an aspect of deterrence.

Firm G did use market research methods, including forecasts by official bodies and trade associations. The results were used to identify how high the interest of buyers was likely to be in Firm G's services, and also to try to forecast any future developments in the market. Marketing and sales promotion were thought to be crucial to stimulating demand for Firm G's products, and this was thought to be true for other firms in the industry. The form of advertising, and the target group for advertising messages, were also thought to be critical to the firm's performance. Rivals' advertising strategies were examined carefully, in relation to the type of service they had on offer. Customers were usually asked how they had found out about Firm G, especially if they were valued American customers. For a small price variation, up or down, of 5 per cent about the established price, given normal business conditions and no responses by rivals, demand was thought to be relatively inelastic. However, for a large price variation (10 per cent), under the same conditions, whilst demand was thought to be relatively inelastic for a price cut, it was thought to be elastic for a price increase. This is the classic case of a 'kinked demand curve' response.[13] If Firm G were to reduce its price it was thought that this would not evoke a price reduction by its strongest competitors, whether business conditions were normal, depressed or buoyant. This lack of reponse by competitors was also thought to be true, were a price to be increased. Consistent with this, the owner-manager felt that he had considerable elbow room in pricing within which a change in Firm G's pricing would not evoke changes in pricing by competitors. This elbow room was estimated to be some 10–15 per cent about the current price. To the extent that price *was* changed, it was reported to be in reponse to cost changes.

Price discrimination was practised by Firm G for different customers. Price rebates were offered in the form of bulk discounting. This pricing stategy was particulary relevant to customers who were companies, and therefore had some bargaining leverage. There was no such thing as a controlled price or a recommended price in Firm G's market. Given the bespoke nature of the package provided, pricing was often unique to a customer. What a customer might wish was only limited by what he might pay. The owner-manager said, 'If the price is right, there is nothing the firm cannot do'. The owner-manager did advertise his SBE's services. This took the form of individual advertising, that is, advertising aimed at promoting Firm G's services over those of its rivals. The owner-manager was prepared to increase advertising during slump conditions, but not to decrease it during boom conditions. Competition in the market was described as 'generally strong', but 'weak' in some aspects. Given the robustness of the industry, in terms of current and expected growth, and the extreme market fragmentation, firms were generally content to exploit their own niches, without infringing upon other firms' territories. The existence of substitutes, conceived of as an extra-industry competitive force, was not thought to be important. If a customer did not buy from within the industry, the only substitute available was for him to organize a tour himself. Given lack of channel access, this was time-consuming, costly and likely to lead to an inferior product. Customers were thought to be aware of the disutility of attempting to create their own substitutes, in effect, by attempting to backward integrate.

'Good' competitors were thought to be important to the functioning of the industry, because subcontracting was common, and often worked on a *quid pro quo* basis. It was necessay to be sure that a subcontracter delivered services of requisite quality. There was some concern expressed about 'pirates' or 'fly-by-nighters' in the industry who could damage its reputation. An attempt was made to marginalize such traders by word of mouth with established rivals of good reputation, suppliers and customers. This was the only sense in which an attempt was made to manage rivals' assumptions, as an aspect of defensive strategy, and was only applied to 'bad' competitors.

At the time of inception of this business the most important sources of information for the owner-manager were, in order of decreasing importance, family and friends, the local enterprise trust and the Scottish Development Agency, currently Scottish Enterprise. The approximate size of the business at inception (January 1984), in terms of total assets (book value) was estimated to be £4,000 at nominal prices. At the time of interview in 1985 the approximate size of the business using the same measure was £15,000 at nominal prices. By 1988 the total asset figure (book value) was still reported to be £15,000 at nominal prices, suggesting that assets had not been revalued appropriately. The owner-manager reported that he had not experienced any difficulty in obtaining financial support at the time of starting the business. He had acquired finance, firstly, from friends and relatives, secondly, by using hire purchase and, thirdly, by borrowing from the bank. To secure this funding he had had to provide financial guarantors. The Enterprise Allowance Scheme had been found to be helpful in the start-up phase of the business.

The gearing ratio (i.e. debt–equity) at financial inception of the business had stood at 3.0. This had proved to be the highest gearing ratio in Firm G's existence. At the time of initial interview in 1985 the gearing ratio figure stood at 0.75, which had also been its lowest figure. In 1985 the gearing ratio was expected to fall for the first year ahead, then to stay the same in the second, and then to rise in the third. It was thought that the gearing ratio would behave this way despite an expected increase in ploughed back profits in the second year. An increase in the owner-manager's personal financial injections was expected in the first year and an increase in debt in the third year.

In the event, this expected future pattern of gearing did occur. At the time of reinterview in 1988, the equity gearing ratio stood at 1.6. Firm G had experienced cash-flow difficulties which were thought to be due to an insufficient overdraft facility, although delinquent debtors were a contributary factor. The owner-manager had resorted to using external finance since starting the business. It had been used to purchase new or expanded business premises and also to deal with the aforementioned cash-flow problems. The owner-manager said he expected to see growth in his business over the forseeable future. It was thought there would be a general expansion of demand for the services of tour agencies, particulary driven by the US buyers, who would become the focus of attention. Along with this, there was likely to be upward price flexibility in the pricing of Firm G's services. For success to be sustained it was felt to be neccessary to establish a direct realtionship with US travel agencies, and to be active on new advertising fronts, like press releases. The owner-manager felt confident about his prospects in an expanding industry, and said, 'It is really just a matter of marketing'. As the industry expanded, it was thought that product demand would become increasingly 'upmarket': average service quality and price were rising. There was little fear expressed of the prospect of losing business. It was felt that provided channels continued to mature, especially for customers who were companies (e.g. from the United States), Firm G would continue to prosper.

Because of this buoyant attitude, deriving from the view that 'there are more than enough customers for everyone', the main emphasis, in terms of business strategy, was on developing and exploiting new niches rather than defending old ones. Thus, filling product gaps by providing new unique tours, which certainly had defensive implications, in terms of market pre-emption, was more stimulated by high demand (and hence high profit-ability) than by a desire to outdo rival firms. Similarly, one could tie up suppliers (e.g. by being the first to arrange exclusive car rental services for a new hotel) with a view to making it easier to meet one's own customers' demands. This would have the beneficial side effect, from a business strategy standpoint, of increasing barriers to entry for rivals, in the sense of raising their input costs. The owner-manager of Firm G was aware that the capturing of large customers (e.g. companies), who might bring high-volume repeat custom, raised exit costs. This, in turn, would increase Firm G's willingness to retaliate if newcomers challenged this part of its business. Such prime customers, along with the channels which were nurtured to capture them, created a stock of goodwill for the firm, which would have to be sacrificed on exit.

In 1988 the owner-manager reported that he had sensed the emergence of an enterprise culture in Scotland. He said that there had generally been 'success in the business area of "tours" for many small firms'.

2.7 PROFILE L: WINE RETAIL DISTRIBUTION

Firm L had been in operation since April 1984. It was a wholesale dis-tributor of wines. At the time of initial interview in 1985, it employed one full-time worker and had an annual sales turnover (excluding VAT) of £72,000 (1985 prices). In terms of legal form, Firm L was a one-man business. Its net profitability in 1985 was 100 per cent. However, other beverage firms (e.g. suppliers of draught drinks) were 'moving into wines', and many small distributors like Firm L were feeling the pinch on profit margins. Within six months, the owner-manager had revised his expected profitability figure downwards to 20 per cent, and then, within two years, to 17 per cent. The owner-manager described his own profit expectations in terms of words like 'modest' and 'realistic'. It was thought that reducing profit targets might decrease the interest of brewer's in Firm L's market segment. The owner-manager was changing his strategy towards one of high sales turnover and high gross profit, abandoning hope of a high profit margin strategy.

By the time of reinterview in 1988, not only had Firm L remained in business, but it had grown substantially. By this point in time it had four full-time employees and two part-time employees. The owner-manager never recruited trainees as such, as 'training was given on the job'. He had never experienced a shortage of any kind of skilled labour. Firm L's sales turnover figure (excluding VAT) had increased to £360,000 (at 1988 prices) by 1988 which represents a real growth in sales turnover of over 90 per cent p.a. Firm L's main product-group in terms of sales value was wine. It had a range of two to five product groups and sold over eighty products in total. In terms of product differentiation Firm L's main product group was thought to be 'similar' to those of its competitors. More remote substitutes like beer had been in decline because wine was regarded as a better alternative for many social occasions on which alcohol was drunk. Wine was particularly popular in hotels and restaurants and tended to be drunk by younger customers. 'Wine coolers' (a mixture of wine and fruit juice) were perceived to be a competitive threat, but it was thought they would not be serious long-term substitutes for wine itself. Indeed, the owner-manager thought that it could be responsible for introducing people to wine in an adulterated form, who would then want to go on to the real thing, thus further expanding demand. Overall, the owner-manager thought such substitutes would operate to his advantage. As a consequence, he had started supplying 'wine coolers' to customers himself, on a limited scale. The owner-manager thought that Firm L had an advantage in the marketplace over rivals in terms of the variety of services on offer. Key features were the extensive range of wines (running to several hundreds), the sale of wine draught pumps, the making-up of bespoke wine lists, and the provision of own-label bottles. No known rival provided more than two of these features. Restauranteurs thought that own-label bottles supplies by Firm L particularly enhanced the quality image of their own establishments.

The owner-manager regarded his principal market as the region in which he was located (western Scotland). Firm L's strategy was to provide reliable and prompt delivery to customers in this region. At its capacity it could not cater for customers outside this region without pushing up the costs too much. In terms of this principal market it was thought that Firm L had a 31–50 per cent market share for its main product group. Over the period 1985 to 1988, the volume of Firm L's main product line changed substantially. The output change of its main product in this period had been an increase of approximately 1,500 per cent. The corresponding percentage change in unit variable cost was a small percentage, where the principal cost contributors were raw materials (+5 per cent) and labour costs. Although output and unit cost had varied substantially over a three-year period, the output mix was rather similar. Firm L did, however, see itself as attempting to fill product gaps (e.g. for wine coolers and draught pumps) which slightly varied its product mix. The owner-manager could not distinguish between major and minor competitors, but he was able to estimate that he had some eleven to thirty competitors in total. He evaluated competition in his industry as being 'intense in every aspect', which covered all the key dimensions like price, quality, delivery, and so on. He said that the industry was becoming more competitive 'day by day'. This was particularly caused by diversification of brewers into wine distributors' traditional markets, which in turn encouraged wine distributors to diversify, seeking new product niche markets and undertaking minor innovations. By 1988 there had been a change in competitiveness in Firm L's principal market and this had been brought about by innovations undertaken by both Firm L and its rivals. Firm L was always striving to stay ahead of its rivals. For example, it was the first to provide draught pumps for wine and 'own label' bottles in its particular market segment. The owner-manager regarded Firm L as 'always on the look-out for new ideas'. He regarded his own innovations as a 'leap-frogging' response to attacks on his market segment by brewers diversifying into wines. He thought that the principal barrier to entry faced by new firms was 'knowledge and experience'. It took three years to build up a business in the wine trade and establish a customer base, during which time little or no profit would be made. Once established, a new firm had to rely on goodwill and efficient delivery to customers to deter further entrants.

Customers in general could not distinguish on technical grounds between the differences in the products sold by Firm L and its competitors. Thus price, brand, advertising intensity, packaging and service all determined these customers' attitudes. A small group of Firm L's customers were fairly expert and could draw upon personal experience and specialist information in making their own judgements about the technical quality of the product. The 'lion's share of sales' was said to come from restaurants, hotels and public houses. They were valued customers as they purchased in bulk and on a steady basis. Typically, customers were well aware of other firms in the industry. In good business conditions loyalty was high, but in bad business conditions the loyalty factor tended to subside and customers became very price sensitive and prone to switching suppliers. In general, customers were perceived to have a great deal of bargaining leverage. Because pricing was so competitive, Firm L tried to raise customers switching costs. This was done by emphasizing the quality of service (e.g. quick delivery, thirty days' credit, wide selection of wines, making-up wine lists for customers). Firm L provided guarantees to customers on the quality of wine. Any unopened bottles from a batch could be returned. If a customer bought a wine pump, it would be guaranteed the right to buy wine from Firm L at a discount. However, it was known that this might eventually encourage the backward integration of some customers. The owner-manager made the following generalization: 'Restaurants are more concerned with what is in the bottle. Off-licences are more concerned with what the bottle looks like'. As customers, restauranteurs were impressed with Firm L's variety of wines and with the knowledge of the owner-manager.

The pricing of a new product would not be determined independently of the amount to be sold. Prices were determined as a flexible mark-up on variable cost per unit. The owner-manager reported that the pricing policy of his competitors was crucial to that of Firm L's pricing, although he was not willing to hold down price to beat his competitors. By contrast, brewers who had newly diversified into his market were dropping prices in an attempt to capture a share of the wine market, a strategy which they were driven to by their own declining sales in beer markets. Some of the big companies were even adopting the short-term strategy of selling wine at cost to deter potential, as well as existing, rivals.[14] Firm L thought it could 'ride out' this short-term strategy. It was well established, had low overheads and a reliable delivery system, and it was felt that this would enable it to absorb the brewers' penetration of the market. However, it was thought that younger, less well established firms might become victims of the brewers' actions.

If a boom in demand were to occur which could not be met from stocks, the owner-manager thought that, firstly, he would increase overtime or shiftwork and, secondly, raise price. Faced with a recession it was thought that, firstly, an attempt would be made to improve efficiency or productivity, then stockholding would be reduced, next price would be cut and finally an increase in sales effort would be made. If demand were to fall for a particular product, it was thought that actions would be undertaken in the following order: an increase in sales effort, an increase in quality, a reduction in price and, finally, a switch to new products.

Costs were split up into fixed and variable costs. The distinction between these costs was found to be useful in the running of the business. The owner-manager did calculate marginal cost and he recognized a maximum capacity output. He thought that Firm L normally operated at less than 50 per cent of its maximum capacity. It was thought that Firm L's approximate cost pattern was one in which the cost of supplying each extra unit initially fell as more units were supplied, but then ultimately rose after a particular point. In other words, it was a typical economist's pattern of U-shaped average costs.[15] Costs were carefully monitored and controlled. In particular, inventory costs were set at a level which was optimal in terms of providing customer choice, yet not blocking cash-flow. Suppliers were not concentrated and had little bargaining power. It was thought that the switching costs of changing suppliers were low. In the past, the owner-manager of Firm L had experienced problems with various suppliers in terms of a poor delivery record and inferior products, and had needed to switch suppliers. It therefore had first-hand experience of the switching costs involved. Out of the fifty or so known suppliers, he had finally settled for just one main supplier who was reliable and who, above all, priced his products very low. Overheads were kept as low as possible, and the owner-manager aimed to spread them over as large a sales volume as possible. His immediate target in 1985 had been to double sales, thereby spreading overheads, a goal which he managed to achieve very rapidly. As sales volume increased, the plan was to increase the volume of directly imported wine from the continent of Europe. This would 'cut out the middle man in London' and reduce costs significantly. However, Firm L would now have to deal directly with import duties, would have to administer the VAT and would have to make sure bulk storage did not become a new source of upward pressure on costs. The transfer to direct continental purchase was planned to be 'a gradual process, justified only by a great increase in sales volume'.

Market research methods were employed by Firm L. These results were used for diverse reasons: to find out how price sensitive customers were; to find out the interest of buyers in Firm L's products; to find out the potential reactions of competitors; and to forecast future developments in the market. Trade magazines and suppliers were used by the owner-manager of Firm L to keep himself informed of new trends, new methods and merchandising, and so on. Customers were found to be a good source of information, particularly when deliveries were being made, at which point it was often possible to observe directly what was happening in the marketplace. On the assumption that Firm L's competitors did not react and that business conditions were normal, it was thought that for a small (5 per cent) price decrease demand would be totally inelastic (i.e. would not increase at all). For a small price increase it was thought that demand would be relatively inelastic (i.e. would fall by less than 5 per cent). For a large (10 per cent) price decrease it was thought that demand would be relatively inelastic, but for a large price increase it was thought that demand would be relatively elastic.[16]

The significance of the costs of purchasing from Firm L in relation to the customer's total costs varied greatly amongst customers. For hotels and restaurants it was thought that supply costs were 'quite insignificant'. This tended to decrease the price sensitivity of such customers. They still had a lot of bargaining power because they were bulk purchasers and tended to exert this power by insisting on a high quality of service (e.g. in terms of reliability). By contrast, public houses and off-licences tended to be more conscious of the purchase costs of wine in relation to their total costs, and were more price sensitive. The owner-manager thought that if Firm L reduced price its strongest competitors would not follow this action in any business conditions be they normal, buoyant or depressed. The same was thought to be true of a price increase.[17] The owner-manager believed that there was a certain amount of elbow room in pricing, within which responses by rivals would be negligible, and this elbow-room was thought to be as large as 15 per cent or more.

Events that the owner-manager thought might lead to an alteration in Firm L's selling price were many. They included the commencement of a new business or new tax year, the occurrence of cost changes, a substantial change in the volume or in the quality of demand, and a change in the price set by the most important competitor. Price discrimination was practised for large and small traders, and price rebates were also offered in the form of bulk discounting. This was done, for example, to purchasers of wine pumps, and the tactic was thought to encourage cooperation and goodwill amongst indirect competitors. Controlled prices were unheard of, but Firm L's goods were sold at recommended prices, and these were paid by 31–60 per cent of its customers. Advertising was not undertaken formally by Firm L, but what the owner-manager described as 'reading between the lines of other firms' advertising' allowed him to gain insight into what was selling well.

The owner-manager did not approach anyone for advice about getting his business started. The approximate size of his business in terms of total assets (book value) at business inception in 1984 was £8,000 at nominal prices. One year later in 1985, this figure had risen to £27,000. By 1988 this figure had grown to £52,000 (1988 prices) representing a real annual growth rate in assets over 1985–8 of about 16 per cent. It was reported that difficulty had been experienced in obtaining financial support for starting the business caused by a lack of personal financial injections. Only personal finance was used in the setting up of the business. Therefore the gearing (i.e. debt–equity) ratio at business inception was zero, and this was also Firm L's gearing ratio at the time of interview in 1985. The highest figure the gearing ratio had reached since inception was 0.43. In 1985 the owner-manager expected Firm L's gearing ratio to rise over the next year, due to an increase in debt, but could not comment further, as his planning horizon did not extend beyond the first year. In the event, the gearing ratio rose in 1986, fell in 1987, and rose again in 1988, by which point it stood at 0.5.

It was found that the Enterprise Allowance Scheme, an employment grant and reduced rental on premises were all necessary to the success of the start-up of the business, which had been located in a custom built industrial estate on the west coast of Scotland. Unfortunately, direct investment grants were not available to this type of firm, though other types of implicit subsidy were, as noted. The owner-manager reported that he had not experienced any cash-flow difficulties. Whilst external finance, in the form of debt, had been sought since the inception of Firm L, it had not been used to stave off cash-flow problems but to increase stock. The owner-manager thought that suppliers' credit terms were important. Firm L was able to command a two-month credit period with suppliers. Given that Firm L insisted on a one-month credit period with its own customers, the net effect was described as 'highly advantageous to cash-flow'. Further, to optimize cash-flow, inventory was tightly monitored and controlled. In 1985, the owner-manager had expected growth for Firm L in the foreseeable future. Behind this expectations of growth was knowledge of a change in taste, away from beers to wines, which was attributed to the cheapness of continental holidays, during which a taste for wines was acquired by new customers. The owner-manager pointed out that wine sales in the United Kingdom were growing at a rate of 24 per cent p.a. It was expected that this growth rate would continue for two years, with the market reaching saturation after five years. This expectation was confirmed in a very tangible fashion by 1988, because by then Firm L had achieved admirable growth in terms of sales, assets and employment. This was all the more remarkable an accomplishment for being in the field of retail distribution.

In 1988, the owner-manager said that he did recognize the emergence of an enterprise culture in Scotland. He commented that 'Government policy has led they way for this culture' and that more people were available 'to have a go' at setting up a small business. He was aware that success was not guaranteed and that established firms had survival advantages over new firms, but felt that generally the market selected fairly against the less efficient firms.

2.8 PROFILE Q: MANUFACTURE OF FILM AND THEATRE PROPS

This SBE had been in operation since February 1985. It had four full-time workers and no part-time workers or trainees. The business was a co-operative managed on a rotational basis by its co-owner. Its sales turnover in the previous tax year (excluding VAT) had been approximately £35,000 at nominal prices. Its product group range was between six and ten and its total number of products was in the range sixty-one to eighty. Scotland was regarded as Firm Q's principal market and its share in this market was 21–30 per cent.

The co-owner interviewed could distinguish between major and minor competitors and it was thought that there were between eleven and thirty major competitors, and between one and five minor competitors. No obvious substitutes for the products of Firm Q were thought to be available outside of this group of competitors. This was so because of the customized or bespoke nature of the products produced by this competitive group of firms. In principle, factory-based manufactures of costumes could be regarded as substitutable for costume supply by a theatrical props firm, but factories lacked the necessary capability for costume research (for period dress) and had little design capability in this area. It was thought that whilst factory production might appear to be cheaper, this was illusory. Supervision and monitoring costs would soar to achieve the necessary quality. High quality was essential to ensure the necessary authenticity of appearance of products used in film and theatre work. It was thought that customers therefore had a low propensity to substitute into factory items.

Product market concentration was perceived to be low. Possibly it was increasing. Firm Q was not taking active steps to increase its market share. The co-owners tended to react to orders, rather than to actively seek work. On the factor market side, supplier concentration was thought to be generally low, though this varied by product. Suppliers were relatively less concentrated than buyers, putting the balance of bargaining power on the buyer side. Also switching costs were relatively higher for customers (i.e. buyers) compared to suppliers. The products of suppliers were generally highly standardized. In most cases substiutes were readily available, though Firm Q might have to go 'further afield' to get an alternative supplier. Seeking out substitute suppliers was common, and it was more motivated by supply limitations than perceived quality differentials. Switching costs in changing suppliers were low.

In general, customers were thought to be expert in determining, by their own judgement, the technical quality of the product. Customer concentration was high. There were about five major customers. They would bear significant switching costs in transferring their custom to other suppliers. There was a significant shared design 'know-how' in supplier–customer relations. It was said that 'filling in the detail is important'. Customers, being well informed, could use this knowledge to exert some leverage over suppliers like Firm Q, though they were generally ignorant of detailed technical specification. The co-owner interviewed reported that Firm Q's main product-group was 'identical' to that of competitors, implying low product differentiation. To the extent that there was differentiation it was in terms of speed, reponse, skill and especially reliablity and range of competence. The co-owner interviewed thought her firm had 'a wider range than most'. This affected the willingness and ability of suppliers to subcontract. Skill was thought to be a major barrier to entry, and it was estimated that it took five years to acquire, to a professional level, the many skills required of a theatrical props supplier. As a consequence, the co-owner thought her firm had high strategic stakes in the industry. It was felt that a source of uniqueness in the value chain of Firm Q was the rich mix of skills which the workforce possessed. In principle, this skill mix could command a high rental. The co-owner interviewed thought that identifying the 'real customer' (i.e. the specific person with the power to initiate a purchase) was important. It was known that some members of production and camera crews had a measure of autonomy in specifying suppliers of props. For this reason it could pay to cultivate specific individuals on a film set. It was thought that irrational factors could work in one's favour. Being liked in the fraught world of theatre was thought to be useful. The 'real customer' particularly valued the quality of the product and the ability to meet deadlines. An example was referred to in which filming was held up for four hours (a very expensive delay) because a rival firm had supplied a jacket of the wrong colour.

Pricing was not influenced by the volume of production the co-owners expected to sell. Price was mainly determined as a flexible mark-up on variable cost per unit of output, though price could be specified by Firm Q's principal customer and/or by reference to price guidelines. The pricing policy of competitors was not thought to be crucial to Firm Q's own pricing. Consonant with this, prices would not be held down to beat those set by competitors. If a boom in demand were to occur, such that demand could not be met from stocks, three courses of action would be taken: firstly, overtime or shiftwork would be increased; then subcontractors would be engaged and, finally, an attempt would be made to increase capacity (this could include the recruitment of more personnel). In a recession, it was thought that the courses of action taken would be, in the following order: to reduce overtime; to increase sales effort; to improve productivity or efficiency and, finally, to introduce short-time working. In the face of a fall in demand for a particular product in the main product group the co-owner felt that increasing sales effort would be her first reaction, followed by switching to a new product.

Costs were split up into fixed and variable costs and these cost divisions were thought to be useful in the operation of this SBE. Fixed costs were low relative to value added (estimated at less than 50 per cent of total value).

The co-owners had deliberately chosen a low-cost location (in terms of rent) on the edge of a major city for this SBE. Rents varied widely by location for the sorts of premises required for Firm Q's work, and choosing a low-cost location was one of the best ways of controlling costs. Many costs were uncontrollable and based on given prices (e.g. raw materials prices, union-determined wages). Even so, the wage bill, which was a major cost-driver, could in some measure be controlled by varying the proportion of overtime to standard hourly work. At the time of interview the co-owners were trying to discourage overtime, except to meet 'short orders' (i.e. customer orders that had to be rapidly met), when the premium price charged for rapidly delivered products could offset higher wage costs. The co-owner felt that costs were already tightly controlled, and that a cost-reduction strategy was not sustainable. In terms of strategy, emphasis on differentiation was thought to be sensible and sustainable, though the idea of this being a 'focus' was viewed with cynicism: demand was thought to be 'too quixotic'.

The co-owner recognized a capacity output and she estimated that the firm 'normally' operated at between 51–60 per cent of capacity. This was an average figure. She explained that the overcapacity was intermittent, but generally Firm Q worked close to capacity. The firm was very adaptive to 'short orders', hence the capacity utilization variation; and much of the work done was of this nature. This pattern of work arose because the production companies, who were principal customers, themselves worked sporadically. They had some in-house theatrical props production facilities, but thought it too risky (in terms of carrying an excessive workforce for dealing with a low average level of business) to backward-integrate fully. This feature of trade encouraged production companies to subcontract to the likes of Firm Q. The co-owner thought that total cost increased in line with supply until the maximum possible supply (maximum capacity) was reached. After this point had been reached, the extra cost of supplying an extra unit rose sharply. For typical ranges of output there were thought to be no scale advantages.

The co-owners of Firm Q did not use formal market research methods of any kind. However, co-owners did attend trade shows. These were used to acquire trade information and to signal the presence of Firm Q to others in the trade network. Trade contacts were cultivated, and the co-owner was aware of the danger of getting isolated from sources of knowledge of technical advance. It was felt that the co-owners were effective in keeping their ears to the ground on such matters. Demand was thought to be inelastic for a small price variation (5 per cent) about the established price. In the case of a large price variation (10 per cent) it was thought that for a price cut there would be no change in demand (i.e. inelastic demand), but for a price increase there would be about a unitary elasticity of demand.[18] The co-owner interviewed did not think that a price reduction by her firm would bring forth a price reduction by its strongest competitors in normal or buoyant business conditions. She was unsure about the reactions of Firm Q's competitors to a price cut in depressed business conditions. The co-owner believed that if she raised Firm Q's price, that its competitors would not follow its action in normal or depressed business conditions. However, given buoyant business conditions competitors would follow a price increase.

It was thought that Firm Q had a significant amount of elbow room in pricing, and it was estimated that it was about 10–15 per cent either side of current price. The reasons for this lack of price sensitivity by many customers had been given careful thought by the co-owners. An important reason for it was that when the customer was producing a film the cost of the props supplied was insignificant compared to film production costs. The principal cost-driver for such customers was time spent on location. It was felt that the more specialized was the product, the less price sensitive the customer would be. For example, the co-owners would be told whether a certain prop would ever be directly 'in shot' of the camera. If it would, then the quality had to be high, if the quality of the customer's product itself was to be kept high. This desire for quality by the customer reduced price sensitivity. Finally, price sensitivity was thought to be less the 'shorter' the order placed (i.e. the more rapidly the order had to be filled or met). If orders were placed at very short notice, as they sometimes were, price sensitivity was much reduced. With less short orders prices would sometimes be set by reference to agreed guidelines. Reliability in the face of short orders was thought to be an important aspect of product differentiation and reputation.

The co-owner reported that the main reasons, in descending order of importance, for altering Firm Q's selling price were: when cost changes occurred; when demand shifted substantially; when demand changed; when a regulatory agency permitted an increase; and when wage bargaining negotiations were concluded. Firm Q did practise price discrimination. Different prices were charged in different marketing areas, in home and foreign markets, for different customers, and for large and small traders. Price rebates were not offered by Firm Q. There was no such thing as a controlled price or a recommended price, though for non-urgent orders pricing guidelines might be referred to. These guidelines were established in line with trade union rates and were adhered to for many jobs which were non-urgent. The use of such guidelines militated against using entry deterring pricing against potential rivals. The co-owner reported that Firm Q did advertise, using both generic and individual advertising methods. Advertising was reported to increase when business demand was low and to decrease when business demand was buoyant. Competition was described in this market as generally weak, but strong in some aspects. The dominant form in which competition expressed itself was 'by getting the order'. This co-owner regarded Firm Q's main competitive advantage as being its capacity to provide a wide range of services. This know-how was regarded as having created a significant entry barrier. The learning curve was thought to tail off slowly. It took years of experience and training to be proficient across the full range of the SBE's activities. Access to channels was also a significant barrier to entry. It took years to cultivate contacts, and to know 'where to get what, and from whom'. By contrast, capital requirements were low and were not thought to constitute a significant barrier to entry. The co-owner interviewed denied a conscious use of defensive strategy against competitors. If custom were lost, Firm Q's personnel might discreetly try to discover why. Retaliatory action might be contemplated. It was said that 'defence would depend upon the attack'. If substitutes from outside the industry were thought likely (e.g. a challenge from factory-based clothes manufacturers in the period costume market niche), a collective industry reponse by props manufacturers was thought to be quite feasible. It was denied that retaliation as such had yet been attempted. There was a willingness to signal a committment to defend Firm Q's market niche and to match guarantees offered by rivals to potential customers. There was no willingness to reduce profit targets to lower the inducement for attack. However, the same aim might be realized by consciously managing competitors' assumptions. The trade network might be used for this purpose.

At the time of starting the business the most important sources of advice, in decending order of importance, were the local enterprise trust, the local government authority and the Scottish Development Agency (now Scottish Enterprise). The approximate size of this SBE at inception, in terms of total assets (book value), was zero and the approximate size of it at the time of interview in 1985 was £7,000 (at 1985 prices). No difficulty had been experienced obtaining financial support at the time of starting the business, though only the personal finances of the co-owners were used to set up the business. The gearing ratio of Firm Q had been 2.5 at the point of financial inception, as distinct from business launch (earlier that year). This was also the gearing ratio figure at the time of interview. This figure had been the only value of Firm Q's gearing ratio. The co-owner expected Firm Q's gearing to fall in the course of the next three years due to an increase in ploughed-back profits.

The following schemes were found helpful in the starting-up of the business: the Enterprise Allowance Scheme, a reduced rental on premises and a local authority interest-free loan. Firm Q had experienced cash-flow difficulties. An inadequate credit policy with suppliers was thought to be the main reason for these difficulties. External finance had been sought to deal with this problem but had not been obtained at the time of interview. The co-owner expected to see growth in her business over the forseeable future. The fact that more feature films were being produced in Scotland was thought to imply potentially rapid industry growth. With this in mind, expansion was being contemplated in 1985. The co-owners were contemplating extending the bundle of skills offered by Firm Q. As the firm expanded, it justified having personnel specializing further in different skills. Imitation of rivals was not being contemplated. There was some enthusiasm for extending activities into theatre wardrobing. Also forward integration into organizing complete wedding events had been contemplated. Three years later the firm was still in business but the co-owners were unwilling to be interviewed. One got the impression that growth expectations had not been fulfilled.

2.9 CONCLUSION

We conclude here our first set of Profiles of SBEs. They are, in a sense, the most typical, for monopolistic competition is very often the market structure within which the SBE operates. The reader will have had an opportunity to relate the instrumentation outlined in the Appendix to the structure of each Profile. He or she might have already become inspired to take evidence from the Profiles as the starting-point for further theoretical enquiry, for certainly they provide abundant material on which the tyro economic modeller can cut his or her teeth. As a guide to this sort of interest, we have included some fairly detailed technical notes, that hopefully can provide an introduction to the rigorous methods of industrial organization theorists.

On another level, more attuned to our intention in writing this book, what we have aimed to do is to lay further groundwork for the comparative analysis of Part III below. The construction of Profiles imposes on us the science-based task of careful data gathering and sifting, followed by presentation within a standardized framework. In and of itself this can be useful. It imposes order on our knowledge, and thus helps in the search for meaning. We pursue the enquiry further in this spirit in Chapter 3.

3 Medium market concentration

3.1 INTRODUCTION

To continue our within-site analysis, we present a further set of seven
Profiles. They relate to SBEs which operate in medium market concentration environments. The SBEs chosen from the parent sample are indicated in Table 3.1. These SBEs have very small market shares (typically < 1
per cent) within large markets, produce goods which are subject to little
product differentiation and enjoy quite high levels of capacity utilization.
We have chosen to view these SBEs as fringe competitors in a dominant
firm/competitive fringe market model.[1] As before, the developments in this
chapter provide a further basis for 'grounding' the theory of the SBE, and
are intended to advance by another step the systematic presentation of
evidence for use in the comparative analysis of Part III.

3.2 PROFILE F: FOODSTUFF MANUFACTURER

Firm F had been in existence since 1982 as a manufacturer of bakery food
products (pies, rolls, buns, etc.). At the time of interview in 1985 forty-seven
workers were employed full-time and there were three part-time workers. In
terms of legal form the business was a private company. It was run by two
brothers, who were co-directors. They were heavily involved in the day-to-
day running of the business, and could reasonably be categorized as owner-
managers. In 1985 the value of the sales turnover (excluding VAT) was
£650,000 at nominal prices. This SBE had a narrow product-group range of
between two and five, and it produced sixty-one to eighty products. The
main product group was pies. The director interviewed described his firm as

Table 3.1 SBEs profiled in medium-concentration markets

F	Foodstuff manufacturer – pies, doughnuts, etc.	K	Electronic instrumentation
I	Computer software	N	Bulk bag manufacturer
J	Cassette tape manufacturer	O	Chestnut fencing manufacturer
		P	Lamination and varnishing for printers

cultivating the image of 'a traditional baker, with good products, sold at competitive rates'. It was felt that differentiation of his products was assisted by an individualized approach arising from trade experience. The director regarded his firm's principal market (for its main product group) as being the region. In terms of this market the firm's market share was estimated at between 1 per cent and 5 per cent. Concentration was increasing over time in this market. For example, a new entrant from another region had just appeared, carrying a lot of excess capacity, with predatory intentions on this firm's market.

The director interviewed could distinguish between major and minor competitors, and it was estimated that there were between six and ten major competitors and over fifty minor competitors. Each competitor was located in his own niche, but there was some overlap in niches. Products in Firm F's main product group were perceived to be similar to those of its competitors. The owner-manager said, 'On the face of it, there are lots of similar products'. They were distinguished by quality and delivery, but otherwise not differentiated. Whilst there was no deliberate differentiation on the physical level, the director thought his own products were readily recognizable. Customers included shops (40–50 per cent), fast-food outlets and large institutions like schools, hospitals and universities. There was low customer concentration and little dependence on any one customer. The most important customer accounted for 15 per cent of sales, and many others for 5 per cent or less. Small customers made small orders on a cash basis, and were good for this SBE's cash-flow. About one-third of the customers did this. The bargaining leverage of customers was generally low. It was thought that customers could not distinguish technical differences between Firm F's products and those of its rivals. They were described as 'conservative and not well informed' and were thought to use rigid purchasing criteria, and to be resistant to change. It was thought important to know the 'real customers', but this took time. A quick 'capture' of customers was sought, and therefore the supermarkets were ruled out as customers. They tended to deliberate too much and too long before agreeing to a deal. Customers' attitudes would be influenced by price, specification, advertising, packaging and quality of service. However, the conservatism of customers meant that even small changes in the product could change their purchasing habits. This meant that introducing entirely new products was very hard and could require a massive marketing effort.

The pricing of a new product was influenced by the volume of sales which the director expected to achieve. Price was set as a percentage mark-up on direct cost per unit and fixed at a level which aimed to achieve a desired gross profit. The director interviewed was also willing to say that price was set at the highest level the market could bear. He admitted to distinguishing between customers by their reservation price (i.e. by the highest price they were willing to pay).[2] The pricing policy of competitors was not considered crucial to this SBE's pricing, though the director said he would hold down price to beat competitors. If a boom in demand were to occur, which could not be met from stocks, the first line of action would be to increase capacity, which could include the recruitment of personnel. Next, overtime and shift-work would be increased, followed by raising price. In a recession, the first line of action would be to increase sales effort, then an attempt would be made to improve productivity or efficiency, followed by reducing overtime. If demand were to fall for a product in the main product group the owner-manager thought that his first action would be enhancing quality, followed by increasing sales effort, and finally, switching to a new product.

Costs were split up into fixed (i.e. overhead, or indirect) and variable (that is, prime or direct) costs and this distinction was found to be useful in the running of the firm. Marginal cost was calculated and a capacity output was not recognized. Remarks made about costs were predicated on the use of sophisticated software for detailed cost accounting of each product line. This facilitated the computation of the relevant 'break-even' points of production for every product, beyond which production would necessarily be profitable. Very often this break-even point was achieved at high volumes of production. A problem in the first year of existence was the inability to achieve such high volumes. This led to a business loss in the first year. A potential disadvantage of high-volume production, once achieved, was that regulations became stiffer as volume increased, especially if packaging was involved.[3] This process was not thought to be too expensive, in terms of compliance costs,[4] and was being contemplated at the time of interview in 1985. It did not involve a departure into unfamiliar areas of food tech-nology.

Using the costing software, the director's computer monitor could display a standard linear break-even analysis, with linear total costs and total revenue, but the director interviewed thought this was not entirely accurate on the cost side. The pattern of Firm F's cost variation was thought to be reflected by the statement that total cost did not increase as fast as the amount supplied.[5] The director did not pursue a cost leadership strategy. The emphasis was rather on product variety and quality. At the time of interview, he worked on an overall costing margin for each product. Gener-ally an attempt had been made to eliminate the least profitable product-lines and, using crude data, some products had been dropped. The director was aware that this practice could be improved, and was starting to use his computer software to improve accuracy by costing every individual item. He identified the principal cost-drivers as labour costs, meat, flour and margarine. His analyses of these cost components was informal but up-to-date and involved various stylized facts. Thus he could tell you: 'Margarine prices have just come down; meat prices haven't moved much; flour prices follow an annual pattern, associated with seasons; labour costs follow the annual wage rounds'. Labour costs were thought to be subject to the greatest inertia, and margarine costs were thought to be the most volatile cost-driver. The business was thought of as 'effectively two businesses:

production and distribution' with the former business having forward-integrated into the latter. Each aspect offered opportunity for reconfiguring the value chain. For example, on the distribution side careful rescheduling of deliveries had been undertaken to minimise fuel costs. On the production side, the wage bill accounted for about one-third of total costs. An attempt had been made to control it more tightly by subtle changes in shiftwork arrangements.

Suppliers were quite concentrated. Because of the limited number of suppliers for each principal input, a deliberate attempt was made to avoid dependence on any one supplier. Three meat suppliers were used, for example. An attempt was made to play off one against the other by being fussy about the quality of the product. There was some scope for a similar bargaining tactic over the quality of margarine. The quality and price of margarine were particulary prone to fluctuations. Flour and meat suppliers had sometimes forward-integrated, but when they had done so, they had often left the downstream firm with considerable autonomy. Switching costs for both suppliers and customers were thought to be low. The directors of this SBE did not use any market research methods of a formal kind (e.g. forecasts by official bodies, trade associations). The directors did go to the relevant trade shows every other year, and found this helped image-building. It was not regarded as a means of beating off potential rivals. Rather, it helped suggest long-term market trends.[6]

Demand was thought to be price inelastic in reponse to a small (5 per cent) variation, up or down, in price. For a larger (10 per cent) price cut it was thought that demand would remain inelastic; though it was thought that demand would be price elastic in response to a 10 per cent price increase. The director interviewed did not think that a price reduction on his part would provoke his strongest competitors into reducing their prices in buoyant or normal business, though in depressed conditions he did expect his competitors to respond by reducing their prices. It was expected that if Firm F were to increase its price, then its competitors would also increase their prices under normal and boom conditions, but would not follow the price increase during a recession. The director thought that he had a certain amount of elbow room in pricing within which a price change did not bring about reactions from competitors. This elbow room was estimated to be between 4 per cent and 6 per cent. However, there was considerable variation in sensitivity to price by the customer type. The most price sensitive customers were hospitals; schools were more quality conscious and also keen on the reliability of deliveries. Quality elasticity could be high in the downwards direction, but this SBE avoided the low-quality end of the market.

The director was aware of the significance of the cost of the product in relation to overall costs for affecting price sensitivity. Thus the relative price sensitivity of hospitals compared to schools was attributed to the greater contribution of the food bill to total costs in the former case. The main reasons for altering this SBEs selling price were reported to be cost changes, demand changes, the conclusion of wage rounds and a price change by the most important competitor. The firm practised price discrimination between different customers and large and small traders, although no price rebates were offered. The director interviewed admitted to consciously using 'different price bands for different customers'. There were no controlled or recommended prices for this firm's goods. This SBE did not advertise.

Competition was perceived to be generally strong, but weak in some aspects (e.g. absence of price competition, but strong quality competition and inter-firm rivalry). The director was aware of many potential competitors, but would not attempt to pre-empt their actions. Rather he would 'take them as they come'. Imitation was not regarded as a threat because 'everyone knows how to make doughnuts'. Capital requirements were high and constituted a barrier to entry. Know-how was important and also constitued a barrier to entry. The directors were knowledgeable because Firm F had forward-integrated from production to distribution, and they also had retail experience. No attempt had been made to raise entry barriers against potential entrants, though this was not ruled out as a business strategy. The directors did not think in terms of retaliation if orders had been lost. However, they would enquire as to how it had happened, and would contemplate change (e.g. by altering a recipe) to suit the needs of a customer. It had been found in the past that this would often 'see off' challengers, leading to a regaining of lost orders. Because they had 'seen challengers come and go' in this fashion, they were not willing to match challengers' guarantees. The director had not thought in terms of lowering the inducement for attack. Indeed, he rarely felt his SBE was under attack, though he admitted that 'This could occur now and then for the odd product'. A typical response to such an attack would be to revamp a recipe. An atypical response would be to lower the profit target for this product-line, though this would not be ruled out: 'It would depend on the current situation'. Deterring attack was conceived to involve more of 'working *with* customers, rather than *against* rivals'. The director was aware of managing his firm's image, and thought this might have a deterrent effect, though this was not consciously pursued. Van drivers were a good source of intelligence. They could also be used to manage competitors' assumptions, though the director interviewed said, 'I did not say this was done'!

At the time of starting the business the directors had not approached anyone for advice. The approximate size of the firm at inception (in 1985) was £130,000 in terms of the book value of total assets at 1985 prices and this had not increased by the time of the 1985 interview. The director interviewed reported that he had experienced difficulty in obtaining financial support at the time of starting the business. The main obstacle in this respect was described as 'conservatism'. The sources of finance, apart from personal finance, used to set up the business were as follows, in decreasing order of importance: a loan from friends, relatives and aquaintances; hire purchase; and a loan from the bank. At financial inception the firm's gearing ratio was 4.0. The highest gearing ratio had been 8.0 and the ratio at the time of interview in 1985 was 3.0 which had proved to be the lowest level. The director expected the gearing ratio to fall over the next three years due to a perceived need to increase ploughed-back profits. Firm F had suffered from cash-flow problems caused by an insufficient overdraft facility. It had required external finance since the business started. This had been used to fund new or expanded premises. The director interviewed expected the overall market to grow over the forseeable future and expected his SBE to share in this growth. He had not prepared an industry scenario and thought it hard to anticipate what competitors might do. For his own SBE, he had made projections for its future profitability. Three years after the initial interview, the directors (brothers) of the earlier interviews were unavailable. They had sold their business to a larger concern, apparently on highly profitable terms.[7] They were now active in retail bakery, an area in which they had had prior business experience.

3.3 PROFILE I: COMPUTER SOFTWARE

Firm I had been in business since December 1983. It employed fifteen full-time workers, but no part-time workers or trainees. In terms of legal form it was a private company. It was run by a group of directors who were also owner-managers. It had an annual sales turnover (excluding VAT) of £250,000 (at 1985 prices). By 1988 Firm I was still in business, and had moved to larger and plusher premises nearby. Its annual sales turnover (excluding VAT) had risen greatly to £3.5 million (1988 prices) representing a real growth rate of approximately 380 per cent p.a. This growth in sales was also associated with a significant shift in product mix. What had been the main product-line in 1985 contributed proportionally very much less to total sales by 1988.

Firm I by this time had also experienced substantial growth in terms of workers. In 1988 the business employed ninety full-time workers and two part-time employees, representing a growth rate of some 170 per cent. The industry was expected to grow at 15–20 per cent p.a., but far higher growth rates had been expected, and achieved, by Firm I, which is to say that market penetration had been sought and achieved. Barriers to entry were thought to be low, with respect to scale, product differentiation and capital requirements. It was said that 'Know-how is the key barrier to entry'. Potential entrants were thought to face difficulties in getting good channels in the trade. Entry deterring pricing was unknown within the industry. 'Skimming pricing' had been tried,[8] but never to the detriment of good margins on profit: this applied to rivals, as well as to Firm I itself. As with entry barriers, exit barriers were low.

The director interviewed said that his SBE had experienced a shortage of skilled labour during the period 1985–8. This shortage was judged to have impeded the growth of Firm I. Difficulties had been encountered in trying to bridge this skill gap. The director was of the view that the two most important problems to solve as a result of this gap were, firstly, identifying the skills required and, secondly, assessing competitors' relative skills' advantages or disadvantages over Firm I. Other difficulties were, in descending order of importance: releasing personnel for training; bearing training costs; paying premium rates for labour possessed of scarce skills; and finally, and quite simply, 'finding the right people'. It was thought that competitors were highly diverse, with skills unevenly spread across firms in the industry. Industry leaders tended to have persistent skill advantages, which were reflected in their very high-quality products. A general feature of the industry was said to be that firms made a point of trying to address different problems, and 'different problems were solved in different ways'.

Firm I had few product groups (between two and five) and sold between eleven and twenty products. The main product group in terms of sales value was software development for subcontracts. It was thought that both Firm I and its rivals had been innovative in this software development, and that small and large firms alike in the industry had been involved in the process of innovation. Products in the main product group were sold on an international market, within which the market share for Firm I's software products was considered to be very small (< 1 per cent). The director interviewed could distinguish between major and minor competitors. He thought that he had between eleven and thirty major competitors and over fifty minor competitors. The industry was characterized as having medium levels of industrial concentration.

In terms of product differentiation, the main product group of Firm I was considered to be 'similar' to that of Firm I's competitors, though once a piece of software was adopted by customers, and then modified to special local requirements by Firm I, substitution for this software development was impossible. Firm I was not, however, emphasizing product differentiation in its marketing strategy. There were always a few substitutes available, and whilst switching costs were quite high, there were usually always some customers who were willing to substitute. They were particularly encouraged to do so if they could be convinced that product differentiation had been pushed so far that a new product was involved. It was admitted that such differentiation could sometimes be superficial. The director admitted 'a demand for gimmicks still exists in the sorts of markets in which we operate'. He aimed to help his SBE develop new products, and commended the company slogan 'new problems, new solutions'. However, Firm I usually did not itself develop new technologies but tried to take 'off the shelf' the latest technology available. It was said that 'The overriding issue is the "time to market" of a new product'.[9] This new product was typically talked of as 'being "high tech"' and it was this that was thought to be an important aspect of product differentiation. It was the major factor in enabling Firm I to keep ahead of rivals. A long-term goal of the director was to see Firm I keep ahead of rivals by continuous use of this high-tech strategy.

It was thought that most customers were well informed or expert and could determine by their own judgements the technical quality of Firm I's products. However, some customers were less expert and needed to be informed about technical features of the product or would themselves consult specialist journals to acquire the necessary information. Each firm in the trade had a limited number of customers. There was medium customer concentration, which was set against medium seller concentration. As a result, there was medium seller dependence. Firm I had to apply more bargaining effort with larger-volume customers. The switching costs of customers were generally high in the trade, though the owner-manager interviewed thought this was less true of Firm I's customers than of those of some of his rivals. Backward integration by customers could occur, but backward disintegration ('putting out work') was a notable counter tendency. Customers were generally not price sensitive: they were more interested in quality and delivery. The customer, viewed as a firm, was generally highly profitable, and this profitability did not crucially depend upon Firm I's product. This largely explains the low sensitivity of customers to pricing variation. On the other hand, the quality of customers' goods was dependent on the quality of goods purchased from businesses like Firm I. The director interviewed said he therefore emphasized quality in bargaining with customers, and that 'pricing is not high on the list of priorities'. The 'real customer' was typically well known.[10] It helped that personnel within Firm I had often worked previously with some of the customer firms.

Pricing was influenced by the expected volume of output. Price was set at the highest level the market could bear. This high price strategy led to a net profitability in 1985 of 24 per cent. The pricing policy of competitors was thought to be crucial to Firm I's own pricing, although the director said that he would not hold down price to beat competitors. If a boom in demand were to occur that could not be met from stocks the director thought that he would try, firstly, to increase capacity (which could include the recruitment of personnel); secondly, to increase overtime or shiftwork; thirdly, to lengthen the order book; and finally, to increase price. In a recession the director of Firm I thought he would, firstly, try to increase sales effort; secondly, cut price; thirdly, reduce capacity (including the laying-off of personnel); and finally, introduce short-time working. If demand were to fall for a specific product, the director thought that he would, firstly, switch to a new product; secondly, increase sales effort; thirdly, cut price; and finally, introduce short-time working.

Costs were split up into fixed and variable costs, and these cost divisions were thought to be useful in the running of Firm I. Marginal cost was understood as a term and was also calculated. A strict capacity limit was not recognized. Though the aim was to work close to the short-run capacity, it was known that capacity could be readily extended. Because of the revenue orientation of the firm, the director did not think in terms of principal cost-drivers. However, he felt that all firms in the market were benefiting from falling prices of factor inputs like computer components. It was said, 'We can now purchase small lots at high-volume prices'. For given plant, Firm I's cost pattern was thought to conform to the standard elongated reverse-S – that is, total cost increasing less rapidly than supply in the first instance, but eventually increasing faster than supply. The output increase over the period 1985 to 1988 had been immense (over 1,000 per cent) and this was associated with a 50 per cent reduction in unit cost. Here, dynamic scale economies were apparent. These were in some measure attributed to learning effects.[11] Suppliers of inputs were quite highly concentrated, but their products were not strongly differentiated. R & D was expensive for them, so most tended to steer clear of this source of differentiation. They emphasized high-volume production with low profit margins on very standardized products. Forward integration was uncommon. Switching costs of customers were generally high, but perhaps less so for customers of Firm I, compared to some of its rivals. Firm I as a customer of its own suppliers had negligible switching costs. Thus suppliers had no bargaining advantage.

The director did use market research methods and these were used to determine four things: the price sensitivity of customers; the interest of buyers in Firm I's products; the reaction of competitors; and the likely future developments in the market. A priority was put on marketing rather than on cost control, though the latter was felt to be good within Firm I. It was said that 'selling is the key', and personnel were encouraged to be revenue orientated rather than cost orientated. Costs were only to be thought of as incurred with a view to producing a marketable product. Attendance at trade shows, monitoring of courses, conferences, and so on, were thought to be important ways of discovering competitors' likely moves. Challengers were always taken seriously, and a response to their actions was always initiated. This response was thought to be part of defensive strategy, but it was 'never in the form of headlong collision'. Rather, response was said to be 'by deflection, especially through changing assumptions and getting into new product lines'. It was generally thought better to keep one step ahead of rivals rather than to engage in litigation. An attempt was made to protect copyright, but it was not always easy, and not always worth it, given the pace of change in Firm I's markets. It was accepted that 'reverse engineering' was an appropriate response to attack. This involves breaking down a rival product into constituent parts in order to work out, firstly, how to duplicate the product, and secondly, how to improve on it – if only marginally. In this way, it was said that one could change from a position of being behind a rival to being ahead. As the director put it, '"leapfrogging" is the name of the game'. However, defensive strategy was thought to be less important than offensive strategy.

Firm I was particularly aggressive in its marketing. It particularly targeted large firms as potential customers. It was willing to form coalitions with firms to arrange 'tie-in' deals. There was an awareness of the notion of a 'good' competitor, this being another firm that through the sharpness of its competition could improve one's own performance. If defensive strategy had to be used, it was not generally in the form of retaliation. It was admitted that some aspects of company development amounted to the accumulation of retaliatory resources, though the director said, 'This is a negative way to look at development'. It was certainly true that 'knocking tactics' would be used to diminish the status of rivals who were threatening to invade market territories. Beyond this, the director of Firm I was prepared to reduce profit targets to lower the inducement for attack by rivals. It was admitted that, in principle, the assumptions of rivals could be manipulated, but the director thought that only the very largest players in the game (of which Firm I was not an example) could do so effectively. For them, it was possible to take actions like managing assumptions which smaller rivals made about new product delivery dates. The director of Firm I thought it was desirable to try to anticipate challenges, both by entirely new entrants, and by entrants diversifying from adjacent market segments. One way of doing so was by constructing industry scenarios, one component of which was an analysis of potential entrants. As if to prove his point, the director turned and referred to an industry scenario sketched on the white board behind him, which had been the focus of the discussion within the company earlier that day.

It was unknown what the sales response would be to either a small (5 per cent) or large (10 per cent) price variation about the established price. It was thought that if Firm I reduced its price, competitors would not imitate this move in any business conditions, be they normal, buoyant or depressed. The same was thought to be true of a price rise. The director believed that he had a certain amount of elbow room in pricing within which a price change would not bring about a reaction by competitors. This elbow room was thought to be more than 15 per cent either side of the current price. Selling price was likely to be altered for a wide variety of reasons. Conventional factors included the start of a new business or a new tax year. Non-strategic economic factors included the occurrence of cost changes or a substantial demand shift. Strategic economic factors included whether or not important competitors had changed their prices, whether Firm I became aware it was selling too cheaply in the market, and how long it was thought an advantageous price change by Firm I could be sustained before detection by rivals. Price discrimination was practised by Firm I with prices being set differently for different marketing areas, for home and foreign markets, for different customers and for large and small traders. Price discrimination was also used to attract new customers. Price rebates were not offered and there was no such thing as a controlled or recommended price in Firm I's markets. Advertising was undertaken by Firm I in the form of individual advertising (i.e. promoting its product over that of its rivals). Advertising was not reduced in buoyant business conditions.

Competition in the market was described as generally strong, but weak in some aspects (e.g. absence of price competition, but strong quality competition and inter-firm rivalry). The main motivation within the company was to 'stay ahead of rivals' in a technical sense. Where imitators existed, the director said that 'The only way to beat such competitors is to outrun them'. Clear 'hunting grounds', as he called them, were set up for competitive endeavours. These were initially broad, but Firm I had steadily focused on narrower targets. Firm I used, referring here to computing terminology, as the director did, a 'bootstrapping' approach. A product was chosen to solve one new problem, which would often suffice to get a toe-hold in a niche market. Then technical developments would be built up on this single new feature, at the same time as building up market interest. The director saw Firm I as adopting a focus strategy based on differentiation. The market segments in which Firm I operated were interrelated, and facilitated diversification into other segments from an existing market position. Firm I, which was basically a software firm, was contemplating moving into an area of hardware manufacturing in a related segment. Here, Firm I hoped that 'bootstrapping' would work, as it had one new design feature for disc hardware which it was thought could give it a toe-hold in this new market segment.

At the time of starting the business, the most important sources of advice were, in decreasing order of importance: existing competitors; the firm's lawyer; family and friends; the Scottish Development Agency (now Scottish Enterprise); the bank manager; and finally, the accountant. The approximate size of the business in terms of total assets at inception (end of 1983) was £5,000. The business had grown substantially by the time of the first interview in 1985, when the approximate size of the business in terms of total assets was £100,000 at 1985 prices. By the time of reinterview in 1988, total assets had increased considerably to the value of £1,776,000, assets measured in each case at nominal book value, net of depreciation. This represents a phenomenal real growth rate in assets per annum of over 400 per cent.[12] No difficulty was encountered in obtaining financial support at the inception of the business since only personal finances were used to set up the business. In the early stages of the business the firm had not used any debt finance, so the gearing ratio had always stayed at zero. However, in 1985 the owner-manager interviewed thought that over the course of the next two years Firm I's gearing ratio would rise to a certain unspecified target value and then stay there. It was expected to behave this way in order to finance the rapid growth expected of the firm. The intention had been in 1985 to increase debt over the subsequent two years with an increase in the owners' injections after the second year stabilizing gearing at its desired level. The net profit (net of taxes and directors' fees) to do this in 1985 was £35,500 at 1985 prices. The possibility of an additional equity injection of outside finance was contemplated for the second year. The planning horizon did not extend beyond two years. In the event, Firm I's equity gearing ratio in 1988 stood at 2.7, having risen in each of the three years since 1985. Borrowing had averaged £150,000 each year. Firm I had suffered cash-flow difficulties mainly due to delinquent debtors. In 1985 the director had expected to see growth in his business over the foreseeable future, and this expectation had been strongly confirmed by 1988. However, despite this success, and the receipt of a prestigious business award for enterprise, the director did not sense an emergent 'enterprise culture' in Scotland in general. There had, in his view, been 'no general upsurge' in enterprise.

3.4 PROFILE J: CASSETTE TAPE MANUFACTURER

Firm J, a light manufacturing enterprise had been in operation since 1975 in the cassette tape duplicating industry. It employed four full-time workers. Firm J's annual sales turnover (excluding VAT) was £200,000 in 1985, at nominal prices. By 1988 Firm J was still in business. It had not grown in terms of personnel but had grown in terms of assets. The book value of assets increased from £100,000 to £180,000 in nominal terms between 1985 and 1988, representing a real increase of approximately 60 per cent. Sales turnover (excluding VAT) had in fact decreased to £150,000, at 1988 prices, which was a real decrease of 42 per cent in value. It was largely due to the collapse of the market for one of the subsidiary product lines. Firm J had just one main product group which was duplicated cassette tapes, and it manufactured between one and ten products within this product group. By 1988 the output mix had changed substantially from 1985, although the main product line still contributed proportionately the same in terms of total sales in 1988. This had been due to a stable core product output, whereas the product mix for other outputs had fluctuated. For example, Firm J had for a time produced computer game cassette tapes, following a perceived market trend. Production of these tapes was stopped when new computer floppy disk technology emerged, largely displacing the old cassette tape technology. The old technology lingered on, but the owner-manager felt he would rather get out before this dwindling market demand collapsed. He said, quite simply, 'The market is finished now'. However, within his principal market, there had not been a change in competitiveness due to innovation between 1985 and 1988. The product was homogeneous, and manufactured accordingly to a world-wide trade standard. There was thus no scope for design change. Rather, effort was directed at productivity enhancement. The owner-manager sought a reconfiguration of his productive machinery which would lower costs and maintain profitablity.

A potential rival product was the digital disk (CD). However, it could not be recorded upon outside of the manufacturing process and was quite expensive. The tape was described as 'a versatile medium'. Digital cassettes were technological substitutes, and had a quality advantage in terms of absence of tape hiss, 'wow', or 'flutter'. There was no obviously preferable digital recording system from a commercial standpoint, although it was felt such systems could appear quite soon. Once they were on the market, it was thought that it would be another twenty years before the audiocassette became obsolete. This led the manager to say that 'There is the technology, but no product'. It was felt that it would be the larger firms, with R & D departments and high profits, that would be the most motivated to make digital cassettes commercially viable. If they succeeded, the owner-manager thought it would be difficult for his firm to make a competitive reponse. He felt that such a development suggested a particularly irrational pursuit of quality by the customer. Existing tape technology already reproduced sound with an accuracy beyond the threshold of the human ear to discriminate. In this sense one could have 'too much quality'.

In terms of legal form Firm J was a partnership. The owner-manager regarded the United Kingdom as his principal market. In terms of this principal market it was thought that Firm J's market share was less than 1 per cent. A distinction was made between major and minor competitors. It was believed that there were between one and five major competitors and no minor competitors. There were three major competitors in Scotland, and the rest were in England. Major competitors could be very large (e.g. Decca, EMI). They were long-established firms and had a strong grip on their customers' loyalty. These firms tended to cater to the needs of large customers only, especially in the pop music industry. The owner-manager said, 'I never get a famous-name pop group'. They would want a million tapes at one month's notice, which was far beyond Firm J's capability. Only a few small firms existed which were willing to provide small batches for customers.

In terms of product differentiation, whilst Firm J's products were physically identical to those of its competitors, differentiation was entirely by service and delivery: the better was the service, and the quicker the delivery, the better was the chance of getting an order. Customers were expert and could determine by their own judgement the technical quality of the product. There were a great many types of customers who placed orders for small batches, like 3,000 tapes. There were also a few larger clients. Firm J was not therefore too dependent on any one customer, and had little worry about losing orders. Its owner-manager felt he got a lot of orders from smaller customers because they had difficulty in persuading larger suppliers to deal with small-batch orders. Once captured, customers tended to stay with Firm J, as switching costs were judged to be high. There was thought to be little threat of backward integration by customers, who typically operated in fast-paced markets which left them little time to get involved in the physical production side of duplicating tapes and associated machinery. In the settling of large contracts, customers often sent out notices to firms, inviting tenders. Interested firms would then submit tenders. Once the bid was accepted by the customer, there was no further negotiation, whether the bidding firm was small or large.

The pricing of a new product brought onto the market would be determined independently of the amount to be sold. Price was set as a flexible mark-up on variable cost and was typically set at the highest level the market could bear. The pricing policy of Firm J's competitors was thought to be crucial to its own pricing. As a consequence, the owner-manager was willing to hold down his price to beat that of his competitors, though in practice there was not much price mobility. Price setting in this way was consciously conceived to be entry deterring, and was felt to be encouraged by the homogeneity of the product. It was thought that one of the most significant deterrents to entry was the fact that incumbent firms already set prices as low as they dared. If a boom in demand were to occur that could not be met from stocks it was thought that the lines of action to be taken would be, in decreasing order of importance, increased overtime or shift-work, lengthened order books and increased capacity. Faced with a recession it was thought that the actions taken, in decreasing order of importance, would be to reduce overtime, to introduce short-time working and to reduce capacity (which might include the laying-off of personnel). If demand were to fall for a particular product, the lines of action taken, in order, would be to reduce overtime, to introduce short-time working and to switch to a new product.

Costs were split up into fixed and variable costs. The distinction made between these costs was found to be useful in the running of the business. Operationally, costs were assigned to the broad categories of materials, labour and machinery. Material costs were in some measure controllable, given that suppliers could be 'tied up' by their desire to avoid potential shortages. For the larger rivals, the investment in fixed plant ran to millions of pounds, but for this firm, and similarly sized rivals, the figure was about £100,000 at 1985 prices. Distribution, marketing and sales were recognized as a potentially important cost category, but costs had been too low to justify consciously recognizing this fourth cost category. Concern was expressed that higher levels of outlays (costs) had not gone on sales promotion. Labour costs were a significant cost-driver. It was felt that further automation could reduce labour costs, but the owner-manager had no desire to disrupt the harmonious functioning that had been achieved with the current workforce. Marginal cost was not calculated though the concept was understood. A maximum capacity output was recognized. It was estimated that Firm J normally operated at 91–100 per cent of this maximum capacity. The owner-manager had no problem of intermittent overcapacity. In fact, in 1985 an increase in capacity was being planned. In the medium term an attempt was being made to increase capacity with a view to being able to cope with larger single orders, rather than more small orders. Firm J's cost variation with output was thought to be represented by the statement that the extra cost of supplying each additional unit fell as more units were supplied. Bulk discounting on supplies helped contribute to scale economies. It was maintained that the scale economies could be significant, and that they could be used by some small firms to compete with larger rivals. However, this was not a strategy which Firm J itself had followed.

A basic component accounting for cost was that of the audiotape itself.

Firm J obtained all its supplies from one supplier on the continent which had a good reputation for quality. Suppliers in general operated in a global market in which quality was paramount. Under this competitive pressure, all UK producers of tapes had gone out of business in recent years. Remaining low-quality suppliers hung on in the global market, but were often being undercut in price by high-quality, high-volume suppliers. Firm J had had bad experiences in the past in dealing with poor-quality supplies. The owner-manager thought that he could initially get away with selling low-quality tapes, because the human ear was not always accurate enough to benefit from certain forms of quality enhancement. However, low quality in the audio sense was often associated with generally low specification of the product. This could lead to unnecessary machine breakdowns, so the firm tended to use only high-quality suppliers. Switching costs attached to changing suppliers were thought to be low, so Firm J was not uneasy about using only one supplier. This supplier was efficient, kept Firm J informed of possibilities of future supply scarcities, and maintained high-quality standards. The owner-manager expressed surprise that suppliers had never forward-integrated, and thought it was logical to do so. That it was unknown suggests he underestimated the extent of firm-specific knowledge. There was a great deal of technical know-how involved (e.g. in electrical engineering) in running this type of business and there were many highly specialized production problems that needed to be solved. These could take up to five years to solve. Further, the owner-manager had worked for a recording company for a few years, which enabled him to identify a market niche which was not being catered for, and to acquire the technical knowledge necessary to run a firm capable of exploiting such a niche.

Market research methods were employed by the owner manger. The results were used to forecast future developments in the market. It was felt that Firm J's strength lay in filling market gaps with respect to small orders that might otherwise go unfilled. On the assumption that Firm J's competitors did not react and business conditions were normal, it was thought that for both a small (5 per cent) and large (10 per cent) price decrease demand would be inelastic. For a small (5 per cent) or large (10 per cent) price increase demand was thought to be very elastic. If Firm J were to reduce its price it was believed that competitors would follow this action in normal or depressed conditions, but not in buoyant business conditions. In the case of a price increase it was thought that competitors would react by matching this price increase in buoyant business conditions, but not in normal or depressed conditions. The owner-manager did not believe that he had any elbow room in pricing within which price could be varied without consequences for demand. This was probably because of the physical homogeneity of his main product. Whilst the cost of tapes in relation to customer costs was typically small, which would tend to foster price inelasticity of demand, the lack of product differentiation in fact made demand very price sensitive. Getting repeat business required quoting very competitive prices, to which was added good customer service. Events which might lead to an alteration in selling price were the commencement of a new business year (or season of production) and a new tax year. Price discrimination was practised. Different prices were set for different marketing areas, for different customers and for large and small traders. Price rebates were not offered, and controlled and recommended prices were unheard of. Firm J did undertake advertising, which was increased in a recession and decreased during a boom. The owner-manager described competition in his principal market as 'intense in every aspect'. It was not thought to be in any firm's interest to encourage 'good competitors' (e.g. through referral). Price was set at rock-bottom levels in most market niches, giving an average profit margin of only 5 per cent. The owner-manager said, 'There is no such thing as a quick profit in this industry'.

At the inception of the business, advice was sought, firstly, from family and friends, secondly from an accountant, thirdly, from a bank manager and, fourthly, from the Scottish Development Agency, later to be Scottish Enterprise. The approximate size of the business in terms of total assets (book value) at inception was £2,000 in 1975 at nominal prices. At the time of initial interview in 1985 this figure stood at £100,000 at nominal prices. By the time of reinterview in 1988, this figure had grown to £180,000, in nominal terms, a real increase of about 60 per cent. The owner-manager had not experienced any difficulty at the financial inception of the firm, as it had been possible to use only personal finance in setting up the business. The gearing ratio at business inception was therefore zero. This was the only value the gearing ratio had assumed in the history of Firm J up to, and including, the year 1985. At that time, the gearing ratio was expected to stay the same one year ahead, but there was uncertainty about what would happen after this period, possibly because of plans for the expansion of capacity. In fact, it was found by 1988 that the equity gearing ratio had remained at zero over the proceeding three-year period. Thus the owner-manager had not used debt at any point in Firm J's history. He felt that part of the success of the firm could be attributed to the fact that there were no outstanding loans to be serviced on the very expensive capital equipment. This absence of debt capital and the existence of adequate working capital had freed the owner-manager of financial worries, and enabled him to make reasonable, but not exciting, levels of profit. The owner-manager had found an investment grant to be helpful in the starting-up of his business. Cash-flow difficulties had been experienced. These had been caused by, in decreasing order of importance, overinvestment, delinquent debtors and inadequate credit policies with buyers. External finance had not been sought since the inception of the business either in the form of debt or equity. The owner-manager expected to see a growth in his business over the foreseeable future. This was largely driven by increases in demands from the large numbers of existing customers, though a few new customers were thought to enter the market afresh each week. To the extent that part of this new demand was created by new small orders, there was no evidence that larger firms were anxious to win such orders. On the other hand, Firm J could meet such demands, and in this context the owner-manager said he would just 'flow with the market'.

In 1988 the owner-manager said that he recognized the emergence of an 'enterprise culture' in Scotland. He commented that enterprise trusts were helping people to start up in business. He added, 'Government policy encourages people to be entrepreneurs.'

3.5 PROFILE K: ELECTRONIC INSTRUMENTATION

Firm K, an electrical and electronic engineering company, had been in operation since May 1984. It employed a total of five full-time workers at the time of initial interview in May 1985, and three months later it employed fifteen full-time workers, and had moved to expanded premises. In terms of its initial legal form, Firm K was a sole proprietorship. The approximate size of its sales turnover in 1985 (excluding VAT) was £25,000. In 1985 Firm K's net profitability was 135 per cent. Three years later, Firm K was still trading and had grown substantially both in terms of sales turnover and personnel. By 1988 its sales turnover figure (excluding VAT) had increased to £750,000 (i.e. £660,000 at 1985 prices). This represents a real growth rate of sales of over 850 per cent p.a. Its workforce had also shown considerable growth, for by 1988 it employed thirty-nine full-time, two part-time workers and four trainees. At no point over the period 1985–8 had Firm K experienced any shortage of skilled labour.

Firm K had a range of two to five product groups, and of one to ten products. In terms of sales value its most important activity was the manufacture and design of electronic test equipment. The owner-manager regarded Scotland as his principal market, and estimated that Firm K's market share for test equipment (his main product line) was under 1 per cent. Within the electronics industry, which was Firm K's broad area of activity, market activity was dominated by a few large firms who allocated work on a subcontracting basis to a much larger number of small firms. It was felt by the owner-manager that the industry offered great potential for growth to small firms willing to provide manufacturing facilities and some design capabilities to large firms. He kept himself informed of demand changes by seeing customers in advance, reading technical and financial journals, and speaking to suppliers of tools and manufacturing equipment. The owner-manager was more concerned with establishing Firm K's market niche in an industry that was enjoying a growth phase than in engaging in retaliatory tactics against rivals. It was thought that rivals who challenged for contracts did not pose a credible threat. They were dealt with 'in a conscious and purposeful manner'. The owner-manager was clear that there was more demand being generated by customers than currently could be met by all suppliers in the industry. Although the output of his main product line had not changed substantially by 1988, Firm K's output mix had changed substantially by this time. In terms of its value to total sales ratio, the main product-line contributed 40 per cent less in 1988 compared to 1985. Numerous new product lines had been introduced over the period 1985–8, but there had been no change in competitiveness in Firm K's principal market due to innovation. Major and minor competitors could be distinguished. It was thought that Firm K had six to ten major competitors and eleven to thirty minor competitors. Competition within the industry was thought to be generally strong (e.g. in terms of delivery) but weak in some respects (e.g. pricing).

Expertise, finance capital and trade contacts were thought to be the main barriers to entry. In terms of degree of product differentiation, Firm K's main product group was thought to be 'similar' to that of its competitors. The scope for product differentiation was thought to be 'nearly limitless'. Ninety per cent of Firm K's business involved the provision of test equipment to large firms. Customer requirements were specific, and orders often had a unique quality (e.g. in terms of the printed circuit board used). Customer location was also important, as it influenced the speed of turnaround on an order. Firm K sought a 'fast turnaround' reputation. The customers of Firm K could be divided up into two groups in terms of their knowledge of the product. Firstly, there were those who could not distinguish between the product and those of Firm K's rivals. For them, price, brand design, advertising, packaging and service were all more important in determining a customer's attitude than technical specification. Secondly, there was a small group of customers who were thought to be expert and who could determine by their own judgement the technical quality of the product. The owner-manager's main concern was with establishing a good reputation for quality and delivery. Customers were a source of information on product modification and they provided the principal means of filling product or market gaps. Complementary to Firm K's manufacturing capability was a design capability for test equipment. This was used more or less continuously to satisfy the needs of customers which were perceived to be 'changing and varied'. This tended to raise customers' switching costs. Thus customers tended to need test equipment for crucial purposes, and very often this need had to be filled 'at the last minute'. The firms who got the orders were those that could promise 'a quick turnaround at the necessary quality'. There was little fear of backward integration by customers because it was thought to be unlikely that they would have the skills necessary to produce test equipment, and that even if they did, their volume requirements would be so low that unit costs would be prohibitive. Firm K, in enlarging its customer base, tried to reduce its dependence on the fortunes of large customers. The owner-manager said that he wanted to get away from the situation in which 'if they are doing well, we are doing well'. It was thought that reputation and experience were important in expanding the customer base. The typical customer was a large firm that needed test equipment. The purchase decision was thought to operate something like this. Firstly, the customer would identify what he required from a product. Secondly, this specification would be put out to tender with between five and ten firms. Thirdly, these firms would vie with one another for the contract, particularly emphasizing quality, volume and delivery, until only one was left. It was known that the firms in the industry who satisfied customers tended to get repeat business.

If Firm K brought a new product onto the market its price would not be determined independently of the amount to be sold. It was thought that each new piece of test equipment was a substitute for previous equipment. The advantage of Firm K's product over substitutes was simplicity of function: 'We don't test for ten different functions when only one is needed'. This kept costs down and raised the product's relative value/price compared to rivals. Price was usually determined as a flexible mark-up on variable cost. However, in special circumstances the price could be dictated by Firm K's principal customer. The pricing policy of Firm K's rivals was considered to be crucial to that of its own. The owner-manager reported that he would at times hold down his price to beat his rivals, but this strategy 'depended very much on the nature of the job'. Potential entrants with the capacity for high-volume production could expect what was euphemistically described as 'artificial pricing' (i.e. pricing below cost) for the most similar products produced by incumbent firms. Such direct confrontations were typical of strategies adapted by larger firms in the industry.[13]

If a boom in demand were to occur that could not be met from stocks then the owner-manager thought that he would respond first by increasing overtime or shiftwork, and then by engaging subcontractors. It was thought that in a recession that the following courses of actions, in decreasing order of importance, would be undertaken: reduce overtime, improve productivity or efficiency and, finally, introduce short-time working. If the demand were to fall for a particular product within the main product group, the owner-manager thought that initially he would react to this by increasing the quality of the product. This would involve enhancing the product specification by what he called 'updating it'. Subsequently, other ways of coping with the fall in demand included switching to a new product and reducing overtime.

Costs were split up into fixed and variable costs and these cost divisions were found to be useful in the running of the business. The owner-manager did calculate marginal cost and he recognized a maximum or capacity output. It was thought that Firm K operated at 71–80 per cent of this maximum capacity. It was felt that high levels of capacity utilization were also typical of Firm K's rivals. Firm K's cost variation was thought to be represented by the statement that the extra cost of supplying each extra unit of the product fell as more was supplied. The main cost-drivers were purchasing, delivery and the payroll. Sustaining low costs was achieved by efficient organization: it was thought to be a matter of 'staying on top of the situation'. Suppliers were numerous, most being big, with a surrounding fringe. The fringe suppliers generally did not hold sufficient stocks to guarantee the fast turnaround on order that Firm K required. Only small items, known to be in stock, tended to be purchased from small suppliers. Typically, the owner-manager of Firm K found switching costs to be low. The cost of switching supplier was said to be 'no more than picking up the telephone'. Rarely was there only one vendor: frequently suppliers could be played off against one another, on price and delivery. Suppliers were primarily distributors, rather than manufacturers, and tended to offer similar prices. Although suppliers could, as described, be played off against one another, it was thought that one ultimately got a better deal on pricing and service by remaining loyal.

Market research methods were not employed by the owner-manager. It was thought to be impossible to estimate what effect a small (5 per cent) or large (10 per cent) price variation around the normal selling price would have on the demand for the main product, given no reaction from rivals. This was true of all business conditions be they normal, buoyant or depressed. The owner-manager's impression was that if he reduced his price then his strongest competition would not follow this action, in normal, depressed or buoyant business conditions. In general, demand was thought to be sufficiently buoyant that Firm K did not have to concern itself with potential retaliation. The same was thought to be true of a price rise. The owner-manager interviewed did believe that he had a certain amount of elbow room in pricing, but he could not estimate how large or small this elbow room might be.

The cost of Firm K's product was an insignificant component of the customers' total costs, which tended to reduce their price sensitivity. Furthermore, Firm K's product had a considerable impact on his customers profitability, as good test equipment ensured the high quality and perform-ance of the customer's product. For all these reasons, one would expect what one discovered: a considerable lack of customer price sensitivity. The main motivators for customers' purchases were therefore not price but quality and delivery. There was also a considerable cost discrepancy between in-house provision and relatively less expensive out-house provision of test equipment, reducing customers' bargaining power over price.

The events that might lead Firm K to alter its selling price were a new business year and cost or demand changes. Price discrimination was prac-tised for large and small traders. Price rebates were offered in the form of bulk discounting. However, recommended or controlled prices were unheard of.

Firm K did advertise and pursued the strategy of 'individual advertising' (as opposed to generic advertising) which was aimed at promoting its own product over that of its rivals. Advertising was increased when business demand was low and reduced when it was high. However, it was thought that advertising played a limited role in stimulating customer demand. Because of the specialized nature of Firm K's products, customers were thought to be best reached through personal trade contacts.

To get Firm K started the owner-manager approached a variety of sources of business advice. They were, in decreasing importance, his bank manager, his accountant, his local enterprise trust and the Scottish Development Agency. The approximate size of the business in terms of total assets (book value) at inception was £2,500 (1984 prices). At the time of interview in 1985, Firm K had increased its total assets (book value) to the figure £20,000. In 1988 this figure had increased again to £70,000. This represents a real growth in total assets in the period 1985–8 of over 70 per cent p.a. The owner-manager reported that he had consciously set up the business using exclusively personal finance. No issue had arisen of any difficulty in obtaining financial support at business inception. Consequently Firm K's gearing ratio stood at zero at inception. The highest the gearing ratio had reached in the life of Firm K was 0.25. At the time of interview in 1985 the gearing ratio stood at 0.08. It was expected that it would stay the same over the next year, but the owner-manager did not find it easy to forecast beyond this time horizon. He guessed he might increase his debt by borrowing in the second year, and possibly the third year as well. He anticipated no increase in ploughed-back profits until the third year. In the event, the gearing ratio subsequently varied very little, and fell slowly over the next three years, until by 1988 it actually stood at zero. The limited amount of external finance Firm K had obtained had been used for several purposes: to expand its premises to purchase equipment and to help in the hiring of new employees. The owner-manager reported that he had not experienced any cash-flow difficulties. It was thought that new entrants to the industry would be confronted with certain financial pressures, like going for three months without receiving payment from large customers, and having to pay for materials 'up front'. In the interview of 1985 the owner-manager said that he expected to see a growth in his business over the foreseeable future, and this expectation was spectacularly realized.

In the interview of 1988, the owner-manager said he did not sense the emergence of an 'enterprise culture' in Scotland, as described on television, radio and in newspapers. He commented that he 'had not seen anything of that nature' in his area.

3.6 PROFILE N: BULK BAG MANUFACTURER

Firm N had been in existence since March 1984. It employed twenty-seven full-time workers and one part-timer. In terms of legal form Firm N was a private company. Its annual sales turnover (excluding VAT) in 1985 was £200,000, and its net profitability was 24 per cent. Firm N had entered the market with high profit expectations. Due to competitive pressures, these expectations were not entirely fulfilled: prices had to be pruned to remain competitive, and product specification had to be modified to accommodate to the customers' diverse requirements. A perceived squeeze on expected profit margins encouraged Firm N to undertake higher volumes of production than had previously been contemplated. By 1988 Firm N was still in operation, and had a sales turnover (excluding VAT) which had increased to £1.6m (at 1988 prices), representing a real growth rate of sales of 170 per cent p.a. It was estimated that the sales turnover figure for 1989 would be approximately £2 million. By 1988 it employed fifty-seven full-time workers and twenty-six part-time employees. The wage bill was a major cost-driver, and within Firm N there was an ongoing pursuit of improved labour productivity.

Firm N's line of business was textile packaging, and its main product-group was bulk bags. These are high performance woven polypropylene bags, used for carrying heavy loads of powders and granules such as chemicals, minerals, fertilizers and grains, and also bulkier products like coal and potatoes. Within this product-group there were about fifty products. The owner-manager regarded the United Kingdom as Firm N's principal market, and he estimated it had a market share of 1–5 per cent. The focus of Firm N's activities was on the UK market, initially seeking large firms as principal customers. Established connections with such large firms had been carried over from previous employment of the owner-manager within a firm that was now a rival of Firm N. Between 1985 and 1988, the output mix had changed substantially, although this did not effect the proportion of the value of total sales attributable to the main product-line. Output of the main product line had increased 120 per cent in volume over this three-year period, which was associated with a 25 per cent reduction in unit variable cost.

The owner-manager interviewed could distinguish between major and minor competitors in his market. He thought that he had one to five major and one to five minor competitors. Within the United Kingdom there were three large bulk bag manufacturers and four smaller ones. The top three in the United Kingdom were textile manufacturers who had diversified into the bulk bag industry. Product gaps were continually being created by new customer needs, and the owner-manager felt that if these gaps were not filled rapidly by his firm's own actions, they would be lost to alert rivals. Firm N's main product-group was considered to be 'similar' to that of its competitors. It was felt that, in order to sustain competitive advantage in the niches in which it was active, Firm N had to be prepared to produce new types of bags. This was, in a sense, creating a new substitute, though the level of innovation was not necessarily great. At the time of reinterview in 1988, there had been a change in the competitiveness in Firm N's principal market which had been brought about by innovation undertaken by Firm N, but not by its rivals.

Customers of Firm N ranged from the expert, who could determine by their own judgement the technical quality of the product, to the relatively uninformed customer, who needed guidance and information about the key technical features of the firm's product. Switching costs were generally only appreciable for customers with specialist needs. However, the largest group of customers was in fact fairly expert about the product and could make a buying decision by drawing on both personal technical expertise and the technical information available in specialist publications like trade journals. The customer base was thought to be continually expanding. This was because goods such as coal and sand, which had previously tended to be transported by ship in bulk containers, were increasingly being carried in durable bags by lorries directly to the customer. This had been proven to lower delivery times and unit costs. Some customer dependence was thought to exist. ICI was the largest customer for the industry, and the owner-manager said, 'If ICI does well, the large firms in the industry do well. If ICI does poorly, all the firms in the industry feel it'. Prompt service, and what was described as 'a fair price' were thought to develop customer loyalty in some degree. However, given the fairly homogeneous nature of the product, customer switching costs were not naturally high. What tended to keep a customer loyal was his desire to avoid disrupting the continuity of the trading relationship. If the service and price were right, continuity would be maintained, and the customer would also not be tempted to contemplate backward integration. Historically, continuity of the trading relationship was typical in the industry. This had the side effect, favourable to the bargaining power of suppliers like Firm N, of limiting customers' knowledge of rival suppliers. It was thought that the typical process by which a customer became involved in a trade connection with Firm N was as follows: (1) customer contact was made, (2) the customer requested a trial sample of bulk bags, (3) the sample was provided and the customer tested the bags, (4) after some bargaining over price the customer placed a small order and (5) if the small order proved satisfactory, the customer placed a larger order. Product quality, easy availability and good service were the attributes that were perceived to create the most valuable differentiation for customers, though their relative ranking varied by customer.

The owner-manager thought the pricing of a new product would be determined independently of the amount to be sold. Price was determined as a fixed percentage mark-up on unit direct cost. An effort was made to set this mark-up to the highest level the market could bear. The owner-manager thought that the pricing policy of competitors was crucial to his pricing. As a consequence, he was willing to hold down his price to beat competitors. If a boom in demand were to occur that could not be met from stocks, the owner-manager said that his first course of action would be to increase overtime or shiftwork. This action would be followed by an attempt to increase capacity (which could include the recruitment of more personnel). Faced with a recession the first action undertaken would be the introduction of short-time working, followed by a reduction in capacity. If demand were to fall for a particular product within Firm N's main product-group, the owner-manager thought that his only option would be to switch to a new product.

Costs were split up into fixed and variable costs. The distinction between these costs was found to be useful in the running of the firm. When the output of a product was increased, marginal cost was calculated. The owner-manager did regard his firm as having a capacity output. He estimated that he normally operated at less than 50 per cent of his maximum possible output. There was perceived to be some intermittent overcapacity. This was caused by the seasonality of some patterns of demand (e.g. from farmers) and by exogenous negative shocks to demand (e.g. periodic hard-currency problems encountered by customers in Nigeria).

Firm N's cost variation with respect to output was thought to be represented by the statement that total cost did not increase as fast as the amount supplied. That is, the cost of supplying each extra unit fell as more units were supplied. Larger firms were thought to enjoy such significant scale economies that this limited their capacity to satisfy small-volume, specialized orders. Whenever it found difficulty in competing head on with large firms on high-volume contracts, Firm N tended to seek out small-volume, specialized demand for its products. It cultivated the skill of flexibly adapting to customers demands, by contrast to the perceived inflexibility of larger rivals. In this way, new, small specialist niches were continually exploited. These niches also offered prospects for healthier profit margins. Firm N was able to minimize delivery costs because its principal customer was located in the same city. There was one major supplier to Firm N, and three others were potentially available. There was perceived to be some dependence upon this major supplier, but it was accepted because this firm was local and therefore greatly reduced the requirements for holding inventory. Many suppliers had engaged in forward integration and now produced bags themselves rather than purchasing from firms like Firm N. The owner-manager thought this tendency 'seemed quite natural'. He understood that suppliers occasionally found that seeking substitutes for available bags was sufficiently expensive that it encouraged in-house provision.

The owner-manager did not use market research methods of any kind, not even as a passive consumer of forecasts by official bodies, trade associations, and so on. On the assumption that competitors did not react and that business conditions were normal, it was estimated that for both small (5 per cent) and large (10 per cent) price variations, the demand for Firm N's products would be completely inelastic. The owner-manager thought that if he were to reduce his price his strongest competitors would not match this action in normal or boom conditions, though they might do so in depressed business conditions. In the case of a price increase it was thought that Firm N's strongest competitors would not follow this action in any business conditions. The owner-manager believed he had a certain amount of elbow-room in pricing which he thought lay between 4 per cent and 6 per cent. The costs of bags were low in relation to the total costs of customers. Further, bags did substantially enhance the service that customers could offer to their own customers (e.g. in terms of packing and transportation).

The owner-manager said, 'Our customers want our bags because *their* customers want them'. These factors would tend to reduce the price sensitivity of customers. When bulk orders were involved and the bags were very standardized, then customers tended to be price sensitive. However, the owner-manager of Firm N said, 'The small guy is not so concerned', for he would tend to seek small lot, specialized orders. Special bags tended to enhance the customer's product quality and/or allowed his product to be handled more easily. Firm N was thought to have the ability to adapt production to any type of bag demanded.

The main events which would lead Firm N to altering its selling price included the start of a new tax year, the occurrence of significant cost changes, the experience of having a substantial shift in demand and the charging of a competitive price by rivals. Price discrimination was practised for different customers. Price rebates were never offered, and controlled or recommended prices were unheard of in Firm N's markets. An aggressive individual advertising strategy was followed – that is, advertising was aimed at promoting Firm N's product over that of its rivals. Very high-quality glossy colour brochures were produced, in three different languages. Advertising was not increased when business demand was low, but was reduced in buoyant conditions. The owner-manager described competition in his market as being intense in every aspect (e.g. price, quality and rivalry). Strategic stakes were high, and the owner-manager of Firm N regarded himself as 'totally committed' to functioning within the industry. Potential entrants into the industry who desired to challenge the high-volume producers of standardized bags would find that they encountered high capital requirements. Even if they surmounted this barrier to entry, they would find that the market niches they were challenging would be occupied by large, long-established, diversified firms that would undoubtedly retaliate. An alternative entry strategy would be to enter the industry on a smaller scale, and to cater for low-volume, specialized demand. Here too, there were entry barriers, including the lack of trade connections[14] and patent protection for the production of a variety of specialized bags. Further, a new entrant would have to arrive with the capability of developing new types of bags already in-house. It was thought that experience was important for success in the industry, and a lack of it constituted a barrier to entry. The necessary experience took some two to three years to acquire.

The owner-manager of Firm N sought advice from many quarters on how to get his business started. In order of decreasing importance the sources used were the accountant, the bank manager, the local enterprise trust and the Scottish Development Agency. The approximate size of the business at the time of inception in terms of total assets (book value) was £5,000 (at 1984 prices). By the time of interview in 1985 this figure had grown substantially to £50,000. By 1988 the firm's assets (book value, net of depreciation) stood at £385,000, a real increase of 164 per cent p.a. Firm N had been set up using both personal and external finance. The owner-manager stated he did not have any difficulty in obtaining external financial support for starting the business, though he thought that the lack of finance did typically constitute a barrier to entry for some potential newcomers to the industry. As the physical capital requirements were high, given the need to exploit scale economies, financial requirements for entering the business were demanding. External finance had been sought for setting up the business from both the Scottish Development Agency and a bank (in the form of a loan), and had been successful in each case, with the Agency playing the most important role. The funding acquired was secured by floating charges (i.e. securities on plant, equipment, stocks, etc.).

At the time of the inception of Firm N its gearing ratio was zero. The gearing ratio at the time of interview in 1985 was 0.5, which had also proved to be the highest value it had reached. The owner-manager expected the gearing ratio to fall the next year and then to stay the same for the following two years. This forecast of the gearing ratio's trajectory was made because of the expectation of an increase in ploughed-back profits in the first year with no increase in debt, followed by an increase in both ploughed-back profits and in debt in the second and third years. In the event, Firm N's gearing ratio actually fell every year over the subsequent three years so that by 1988 it had fallen to zero. The owner-manager claimed that, of the various forms of financial assistance which had been obtained, an investment grant had been the most necessary for successfully starting up in business. Other helpful schemes had included the Enterprise Allowance Scheme, an employment grant and reduced rental on his premises. Firm N had not experienced any cash-flow difficulties since its inception. The owner-manager put this down to the effective trade credit terms he had agreed with suppliers and buyers, which enhanced cash-flow. Forms of external finance had been sought since the start up of the business for a variety of reasons. These included funding for expanding premises, purchasing new plant and equipment, increasing inventory and hiring new employees. In 1985 the owner-manager said that he expected to see a growth in his business over the foreseeable future, and this expectation was realized. The industry as a whole experienced a fairly stable demand for its products, and was thought to have some growth potential. This growth was thought likely to be fuelled by a trend to cheaper and non-returnable bags. Firm K hoped to diversify into producing these new types of bags, but had no plans for forward or backward integration.

In 1988, the owner-manager claimed that he sensed the emergence of an 'enterprise culture' in Scotland, especially in the Dundee area, where he commented there had been 'a definite growth of such a culture'.

3.7 PROFILE O: CHESTNUT FENCING MANUFACTURER

Firm O had been in existence since October 1983 and manufactured chestnut fencing. At the time of interview in 1985, it had three full-time employees. Firm O was a one-man business. The approximate size of its sales turnover in the previous tax year 1984 (excluding VAT) was £96,000. Its net profitability was 15 per cent. At the time of reinterview in 1988, Firm O was still in operation and had grown in terms of both personnel and sales turnover. By 1988 it had six full-time employees, one part-time employee and a trainee. The owner-manager had not experienced any shortage of skilled labour. The sales turnover figure (excluding VAT) was estimated to be £160,000. This represented a real growth in sales turnover of approximately 8 per cent p.a. Firm O had a very narrow product group: it sold just one product group, which was chestnut fencing. There were approximately thirty individual products within this group. The product mix was stable over the three years from 1985 to 1988. The owner-manager regarded his principal market as Scotland, and thought that within it his market share was 1–5 per cent. However, it was believed that Firm O's potential market was much greater.

The owner-manager could distinguish between major and minor competitors and thought that he had between one and five major and between six and ten minor competitors. There were only two other firms manufacturing chestnut fencing in Scotland. An English firm in Kent was also identified as being a significant rival, for it had the advantage of being close to a chestnut growing area. However, delivery costs limited its competitive threat in Scotland. In a similar way, delivery costs limited the extent of Firm O's markets, in this case, to Scotland, Northern Ireland and northern England. In terms of product differentiation, it was thought that Firm O's product group was 'similar' to that of its competitors. Chestnut was a traditional material for fencing ('it has always been used'), was cheap when supply problems were absent and had a reputation for great durability (seventy years or more, for fencing). Strict substitutes did not exist, given the uniqueness of the wood, but there were technological substitutes available, which the owner-manager described as 'expensive and inferior'. However, they had not been dogged by supply difficulties, as had chestnut products. Softwoods offered a cheaper substitute in some uses, but lacked longevity for many uses. This was perceived as a great disadvantage by customers like local authorities, who valued longevity. Only building contractors would readily switch to softwoods, having shorter time horizons. Given chestnut's traditional position, and its technical advantages, the owner-manager thought that softwoods would only ever be favoured if chestnut were in short supply.

The owner-manager thought generally that his customers could not distinguish on technical grounds between his business's products and those of his rivals. In his view, it was not technical specification but price, design, advertising and service which determined most of his customers' attitudes to his products. He thought that a minority of customers, while perhaps not technically minded, did at least have in mind a few technical features that the product should possess. The principal customers were regional, district and local authorities, and building contractors. The motivation for government authorities to buy chestnut fencing was that it was cheap, reusable and provided work for unskilled labour. Building contractors were mainly motivated by the urgency of completing a job. They were less price sensitive than government contractors and less concerned with technical features like the longevity of the fencing. Firm O was not dependent on any one customer and found it easy to acquire new customers if some were lost. Typically, individual customers accounted for some 5 per cent of sales, with the largest customer, in Northern Ireland, accounting for some 20 per cent of the sales. Customers were generally well informed about rival suppliers to Firm O (barring, perhaps, building contractors), so they needed to be treated well to be retained. Except for obviously one-off sales, Firm O had not lost an account from a customer who had been operating on a continuous repeat-purchase pattern. This success was attributed to the owner-manager's ability to develop a personal relationship with customers. He was willing to extend this beyond business to a social connection and was aware that this would increase customers' switching costs. Prompt delivery (e.g. within two days of order) was thought to be more attractive to customers than a competitive price. The loyalty that Firm O had built up with its customers meant that the firm would tend to be given the right of being the last bidder for a potential new contract.

If the owner-manager were to launch a new product onto the market, price would be determined by the volume of sales he expected to achieve. It was thought to be difficult to launch new products. Customers 'needed to be re-educated' into the use of chestnut products and reassured that there would be no supply problems. Generally, price was consciously set as a flexible percentage mark-up on variable cost per unit. Flexibility was used in a profit seeking way, and on occasions price was set at the highest level the market could bear. The pricing policy of competitors was thought to be crucial to Firm O's own pricing policy. However, the owner-manager stated that he would not be willing to hold down his price to beat his competitors. If a boom in demand were to occur that could not be met from stocks the owner thought that he would take actions in the following order: increase overtime or shiftwork, increase the price of the product and, increase capacity (which could involve the recruitment of more personnel). In a recession it was thought that the actions taken would be, firstly, to increase sales effort, followed by attempting to improve productivity or efficiency. If demand were to fall for a particular product within Firm O's main product-group, then it was thought that the first reaction would be to increase sales effort, followed by switching to a new product.

Costs were split up into fixed and variable costs and these cost divisions were found to be useful in the running of the business. The owner-manager did calculate marginal cost and he also stated that a maximum capacity output was recognized. He thought that his business normally operated at 81–90 per cent of maximum capacity. It was thought that high capacity utilization helped to control unit costs. A careful watch was kept on labour productivity, and delivery costs were tightly controlled. It was thought that if softwoods were substituted for chestnut, a 10 per cent higher output of fencing could be obtained for the same cost. Total cost was described as not increasing as fast as the amount produced. That is, the extra cost of producing each extra unit fell as more was produced. The basic raw material was chestnut timber, and the owner-manager made what he called 'a pilgrimage' every year to Kent and Sussex to make arrangements for supply, this being the major area for chestnut in the United Kingdom. Suppliers had to be able to provide at least twenty tons of timber for each order, in order to make contracting profitable. As Firm O typically required a much greater tonnage than this, it had organized supplies such that up to seven firms could be called upon. Suppliers knew that once they had acquired over twenty tons of chestnut timber, it was worth giving Firm O a call, with a view to agreeing a contract. Suppliers were unlikely to forward-integrate in the Kent and Sussex area, because there were already so many chestnut fencing manufacturers in operation there. Within Scotland lack of trade connections would impede forward integration. It was found that developing a personal relationship with the supplier was very important to ensuring continuity of supply. It was known, for example, that suppliers were very reluctant to deliver chestnut to unknown customers. This marked supplier loyalty went hand in hand with a rich flow of trade information from suppliers. This was a significant barrier to entry for those contemplating setting up in the industry. Futhermore, the inventor of the standard industry machine for making chestnut fencing had promised not to make it available to any firms contemplating entering the industry. Hence, near monopoly and exclusive supply of both materials and physical capital constituted major barriers to entry.

Firm O did not use formal market research methods of any kind. For both small (5 per cent) and large (10 per cent) variations of price, and given business conditions were normal, demand was thought to be elastic. If Firm O reduced price it was thought that its strongest competitors would follow this action in normal and depressed conditions but not in boom business conditions. In the case of a price increase it was thought that competitors would not follow Firm O's increase in depressed or normal conditions, but that they would do so given boom conditions (i.e. in a seller's market). The owner-manager believed he had a certain amount of elbow room in pricing. This elbow-room was thought to be 4–6 per cent. Its existence and magnitude could be partly explained by the lack of customer concentration, which would limit customer bargaining power over price. Price discrimination was practised by Firm O on a number of bases. Different prices were set for different marketing areas, for different customers and for large and small traders. Price rebates were not offered and controlled or recommended prices were unheard of. Advertising took the form of individual advertising – that is, it aimed to promote Firm O's products over those of its rivals. It was increased in depressed conditions and reduced in buoyant conditions. The owner-manager described the competition in his market as generally strong, but weak in some aspects (e.g. strong in quality competition, but weak in price competition). The main new competitive threat was in Firm O's principal market, Northern Ireland. Firm O was the sole supplier to the market, but government support was being sought by local firms to help them get a toe-hold in the local market. The owner-manager of Firm O was contemplating extending his production operations directly to Northern Ireland to attempt to protect his market there. He was aware that a counter-threat existed of a manufacturing capability developing in Northern Ireland, which might then benefit from a government export subsidy, putting Firm O's own Scottish market under threat. To some extent, therefore, Firm O's desire to be the dominant supplier in Northern Ireland was a pre-emptive strategy.

The owner-manager had sought advice on how to get the business started. Most important to him at this stage had been his local enterprise trust, followed by the Scottish Development Agency, and then his bank manager. The approximate size of the business at the time of inception in 1983, in terms of total assets (book value) was £15,000. At the time of the first interview, in 1985, the approximate size of Firm O, by the same criterion, was £50,000. In 1988 the owner-manager reported that this figure had fallen to £46,000, a real decrease of 22 per cent. The owner-manager explained that he had had difficulty in obtaining financial support for starting his business. The two main difficulties encountered in obtaining financial support were, firstly and most importantly, lack of personal financial injections and, secondly, difficulty in establishing the idea that a market existed for his products. The owner-manager had sought, and obtained, external sources of finance to help him set up in business. His most important sources were borrowing from family and friends, but he also borrowed from his bank. Unusually, he was in an area where the local enterprise trust would advance loan capital, and he benefited from this, and from a loan provided by the Scottish Development Agency. Finally, he got some industry backing in the form of loan finance. The owner-manager felt that he still lacked the financial resources he required, and that this had deterred him from expanding into the lucrative market in Northern Ireland. Firm O's gearing ratio had stood at 10.0 at the inception of the business, perhaps not surprisingly in view of the interest raised amongst many providers of debt finance. This had also proven to be the highest value of the gearing ratio. At the time of interview in 1985 it stood at 1.0, which had been its lowest value in the short lifetime of Firm O. Then, the owner-manager expected the gearing ratio to fall even further over the next three years. It was expected to behave like this due to both an increase in ploughed-back profits and a reduction in debt. In the event, the gearing ratio fell in the first year, rose in the second and remained the same in the third year. Thus by 1988 the owner-manager was able to report a gearing ratio of one-third.

The owner-manager of Firm O had found that several special financial schemes had been useful when he was starting up his business. Strictly necessary to his success had been a reduced rental on his premises. It was also found that the Enterprise Allowance Scheme, an employment grant and an investment grant were helpful at the stage of business inception. Cash-flow difficulties had been experienced by Firm O. They had been due primarily to an inadequate credit policy with suppliers, but delinquent debtors and an insufficient overdraft facility were contributory factors. External finance in the form of debt had been used since the start-up of the business, partly to ease the cash-flow problems but also to increase stocks. In 1985 the owner-manager had expected to see a growth in his business over the foreseeable future, and in a modest way this proved to be the case. However, his earlier prediction that potential market growth was 'huge' was clearly optimistic. The industry as a whole had been contracting in recent years because of supply difficulties and the subsequent disillusion of customers, either at rising prices or at shortages. Against this background, any individual firm growth was impressive.

In the 1988 interview, the owner-manager said that he had sensed an 'enterprise culture' emerging in Scotland. He commented that the current high unemployment figures had 'created a situation where people have to start up their own business to generate an income'. He also reflected that 'more economic help is available for people who are starting up'. He thought these 'new' entrepreneurs were being financially helped, and were generally being 'pointed in the right direction'.

3.8 PROFILE P: LAMINATION AND VARNISHING FOR PRINTERS

Firm P had been operating for two-and-a-half years at the time of interview in 1985. It employed five full-time workers and two part-time workers. The business was a partnership and had a sales turnover in the tax year prior to interview of £240,000 (approx.) at 1985 prices, excluding VAT. It had a narrow range of product groups (between two and five) and no more than ten products in total. The main product group in terms of sales value was lamination and varnishing. It was a market in which demand was strongly seasonal (e.g. in terms of treating printers' products like calendars and post-cards). The principal market for this product group was regarded, by the partner interviewed, as the whole of Scotland. Firm P had initially captured the local market in one of Scotland's major cities and had then gone on to capture the market of another major city in Scotland. In terms of the Scottish market, Firm P's share was in the 11–20 per cent range. The partner interviewed could distinguish between major and minor competitors, and estimated that there were between one and five of each. There were eight firms in the lamination and varnishing industry in Scotland, including one multinational and seven average-to-small firms. Firm P, and the multinational, with which it had most-favoured status, used the most up-to-date machinery. This was available to Firm P on especially favourable leasing terms from the multinational. The partner interviewed admitted in the interview that because of this arrangement 'the multinational is effectively subsidizing our lamination business'.

In terms of product differentiation the products in Firm P's main product group were said to be 'identical' to those of competitors. The partner argued that whilst varnishing appeared an alternative to lamination, it was better to regard a move to undertake varnishing as a form of diversification. The desired product itself determined whether lamination or varnishing was the more suitable process. The partner said that he intended first to consolidate Firm P's place in the lamination market, then hoped after two years to purchase a varnishing machine.

The partner thought that customer knowledge varied considerably. One (smaller) group of customers was not technically minded. Another larger group was considered expert, and customers in it could determine by their own judgement the technical quality of the product. The technical differences between Firm P's products and those of its rivals were too small for most customers to distinguish, and therefore in part customers' attitudes were determined by price, product differentiation and service. There were a large variety of customers, but the principal ones were in the printing industry. For them, lamination was a necessary attribute of many of their products, and the process was essential to quality.

Firm P had only been in operation for two years, but in that time had enjoyed much success at the expense of its primary rival, a multinational firm using the same latest-practice technology. The relative success of the smaller firm, as reflected in sales, profits and growth, was attributed to the more personal relationship which Firm P could build up with its customers. This firm was finding it had a growing number of new, small customers. However, customer concentration was high, and if one of the larger customers dropped out, it was thought to be hard to offset this loss by the trade which new customers generated. Given the high capital costs of lamination equipment, customers faced severe barriers to backward integration. On the supply side, there had been no known attempts to forward-integrate, presumably because trade contacts were difficult to acquire and sustain. An attempt had been made to increase customers switching costs through developing Firm P's reputation for reliability and trustworthiness. The dominant multinational rival lacked a personal approach and therefore could not use this strategy. This made the partner of Firm P that we interviewed worry about how the multinational would react to a constant erosion of its customers. He feared a price war might result.

Price was mainly set as a fixed percentage mark-up on direct cost per unit of output. The mark-up was set at a level designed to achieve a desired level of gross profit. However, some flexiblity in the mark-up on direct cost per unit was deployed if there was thought to be a possiblity of enhancing the level of gross profit. Pricing was not thought to be influenced by the volume of products the firm expected to sell. The pricing policy of competitors was not thought to be crucial to Firm P's pricing, although it was certainly important and price might be held down to beat the price of competitors. The partner interviewed said that his firm steered clear of the more adventurous customers, who were often working on very tight margins and expected a special cut-price deal. He said, 'We are not interested in buying business'. There was some fear that the dominant multinational competitor, which had lost business through lack of a personal service, might attempt to regain lost market share by price cutting. It was even thought that the multinational might cut price below cost. If it did so, Firm P was unlikely to follow: 'We would ride out such action'. It was felt that customers would realize this was a short-run strategy and would be unlikely to switch suppliers.

The courses of action to be undertaken if a boom in demand were to occur, and this demand could not be met from stocks, would be, firstly, to increase overtime or shiftwork, and, secondly, to increase capacity (which could include the recruitment of more personnel). The actions taken in a recession were thought to be, firstly, to improve productivity or efficiency, secondly to increase sales effort and, thirdly, to reduce stockholding. It was thought that if demand were to fall for a particular product within the main product group, then the partners of Firm P would take three courses of action, in the following order: switching to a new product; reducing over-time and introducing short-time working.

Costs were split up into fixed and variable costs and these cost divisions were found to be useful in the running of the firm. Marginal costs were not calculated for Firm P. A capacity output was recognized, and it was thought that this SBE normally operated at 61–70 per cent of capacity. The partner interviewed felt that for normal output variation the total cost increased in line with the amount supplied (i.e. that marginal cost was constant). Firm P was thought to be the lowest-cost producer in the industry. As a result, it had what the partner interviewed regarded as a very healthy gross profit margin of 54 per cent. Low unit costs were thought to have been achieved by exploiting scale economies, by using modern, efficient machinery and by tightly controlling overheads (i.e. support activities). Further, the wage bill was tightly controlled by limiting the number of employees. Making deliveries in a prompt and reliable fashion was thought to control costs as well, presumably by avoiding the high extra cost of urgent delivery sevices. It was anticipated that another lamination machine would be purchased to meet the growing new orders, and that this would help to reduce unit costs further.

Market research methods were used to find out how price-sensitive customers were, how interested buyers were in the firm's products, the form of competitors' reactions and what developments in the market could be expected in the future. Demand was thought to be inelastic in response to both small (5 per cent) and large (10 per cent) variations of price, assuming no reaction from competitors and normal business conditions. This inelasticity would have been partly a consequence of the fact that the cost of this product was but a small part of the customers' total costs. The partner did not think that a reduction in price by his firm would evoke a reponse from his strongest competitors, irrespective of whether business conditions were normal, buoyant or depressed, and the same was thought to be true in the cases of small and large price increases. Consistent with this, it was thought that Firm P had a certain amount of elbow room in pricing, within which a price change by it would not bring about a reaction from its competitors. This elbow room was estimated to be more than 15 per cent. The events that might lead the partners of Firm P to alter its selling price included, in decreasing order of importance, the occurrence of cost changes, a substantial shift in demand and a change in competitors' prices. Price discrimination was practised by Firm P, involving different prices being set for different customers and for large and small traders. Price rebates were offered in the form of bulk discounting. Firm P's goods were not sold at controlled or recommended prices. The firm's advertising took the form of both generic and individual advertising. The partner was prepared to increase the advertising of his firm when business demand was low, but not to reduce it when there was a boom in demand.

Competition in Firm P's principal market was described as 'strong, but weak in some respects'. The multinational firm was the only major rival, and it used the same modern technology. However, its competitive edge was limited by poor customer relations. Firm P, with the same modern machinery, but a more personal approach to customers, was known in the trade to be capable of winning customers from the multinational. This helped to give other small rivals more heart for competition. There were thought to be 'good' competitors in the trade, to whom one could sub-contract if demand could not be immediately met. Not all rivals had this status, and there was some fear of 'giving customers away' by subcontracting. 'Good' competitors were thought to share a healthy understanding of the need to maintain a healthy profit margin in the industry.

Barriers to new competition were significant. In particular, there were high capital requirements. New lamination machines were priced at £120,000 (in 1985 prices) and there was an eighteen-month delivery lag. Suppliers to the industry have become aware of their market power. Earlier, there had been a favourable leasing agreement for lamination machines which required payment after six months of starting the lease. At the time of interview in 1985 a new scheme operated which required all the money to be put up front for lamination machines. The partner interviewed thought that the high gross profit margin of Firm P (54 per cent) could be attributed to superior machinery. Business knowledge as well as technical knowledge about printing materials were also thought to be a barrier to entry.

Advice was not sought at the time of starting the business. According to the partner interviewed, the size of the total assets of Firm P at financial inception was a nominal £2. The approximate size of Firm P, in terms of book value of assets, in 1985, was £180,000. The main obstacle to obtaining financial support to start the business had been a lack of personal financial injections. A secondary obstacle had been difficulty in producing satisfactory financial statements of the proposed business (e.g. in terms of a projected cash-flow budget). Obtaining financial support for starting the business had been found difficult and only personal finance was used to set up the business. The initial gearing ratio had therefore been zero. The equity gearing ratio at the time of interview was one-third, which was the highest value it had attained. The partner expected the gearing ratio to stay the same over the next year, due to an increase in ploughed-back profits and a parallel increase in debt. He then expected it would fall for the following two years due to a reduction in debt and an increase in ploughed-back profits.

Firm P had experienced cash-flow difficulties, with overinvestment being the main causal factor, aggravated by an insufficient overdraft facility. External finance had been sought since inception to fund the purchase of plant and equipment. The partner expected to see growth in his SBE over the forseeable future. This was both because demand for the main product was thought to be growing, and because it was thought that the benefits of this growth would be evenly distributed over all the firms in the industry, including Firm P itself. There was some confidence that no new technologies would change the market order. It was thought that at least three years would be required to develop new machinery. The current (in 1985) best-practice technology had taken twenty years to develop. Trade magazines and journals and suppliers themselves, provided good information on new developments. Three years after the initial interview, Firm P was still in business, but its partners at the time of interview in 1985 were unavailable for interview. The firm had become a private company limited by guarantee. From what we were able to determine indirectly, the original partners of Firm P had sold a share of the company to an outside party, and were in due course bought out. The new major shareholder then ran the same business from the same address, apparently with customer goodwill intact.

3.9 CONCLUSION

We have now concluded our second set of Profiles of SBEs. Again, as well as providing evidence in a form which aims to be scientific, we hope to have stimulated a taste for theoretical enquiry. For example, Firm F (foodstuff manufacturers) illustrated the entrepreneurial theory of Holmes and Schmitz (1990) according to which high-quality entrepreneurs set-up and then sell-on high quality SBEs. As another example, Firm I (computer software) illustrates the importance of learning by doing, and the dynamic scale economies it generates.

More humbly, we have steadily accumulated and sifted further evidence in a unified framework. Knowledge is thereby advanced, and meaning is attached to SBEs' actions. We thus move one step further towards the possibility of cross-site analysis.

4 High market concentration

4.1 INTRODUCTION

Here we present for the reader the third and final set of Profiles. They relate to small business enterprises (SBEs) which operate in high market concentration environments. The SBEs chosen are indicated in Table 4.1.

These SBEs are all subject to marked product differentiation, higher entry and exit barriers, and on the evidence available, have significant market shares. We have chosen to view these SBEs as essentially subject to the forces of oligopoly, in a market-models sense. This leaves relatively open to us the specific choice of oligopoly model. A familiar way to proceed would be to examine price-setting oligopolists, each of which maximized profits independently in a market for differentiated products.[1] Depending on the belief of an oligopolist about how rivals' prices will change if his own price changes, one gets a different type of oligopoly model. However, there are some general results to which one can appeal for guidance on how real oligopolies might be expected to function. The mark-up of price over marginal cost for a specific oligopolist will depend inversely on the industry or market elasticity of demand, other things being equal. This mark-up will also be negatively associated with the number of rivals: larger numbers of rivals, other things being equal, lower margins. Further, the mark-up is negatively associated with the individual oligopolist's partial elasticity of demand, other things being equal. Finally, the mark-up will depend negatively on 'conjectural variation', an oligopolist's belief about the effect his price change will have on rivals' behaviour. This can be 'packaged up' into a kind of portmanteau effect for the market as a whole. For example, if the oligopolists simply colluded, this portmanteau effect would have a value of unity. We have only three oligopoly markets to examine and are not appealing to econometric evidence to try and determine what conjectures

Table 4.1 SBEs profiled in high-concentration markets

B	Security printers blankets
H	Retail cosmetics
M	Aerobatic aircraft construction

are for each market. In principle this can be done,[2] but we do not have the data on rivals necessary to achieve this. Therefore, we have to proceed by being prudently aware that the conjectures made by oligopolists have an appreciable effect on market outcomes. Fortunately, for Firms B, H and M we have rich information on these SBEs' conjectures or beliefs, particularly so far as pricing is concerned. The advantage of our method is that the instrumentation has permitted us to investigate these conjectures or beliefs directly.[3] We turn now to an examination of this, and many further issues, in these our last three Profiles.

4.2 PROFILE B: SECURITY PRINTERS BLANKETS

Firm B had been formed as a result of a managerial buy-out in August 1982. The firm in its original form had been in existence for over one hundred years. It produced a highly specialized product which was subject to patent protection. There were eleven full-time workers, two part-timers and two trainees. In terms of legal form, the firm was a private company. In 1985 the value of the sales turnover (excluding VAT) was £600,000 at 1985 prices.

The main product produced was security printers blankets. These were used for printing currency and travellers cheques. Briefly, the product is a blanket of 0.50mm thickness, made up of a pure cotton woven fabric of 0.35mm thickness and faced with a higher-quality synthetic rubber of 0.15mm thickness. The firm produced from two to five product groups (e.g. security printers blankets, letterpress blankets, rubber proofed fabrics, etc.) and a total of between twenty-one and forty products. The firm could have produced a much broader range of products. However, this had been the strategy of the previous incarnation of the firm and had led to poor performance. This had been because some products were being marketed in areas of particularly stiff competition, and little attention had been paid to analysing which were the high-value product lines. The new strategy was to keep out of areas of stiff competition and to concentrate on high-value-generating products. A way of doing this was to pounce on new opportunities in related market segments as soon as they appeared. This had been done very successfully. In established markets Firm B strenuously repelled new entrants. Here it was helped by patent protection. The SBE was aware that getting into new lines could foreclose options for rivals. This might include foreclosing on a technology.

The principal market was perceived to be the international economy and the market share of world business was estimated at 11–20 per cent. There were no minor competitors and major competitors numbered no more than five. The global industry was highly concentrated. Firm B was the sole producer of the main product range in Europe and the only producer of a certain product in the world. It believed itself to be competitive, even against large multinational enterprises. The main product, compared to that of rivals, was perceived to be mildly differentiated. Product differentiation, whilst recognized, was not a preoccupation, though it was seen to be valuable. The firm aimed to achieve costless differentiation, but had not yet explored costly differentiation. An attention to detail was important. Detailed design characteristics, which were an aspect of differentiation, and which were not costly to modify, could significantly influence demand. An example given was the colour of sheeting used for a main product.

Suppliers were quite concentrated. For some specialized inputs there was little choice of supplier, and sole suppliers were not unknown. In such cases, the firm sought, and tried to encourage, the emergence of substitutes. Many suppliers produced a standardized product, but a few special items were almost like prototype work. Forward integration had been attempted by one supplier, but with no success, due to lack of know-how.

Regarding the knowledgeability of customers, three types were distinguished, all of which could be regarded as relatively well informed. Firstly, there were the customers who needed to be informed on the technical features of a product, and were guided by such matters. Secondly, there were the fairly expert customers who could draw on personal experience in evaluating the product, as well as on technical information available in specialist publications and trade journals. Thirdly, and most typically, there were the customers who were experts, who could exercise independent authoritative judgement on the quality of the product. Given the importance of national governments as customers, who would employ expert advisers as buyers, the very knowledgeable characteristics of these channels to purchasing was understandable. Whilst customers were well informed, they still lacked vital inside information. This lack buttressed by patent protection of key formulas, removed the threat of backward integration. Customers tended to be conservative. They were aware of technical substitutes (e.g. man-made fibres) but preferred traditional materials. A major rival, a multinational enterprise, had tried to use man-made fibres, but customers rejected the product, considering it to be of lower quality. Customers had a low propensity to substitute (between traditional and new rival products) if the quality of traditional products was high and service was good.

Firm B recognized the concept of the 'real' customer, this being the specific person in an organization who had authority over purchases. It was said that 'person-to-person contact is vital'. Senior staff travelled extensively to make personal visits, and carried out a form of market research at the same time. Some customers possessed, and exercised, bargaining leverage on this SBE. Whilst Firm B aimed to reduce seller (i.e. supplier) dependence, it recognized that loss of any single customer could be viewed as a problem. Fortunately, switching costs were high for some products, for some customers. This made negotiation more likely than loss or non-renewal of contract. Replacement demand was an important generator of orders. These were often placed by government agencies, but the firm did not attempt to influence such institutions once they had become clients. They aimed, rather, to be adaptive to the demands of clients.

Price was determined as a flexible mark-up on variable cost, and the aim was to set the mark-up at the highest level the market would bear. Volume considerations were taken into account when setting price. The pricing policy of competitors had a significant impact on the firm's price setting, and price would be held down, if need be, to beat competitors. However, recourse to this strategy was approached cautiously. There was a considerable resistance to reducing profit targets, and a fear that price cutting might precipitate a price war. A preferred device to beating customers on price was beating them on delivery, on a fast turn-around. The firm did not use entry-deterring pricing, which it tended to regard as unethical.

In the face of a boom in demand which could not be met from stocks, the first reaction would be to increase overtime or shiftwork, followed by increasing capacity, possibly by recruiting more personnel. Faced with a recession, the first reaction would be to reduce overtime, followed by an increased sales effort, with the final resort being to reducing capacity, possibly by laying-off personnel. If demand fell for a product within the main product group, not necessarily associated with a recession, the first reaction would be to increase sales effort, the second would be to try to establish the underlying cause (e.g. quality, delivery, technical specification), and the third would be to cut price.

Costs were split up into fixed costs and variable costs, and these categories were thought to be useful in running the firm. Firm B aimed to achieve cost leadership on its standardized run-of-the-mill product. The target was to achieve a given high specification at least cost. Firm B was not willing to produce to a lower specification of its products at lower costs. This would be perceived as a neglect of quality and of potential damage to this SBE's image and reputation. It wished to be thought of as a major supplier of top technical specification goods. The principal cost-drivers were materials and salaries. Of these, materials costs were difficult to control. It was found to be possible to reconfigure the value chain by juggling with job scheduling. All employees were salaried which meant treating wages as a fixed rather than variable cost. This was found to be good for productivity when put alongside a twice yearly bonus. Marginalist mentality was indicated by the claim that the firm could calculate the additional cost of increasing the output of a product by a given increment. There was an output which was recognized as the capacity, or maximum possible output; and actual output was estimated, in normal conditions, to be 61–70 per cent of capacity output. The firm aimed to carry a certain amount of capacity for competitive advantage. The pattern of cost variation with output variation was thought to satisfy a concave total cost schedule, indicating a declining marginal cost, and a declining average cost as output increased.[4]

No formal market research methods were used, though this SBE did have good sources of trade intelligence established in over a hundred years of world-wide operations of its previous incarnations. Firm B found that much the most useful market research was obtained by face-to-face contact with actual and potential clients. It aimed to keep an active interest in ideas relevant to the industry. Thus trade shows were thought to be both good for the company image, and of help in finding out about new developments.

In the face of a small (5 per cent) price change up or down, assuming no response by rivals, it was felt that there would be no difference in the amount purchased of the main product. In the face of a large (10 per cent) price increase (again assuming no rivals' responded) it was felt that demand would not fall at all; but in the face of a 10 per cent price decrease it was felt that demand would increase less than 10 per cent. That is, for large price variations demand was thought to be totally inelastic upwards, and relatively inelastic downwards. This is part of a general tendency in the parent sample of SBEs for price flexibility to be relatively unimportant in influencing demand in markets where the product was differentiated and technical specification was important. The price sensitivity of customers was analysed in a very sophisticated way. Two main product groups were identified: printing and rubberized sheeting. In the case of printing, the product, while important to the customer (even, arguably, indispensible) and of an exact technical specification, was a minimal component of total cost. Customers of this product group therefore displayed little price sensitivity. In the case of rubberized sheeting, the cost was likely to be a large component of the customer's total cost. Such customers were more price conscious. Impressed by the detail of this analysis, the interviewer asked the respondent how he knew customers behaved like this. He replied, 'They let us know'. As a general proposition he felt that low profitability of the customers' products increased their purchasing price sensitivity. It was also thought that product differentiation affected price sensitivity. An example given was that the demand for a 'designer' (i.e. highly fashionable) mail-order product was not price sensitive, though it was very quality sensitive. In fact, a client had come to Firm B seeking supplies for this market precisely because the necessary quality was not available elsewhere.

In terms of conjectural variation in price, this SBE thought that if price were reduced then the major rival would also reduce price in boom or recession conditions but not in normal conditions. For a price increase it was felt rivals would not match it, in normal or recession conditions, and no judgement could be made on what would happen in boom conditions. Consistent with this general picture of demand inelasticity was the belief held by this firm that it had a considerable degree of elbow room in pricing, within which no price reaction would be forthcoming by its competitors. The magnitude of this elbow room was estimated to be in the range of 10–15 per cent. Reasons for altering the selling price were particularly identified as the arrival of a new business year and substantial shifts in demand. These reasons are really distinct. Presumably if nothing had changed, price would not be changed, even if a new business year had started. It amounts to saying that price is usually not changed until a new business year commences, and that typically the reason for doing so is a demand shift. Price discrimination was practised between different customers and price rebates were offered on a bulk discount basis. There were no controlled or recommended prices for this firm's products. Advertising was used, of the type described as rivalrous (i.e. it aimed to promote this firm's product over that of its rivals). This SBE was aware that maintaining a high profile helped to put off rivals. Advertising was increased when business demand was low in order to drum up more trade, but was not reduced in a boom. Concerning the latter behaviour, it is clear that Firm B was not willing to act under the dangerous presumption that custom was there for the taking. It was very sensitive to the long-term nature of its business connection with most of its principal clients. Competition was thought to be generally strong, though weak in some aspects.

No outside advice was sought at the stage of inception of Firm B. This had been accomplished three years earlier by a managerial buy-out of a long-established firm with a stable customer base. As financial inception the approximate size of the business (at 1983 prices) was £70,000, measured by the book value of total assets. In 1985 (at nominal prices) size by assets was estimated to lie in the range of £100,000 to £110,000. Firm B used largely personal finance at inception and experienced neither difficulty in raising it nor in raising outside debt finance. At financial inception the gearing ratio was one-half, which had proven to be its highest level. This had been reduced to zero in the three years since financial inception. Over a three-year future time-scale, Firm B's intention was to keep the gearing ratio at zero. It was reported in 1985 that 'The company set-up at the present time is quite satisfactory'. No special financial schemes had been necessary or helpful at the time of financial inception. The firm had experienced cash-flow difficulties caused by overinvestment, but had not resorted to debt finance to alleviate the problem. The expectation was that growth of the business would occur over the forseeable future.

Three years later, by the time of the reinterview this expectation had indeed been confirmed. Firm B was still in business at the same location, producing similar products, with the same core personnel. In 1985 a market growth of 10 per cent per annum and a company growth of 20 per cent per annum was anticipated. Growth indeed had been rapid since 1985 with sales turnover having risen from £600,000 in 1985 to £927,000 in 1988 (both at nominal prices, exclusive of VAT). This represents a real sales growth of 37 per cent. Real asset growth (net of depreciation) had been 42 per cent. The number of full-time employees had risen from eleven to sixteen. Firm B no longer had part-time employees and still employed two trainees. Profitability in 1985 was 23 per cent, net of taxes and directors' fees; and gross profitability[5] was 41 per cent. Both these figures are high compared to the average for the sample as a whole (9 per cent and 29 per cent, respectively). There had been no change in competitiveness due to innovation over the three years from 1985 to 1988. The output of the main product-group had increased substantially (by an estimated 35–40 per cent), and unit costs had risen quite markedly (by about 25 per cent). The output mix had changed substantially, resulting in an estimated 6 per cent increase in the relative sales value attributable to the main product-line. Since 1985 the firm had experienced a shortage of skilled labour, but Firm B did not think this had had a serious impact on its growth. Attempts to fill the skills gap at the wage Firm B could best afford, had resulted in difficulty in recruiting people with previous employment experience.

Unusually for the sample, Firm B had quite well articulated defensive strategies, possibly because the earlier SBE from which this one rose as a 'phoenix enterprise' had been in business for many decades. Further, to some extent the vulnerability of the earlier SBE had driven home to those who participated in the management buy-out how important it was not only to create and exploit niches, but to defend them as well. Firm B enjoyed significant defensive advantages from barrriers to entry. These had been facilitated by priviledged contact with a major UK institution, which created many exclusive channels of access for Firm B. A lack of these would be very hard to overcome by any rival contemplating entry. As the respondent for the semi-structured interview of 1985 put it in this interview, 'Channels are vital'. Capital requirements were important, as a barrier to entry, because the machinery was specialized and expensive. The plant was valued at over £1 million at 1985 prices. Know-how was also mentioned in interview as being a barrier to entry. It was claimed that exit barriers were low.[6]

Firm B had high strategic stakes and signalled its commitment to defend its markets. For example, it had to consider its defence against a large multi-national product which had imitated both its product and price list. Early response was thought to be vital. In view of the exclusive nature of the product, challengers had to be taken very seriously. In the case of the threatening multinational, a lawyer's response was sent off the next day, conveying that Firm B was prepared to pursue litigation. The respondent felt that this multinational's attack was in some sense a compliment to his SBE's strong competitive position. The attack could not be allowed to go unchallenged, as it would have damaged the intended image of Firm B as a tough defender. The respondent took an individualistic line on this, saying, 'We don't let others speak for us: we speak for ourselves'. The idea of a collective industry response was not thought to be desirable or probable.

The respondent in the 1988 reinterview had sensed the emergence of an enterprise culture in Scotland since 1985. He had witnessed many SBEs growing and moving into larger premises. On the industrial estate on which his own SBE was located, he knew of only one firm which had closed down in the previous three years.

4.3 PROFILE H: FRANCHISE RETAIL OUTLET FOR NATURAL HAIR AND SKIN PRODUCTS

Firm H had been in existence since December 1984 as a retail distributor of cosmetics. It employed eight full-time workers and five part-time workers. In terms of legal form the business was a franchise. In 1985 the value of the sales turnover (excluding VAT) was upwards of £245,000. Firm H had grown rapidly since inception and was participating in an industry-wide growth trend. The owner-manager attributed a lot of his SBE's growth to its central city location. He said, 'Because the typical customer spends just £3 you need a lot of "traffic", and a good site provides the best indictor of the firm's established position in the market'. This trend in Firm H's growth was confirmed in 1988, as it was still in business and had grown both in terms of personnel and sales turnover. By 1988 it employed fourteen full-time workers, six part-time workers and two trainees. The sales turnover (excluding VAT) was £1.06 million (at 1988 prices), representing a real growth of sales of over 280 per cent. The business had a wide product-group range, over fifty, and it stocked over eighty products. This was typical for the market as a whole, for which the owner-manager estimated that over a hundred different products were marketed.

The franchisor provided 70 per cent of the products to this franchisee. Multiple suppliers catered to the remaining 30 per cent of product requirements. An ongoing concern of Firm H was with 'filling product gaps'. Firm H introduced between twelve and fifteen new products each year. It was felt to be important to keep the staff abreast of changing customers' wants and needs. The 'formula for success' expressed by the owner-manager was 'good staff, good products and customer rapport'. It was felt that a good staff made the success of the firm less dependent on the continuous presence of the owner-manager. This could free up his time to open other retail outlets on the same model. By 1988 the output of Firm H's main product line had not changed. However, the output mix had changed substantially, with the importance of the main product-line having increased by 20 per cent, in terms of proportion of value of total sales.

The owner-manager regarded his principal market as the region, although the franchisor's operations were national and plans were afoot to extend operations to the United States. In terms of this regional market the owner-manager estimated that his market share for natural hair and skin products was over 50 per cent. The manager could distinguish between major and minor competitors and estimated that there were between six and ten minor competitors but no major competitors in his regional market. Of course, there are many large firms in the cosmetics industry, taken as a global industry. By 1988 there had been no innovation in the principal market, therefore, on this dimension, competitiveness had been unaffected.

The main product group of Firm H was perceived to be 'different' from that of its competitors. Generally, packaging partly achieved this perceived product differentiation, but Firm H deliberately did not use the glamorous packaging so typical of cosmetics' marketing. Where products offered were similar to rivals this would always mean a matching of quality, though price might be lower for Firm H. A unique container refill policy helped keep down costs to customers. An emphasis was placed on the natural ingredients used in the products: 'There is no substitute for the real thing'. The location of the retail outlet was felt to be an important dimension of product differentiation.

There were three main customer types. Most typically, customers buying Firm H's products generally needed to be informed on the technical features of a product and were guided by such factual matters. Firm H strongly believed in keeping customers informed about both established and new products. This was done by providing information about them on the shelves below the particular products. Staff were also kept informed about products, and a *Product Information Guide* was provided at the sales counter. The sales ethos was that customers should not be pressurized into a sale, but rather that sales staff should be present to facilitate a sale when required, and to provide useful information otherwise. Less typically, some customers of Firm H could not distinguish the technical differences between its products and those of its rivals. They were influenced by price, brand, design and packaging. Finally, there was a third group of customers who were fairly expert about the products and could draw on personal experience, as well as technical knowledge available in specialist publications, in making their purchasing decisions. Customers of this SBE were thought to be largely '*all* women regardless of age, income level or social status'. Contrary to many other firms, who targeted market segments more narrowly, Firm H aimed at wide appeal. The average customer purchase was valued at only £3 in 1985, and Firm H was not dependent on any one customer type. Customers had in common that they were looking for products to improve their health and beauty. Firm H had a role in solving what the customer very often perceived as a health or beauty problem.

If a new product were brought onto the market its price would be set without regard to the potential sales volume. Up to 15 per cent of products were new each year. Price was partly set by the franchisor, who determined price by a flexible mark-up based on variable cost per unit. Costs (manufacturing and distribution) were kept as low as possible by the franchisor. Further, Firm H, as franchisee, benefited from low marketing and sales costs because of using the nation-wide image of the franchisor. The pricing policy of competitors was not considered crucial to Firm H's own pricing and the owner-manager thought that his SBE would not hold down price to beat its rivals. It was recognized that, given the multitude of differentiated products in the industry, price differentials would be widespread and persistent. It was felt that Firm H already provided quality products at very competitive prices. Should a boom in demand occur that could not be met from stocks, the first line of action to be undertaken would be to lengthen the order books followed by increasing capacity (which could include the recruitment of more personnel). In a recession the first reaction would be to reduce overtime, followed by an increase in sales effort, then stockholding would be reduced and lastly a price cut would be considered. If demand were to fall for a particular product within the main product group, the only action would be to cut price. Much of the price discretion was exercised by the franchisor in response to national trends in demand. At the regional market level, of some relevance to Firm H, the range of products provided some extra discretion.

Costs were split up into fixed and variable costs and these cost divisions were found to be useful in the running of the firm. Additional costs would be calculated if Firm H intended to increase output. The manager did not recognize a level of output which he regarded as the capacity or maximum possible output. Regarding the form of the cost curve, it was thought that at first total cost did not increase as fast as output, but that it then increased faster than output. The point at which marginal costs started to rise was presumably high, as the owner-manager talked of scale economies being important. The franchise as a group exerted a powerful bargaining pressure on suppliers, which helped to keep costs low. Small-scale new entrants would not have this bargaining advantage with suppliers, and a lack of it constituted a barrier to entry. Other barriers to entry mentioned by the owner-manager included trade experience, scale economies, capital, trade contacts and location. In addition, the franchisor held a number of patents which protected its franchisees' markets.

Firm H did use market research methods – for example, forecasts by official bodies and trade associations. These were used to discover the importance of price changes to customers, the interest of buyers in Firm H's products and the way in which future developments would affect the market. Apart from the systematic market research, suppliers and customers were important informal sources of market information. Suppliers kept Firm H informed about new and popular products. They would provide trial samples to support their view of the market. The more adventurous customers would also keep Firm H informed about prices and products offered by similar franchises. Finally, trade shows were also a good source of information on new suppliers and products.

Given the low costs per item, and the low costs compared to the customers' total outlay on products for well-being, it would be unlikely that customers were highly price sensitive. For a small (5 per cent) increase or decrease in price, given no response by competitors and normal business conditions, demand was thought to be totally price inelastic. For a large (10 per cent) price increase or decrease, demand was thought to be relatively inelastic although not completely. The manager thought that if he reduced his price, his strongest competitors would not follow this action in normal or buoyant business conditions, but that they would given depressed conditions. It was thought that competitors would not raise their prices if Firm

H did so first, in any business conditions, normal, buoyant or depressed. Consistent with the belief that demand was inelastic for both large and small price variations, a certain amount of elbow room in pricing was recognized and this was estimated to be 7–8 per cent. Customers were described as being 'obsessed with the enhancement of their health and looks'. Consequently customer motivation was high. Switching costs were thought to be quite high. If the product worked for the customer, they were unlikely to be swayed by the 'fancy packaging and high prices' of rivals. It was felt that rivals in the health products industry would not be taken seriously until they abandoned their 'glamorous packaging' strategy. This seemed unlikely as this strategy was aimed at such specialized marketing segments. If rivals deviated from their existing strategies, they would lose even their present clientele.

Events which might lead to an alteration in selling price included the commencement of a new business year or season of production, the occurrence of cost changes, a shift in demand and the granting of permission for price adjustment by the franchisor. Firm H did practise price discrimination, with the franchisor specifying some prices, but not all. Price rebates were offered, but the firm did not practise bulk discounting. Products were sold at prices controlled or recommended by the franchisor. The volume of customers who ended up paying this recommended price lay between 91 per cent and 100 per cent. Advertising was undertaken and this took the form of both generic and individual advertising. Potential entrants could expect retaliation in the form of advertising. Advertising was not increased if demand was slack and it was not reduced if demand was strong. Competition in the market was described as generally weak in all its aspects. 'Good' competitors were encouraged by sending customers to rivals that supplied products which Firm H did not stock. Such products were typically complementary to Firm H's, hence both firms would benefit from the referral.

At the inception of the business the owner-manager sought advice firstly from family and friends, followed by his accountant, then the local enterprise trust and finally the Scottish Development Agency. At inception, the approximate size of Firm H in terms of total assets (book value) was £16,000 in 1984 (at nominal prices). There had been a rapid growth in the size of this SBE. At the time of interview in 1985 assets were £65,000 at 1985 prices. By 1988, assets had grown to £1,500,000 (at nominal prices) representing a real annual growth rate of approximately 650 per cent p.a. The owner-manager hoped to open another shop in the same large city within the same franchise network, and then possibly a third in another city about 50 miles away. Market segments were thought of in geographical terms.

The owner-manager had encountered difficulties in obtaining financial support for starting the business. Firstly, it had been thought that the owner-manager's employment experience was not a good preparation for small business ownership. Secondly, it had been difficult to persuade potential backers that a market existed for the firm's products. Thirdly, difficulties had been encountered in producing satisfactory financial statements of the proposed business (e.g. in terms of a cash-flow budget). Only personal finance was used to set up the business (i.e. the gearing ratio had initially been zero). At the time of interview, in 1985, the gearing ratio was still zero. The owner-manager expected the gearing ratio to rise over the next year due to an increase in debt, and then to 'stay the same' over the next two years. He had expectations of an increase in ploughed-back profits; a reduction in debt, and profit-taking (in the second year); and ploughed-back profits (in the third year), which should *lower* gearing. In the event the gearing ratio did fall over the first two years and then rose, presumably to fall again to zero during the third year. At the time of reinterview in 1988, Firm H's debt gearing ratio was zero. Based on figures provided in 1988 for three years earlier the rate of profit in 1985 was estimated to have been 10 per cent. However, other evidence indicates it may have been as high as 77 per cent. The owner-manager had never suffered cash-flow difficulties and had not sought external finance since starting his business. He expected to see growth in his business over the foreseeable future.

In 1988 the owner-manager said that he had not sensed the emergence of an enterprise culture in Scotland since 1985. He commented, 'Small firms are still suffering from a lack of professional expertise'.

4.4 PROFILE M: CONSTRUCTION OF FULL-SCALE AEROBATIC AIRCRAFT FROM KITS[7]

Firm M had been in existence for nine months at the time of interview in 1985, though an earlier form of the business had operated for five years. Firm M employed one full-time worker and two part-time workers. In terms of legal form, it was a private company. Because Firm M was so close to financial inception at the time of interview in 1985, no figures were available on current turnover. However, the value of the sales turnover (excluding VAT) was expected to be £100,000 over the next twelve months.

The main product group of Firm M was light aircraft; this was also the only product group. The total number of products was small, in the range one to ten. Barring bespoke aspects of particular orders, there was in essence one product, a low-cost alternative to the market leading brand of aerobatic aircraft (namely, the Pit Special). Low cost was being achieved by assembly from a kit form. This was a single-seater aircraft, highly manoeuvrable, which could fly for about two hours at 100 mph. Firm M was a competitor in what was perceived as an international market. Its market share for light aircraft was unknown but very small. There were known to be 21,000 pilots in the United Kingdom, which was a starting-point for an analysis of the domestic market, but only a fraction of these would be able to purchase an aircraft. Some 2,500 pilots in the United Kingdom gave up flying each year because it was too expensive, and Firm M offered a kit aerobatic aircraft at half the price of the main rival product aimed at such potential customers. Both domestically and internationally the aerobatic aircraft niche in the aviation industry was known to be a very small and specialized one. The owner-manager could distinguish between major and minor competitors but was not prepared to hazard a guess at how many major competitors his firm had. The aerobatic aeroplane industry was dominated by a number of large American companies producing expensive high-performance aircraft. The only rival product to theirs had previously been second-hand military aircraft. The owner-manager of Firm M thought he could provide more effective rivalry than this. Military aircraft tended to be unnecessarily large for aerobatics and hence expensive to run. They were also rather old (twenty to thirty years) and could present difficulties in sourcing spare parts. Furthermore, because they were usually metal, rather than wooden, they were less manoeuvrable. It was thought that there were between one and five minor competitors.

In terms of product differentiation, Firm M's products were thought to be 'different' from those of its competitors. However, these differences did not involve significant technological innovations. High-technology rivals were not expected to emerge in the near future. New technology was thought most likely to be introduced from outside the industry. The suppliers did not contribute to technical change. A certain conservatism in the industry was fostered by heavy government and safety regulations. Thus suppliers would provide customers with very standardized information on existing products, with no hint of what was to come in terms of innovation. The owner-manager said, 'Looking back over the industry, not much has changed in the last thirty years'. It was thought that the volume of customers who could afford to buy an aerobatic plane, even a relatively low-cost one, was small. The 'time to harvest' was thought to be short: 'It may be that everyone who wants to purchase such a plane will have purchased one within three years'. Customers were recognized as having fairly expert knowledge about the firm's products and could draw on personal experience (e.g. of flying and of airshows) as well as on technical information available in specialist publications and trade journals. An aim of the owner-manager was to display Firm M's products at airshows and flying clubs, and to advertise in the right journals.

Pricing was not influenced by the volume of products the owner-manager expected to sell. It was such a low-volume operation that such considerations were unlikely to be important. Price was set as a fixed mark-up on variable cost per unit. The aim of this pricing policy was to achieve a desired level of gross profit. The owner-manager thought he had set a 'realistic and fair' mark-up of 20 per cent. In terms of low-cost producers of high-performance aerobatic planes, he did not fear rivals. Thus, rather than worry about deterring rivals, his main concern was to expand the market by appealing to customers who were highly motivated to fly aerobatic aircraft. There was no mass market, so competitive threats from broadly targeted competitors in the aviation industry were non-existent. It was thought to be too early in Firm M's development to worry about the prospect of retaliation by rivals. The pricing of competitors was not regarded as important, although the owner-manager reported that his SBE would hold down its price to beat that of its competitors. The Pit Specials were not thought to be realistic economic rivals as they were priced at around £55,000, almost twice what Firm M would charge for its low-cost technological substitute. However, cheap, second-hand military aircraft appeared to be possible economic substitutes, though they were poor technological substitutes being too old, too heavy and lacking in manoeuvrability. If a boom in demand were to occur which the firm could not meet from stocks, the first reaction would be to try to increase capacity (this could include the recruitment of more personnel) followed by a lengthening of the order books. Only one course of action would be undertaken in a recession and this would be to reduce capacity (including the laying-off of personnel). In the face of a fall in demand in the firm's main product-group it was felt that the only option would be to switch to a new product.

Costs were split up into fixed and variable costs. These cost divisions were thought to be useful in the running of the business. The firm was conceived as a low-cost operator. Very cheap premises were rented and only two persons worked on construction. The design itself was established, so no development costs were incurred. Marginal cost was calculated for an increase in output. The owner-manager did recognize a capacity output though not in the conventional sense. Expected capacity was governed by the expected size of the market, which was very small, and by the availability of a specialized aero-engine that was fuel-injected, had a lot of power for its capacity and was very fuel efficient. Only eight of these engines could be produced each year by a specialized supplier. It was felt that without this engine, the product produced would be inferior. Hence, in principle, the annual capacity production was just eight aircraft. The target production each year was four aircraft, which would provide a handsome profit, and three would have to be produced to make a reasonable profit.[8] The owner-manager felt that Firm M normally operated at less than 50 per cent of capacity. Total costs were thought not to increase as fast as the amount supplied (i.e. the extra cost of supplying each additional unit falls as more is supplied). The intention was that units would be produced seriatim, with each aircraft requiring four months' work.

Market research methods were used as a tool to find out how interested buyers were in Firm M's products. Air displays were a good source of trade intelligence. The typical customer was 'very self-indulgent' and had 'flying in his blood'. The customer was collective: 'he' was typically a syndicate of five or six pilots. The customer did not want cheap flying as such, but cheap aerobatics. The owner-manager said, 'My firm is essentially selling performance at an affordable price'. His product would sell at £25,000 per aircraft, whereas for comparable performance the customer would have to go upmarket and purchase the expensive, high performance Pit Special at £55,000 (1985 prices). The one-seater design of Firm M's product allied to a high-performance aero-engine made the aircraft very suitable for its specialist purpose, aerobatics, but of little use as a general-purpose flying machine, hence the focus on highly motivated customers. They were typically experienced ex-fliers.

Demand was thought to be inelastic in response to both small (5 per cent) and large (10 per cent) variations in price about the established price, assuming that business conditions were normal and that there were no reponses from competitors. The owner-manager did not think that a price reduction by him would bring about a price reduction by his strongest competitors in normal, boom or depressed business conditions, and the position was thought to be similar with respect to price increases. Consistent with this, it was believed that Firm M had a considerable amount of elbow-room in pricing such that a price change by it would not evoke a reaction by its competitors. This elbow room was estimated to be large, over 15 per cent about the current price. This lack of customer price sensitivity arose from the fact that most purchasers would ideally like a Pit Special, an upmarket, expensive, high-performance aerobatic plane, but few could afford it. What Firm M offered was something similar, constructed from a kit, offering almost the same performance at half the price. A customer might buy Firm M's product as an end in itself, or else to gain further experience, with a view to eventually purchasing a Pit Special. Customer motivation was thought to be significantly increased after the kit-based product had been demonstrated actually flying.

Selling price would be altered by the SBE if cost changes were to occur. Price discrimination was not practised by the owner-manager of Firm M, and no rebates were offered to customers. There were no such things as controlled or recommended prices for Firm M's product. An aggressive advertising campaign had been adopted in the form of individual, rivalrous advertising. An important promotional device was the first aircraft produced, which was used for demonstration purposes and was not for sale. The only restriction on this medium of advertising was 'finding the airfields'. Specialist flying journals were also used for advertising messages. Advertising was reduced in boom conditions but it was unknown whether advertising would be increased in depressed conditions.

The competition in the market was described as generally weak, but strong with respect to price and quality. The owner-manager claimed he would welcome competition 'to increase customer awareness.' However, competition was slight. Barriers to entry limited competition. Capital requirements were high, and there was a long average period of production (four months for each aircraft) during which there was no tangible return on investment. Suppliers were highly specialized and few in number. Because of stiff government regulations and patent protection, all materials had to be tested, approved and licensed before being sold. Supply channels were hard to access and exerted considerable bargaining power. Because Firm M had suffered at the hands of its main supplier, through production hold-ups caused by slow delivery of components, the owner-manager had contemplated (possibly unrealistically) the prospect of backward integration. Certainly knowledge of such potential supply difficulties by potential entrants would constitute a significant barrier to entry. The business was also highly risky. Getting a good demonstration aircraft built first was a prime requirement for success. A considerable investment in production expertise was necessary to be 99 per cent certain that the aeroplane would fly well before it was built. This required tremendous experience in the aviation industry.

At the time of starting the business, advice was sought from the local government authority, the local enterprise trust and the Scottish Development Agency, respectively. The approximate size of the business at inception in terms of total assets (book value) was £35,000, and its size was the same at the time of interview. The owner-manager did not experience any difficulty in obtaining financial support for starting the business. Apart from personal finance the owner-manager used a Scottish Development Agency loan, a grant and a borrowing facility from a bank (in decreasing order of importance) in setting up the business. The security the owner-manager had to provide for this funding was a personal guarantee (implying a liability to repay loans) and a floating charge (i.e. securities on plant, equipment, stocks, etc.). The initial gearing ratio of Firm M was 2.5, which was the ratio at the time of interview. This figure had not been altered in the history of Firm M's operations. The gearing ratio was expected to fall over the three years 1985–8 due to an increase in ploughed-back profits and a reduction in debt over this period. Two special financial schemes, an investment grant and reduced rental on premises, were found to be helpful to Firm M at the time of starting the business. The owner-manager reported that his business had experienced cash-flow difficulties and the major factor that had contributed to these difficulties had been delinquent suppliers. Dependence on one supplier had imposed severe strains ('We've had to live on air') and had caused production delays of six months. Firm M had not sought external finance since the inception of the business. The owner-manager expected his business to grow over the forseeable future. In the event, Firm M was no longer in business in 1988, and had not been the subject of a trade sale. The owner-manager had shifted location and was still running a business: he had not gone into waged employment or become unemployed.

4.5 CONCLUSION

We have now concluded our final set of Profiles, those relating to oligopolistic, high-concentration markets in which there is conjectural dependence amongst SBEs. Thus the within-site analysis of SBEs is completed, when the material of this chapter is considered along with the seven Profiles of

Chapter 2, emphasizing monopolistic competition in low-concentration markets, and the further seven Profiles of Chapter 3, emphasizing fringe competition against a dominant group in medium-concentration markets.

These seventeen Profiles are the evidence of this study. They support the much larger body of evidence analysed in the companion volume (Reid 1993) and in their own right provide the newcomer with a new picture of modern small business enterprises in the recent past. This picture has been presented within an analytical framework which is consistent between Profiles. This facilitates the task of cross-site, or comparative, analysis. It is to this task that we now turn, carrying with us the industrial economics and business strategy inspired framework, and also further utilizing the division of Profiles into low, medium and high market concentration cases.

Part III
Comparative analysis

5 Competitive forces

5.1 INTRODUCTION

Strategic behaviour on the part of the SBE is often fraught with uncertainty and misdirection. Typically, small business is forced to operate in market niches which larger rivals may be inclined to abandon or ignore. These niches are often market segments which are relatively small in size and may be lacking in adequate growth or profitability opportunities, unless skilfully exploited. Limited physical, financial and human resources, a lack of industrial experience and of business acumen on the part of owner-managers of the SBE are frequently to blame for poor exploitation of these fragile niches. Nevertheless, if an SBE is to grow and prosper, rather than simply to survive,[1] over a non-trivial period of time (say more than three years), it must properly identify, develop and implement the requisite business strategy.

A logical first step towards discovering this strategy is to analyse the industrial structure within which the SBE is located, and thereby to determine the industry's long-run profit potential as well as to identify potentially profitable strategies. In the competitive strategy/competitive advantage framework of Michael Porter (1980, 1985, 1990), adapted to the small firms' context, five competitive forces are the essential determinants of the industry structure. If these forces are properly assessed, individually and collectively, this will lead to the identification and subsequent deployment of appropriate (i.e. profitable) strategies. The approach should make transparent the SBE's strengths and weaknesses.

This chapter undertakes a cross-site, or comparative, analysis of the Profiles of SBEs analysed in Part II, utilizing Porter's 'forces of competition' analytical framework. An introduction to that approach has already been provided in Chapter 1. As a means of injecting order, and hopefully clarity, into the analysis, the SBEs are examined within the same categories of market concentration (namely, low, medium, and high) that were used in Part II. The fruits of this analysis suggest to us that this approach is valuable. Certainly, to group SBEs by the level of concentration of the markets in which they function does not militate against the efficacy of the Porter schema. Indeed, it is believed that a more robust assessment of the SBEs' strategic options is achieved thereby. This assessment of competition within a classification of market concentration will set the stage for Chapter 6, where within the same groupings by market concentration we consider the competitive alongside defensive strategies for the SBE.

As analysed in Chapters 2, 3 and 4 of this book, the Profiles of SBEs to be examined in a comparative way are assigned to particular market models, which in turn are connected to particular degrees of market concentration. The seventeen SBEs of the Profiles are placed in low, medium or high market concentration categories using a subjective, aggregate consideration of the evidence. Thus we have paid attention to significant structural characteristics like the number of rivals, market share, entry/exit barriers, and product differentiation. Our general approach (see ch. 1) is to consider SBEs in low-concentration markets to be monopolistically competitive; SBEs in medium-concentration markets to be members of a competitive fringe dominated by a group of larger firms; and SBEs in high-concentration markets to be competing intimately with rivals in particularly specialized and/or exclusive markets.

5.2 LOW-CONCENTRATION MARKETS

In Table 5.1 we have identified those SBEs which operate in low-concentration markets (Firms A, C, D, E, G, L and Q). The key characteristics identified for each SBE are the product, the market extent in a geographical sense, the market share, the degree of product differentiation and the extent of entry/exit barriers.[2]

These seven SBEs all sell their products in highly fragmented market segments in which product differentiation, whilst slight, is real and pervasive. Whilst little physical differences may exist between competing products, differentiation is achieved by means like personal service and quick delivery. Barriers to entry and to exit are virtually non-existent for

Table 5.1 Features of SBEs operating in low-concentration markets

Firm	Product market	Geographical market	Market share (%)	Degree of product differentiation	Extent of entry/exit barriers
A	Blind cleaning	Regional	<1	Little	Low
C	Knitwear manufacturer	International	<1	Little	Low
D	Automotive repairs	Regional	<1	Little	Low
E	Industrial cleaning	Scotland	<1	Little	Low
G	Holiday tours	Scotland	1–5	Little	Low
L	Wine retail distribution	Regional	31–50	Little	Low
Q	Theatrical props manufacturer	Scotland	21–30	Little	Low

potential entrants and incumbents alike. The second column of Table 5.1 indicates that SBEs from diverse sectors display these characteristics, ranging from services and distribution (A, E, G, L) to manufacturing (C, D, Q). Expressed briefly, Table 5.1 indicates that SBEs which are monopolistically competitive may be in services or manufacturing, have low market shares, sell mildly differentiated products and are subject to low entry/exit barriers. We now move to more detailed analysis by reference to rivals, entrants, substitutes, buyers and suppliers: that is, to 'extended rivalry'.

Existing rivals (low concentration)

Competition amongst existing rivals is considered to be 'generally strong' to 'fierce' by these SBEs. Existing rivals are numerous and similar in size and all market shares are small. Competition may therefore be characterized as 'atomistic'. Despite the numerous and equally balanced nature of competitors, existing rivals do not necessarily view competition as divisive or unstable. There is an absence therefore of confrontational marketing strategies (e.g. 'knocking' advertising) or aggressive pricing strategies (e.g. predatory or skimming pricing). Rather, these SBEs are intent on discovering or creating market niches which are adjacent to, but not overlapping, their rivals' niches. Competition between niches is nevertheless vigorous, which is reflected in the generally small market shares of most SBEs. As indicated in Table 5.1, all these SBEs, apart from Firm C (knitwear manufacturing), serve market segments which are limited in geographical extent. Despite the indication that Firm C (knitwear manufacturing) perceives itself as operating in an international market, few of its customers are outside the United Kingdom and its main customer base is local. Its few international customers are all department stores in New York.

Firms L (wine distribution) and Q (theatrical props) did not necessarily overstate their relative market shares (up to 50 per cent and 30 per cent, respectively) within the very narrow confines of their region, but arguably their economic markets are much larger. Firm L operates in a small and well-delineated regional market in the west of Scotland, but arguably is subject to competition from further afield. Firm Q's market segment is proportionally large, on a Scottish dimension, but is actually rather small in both absolute terms and in relation to the UK market as a whole. In short, the market shares for Firms L and Q may be overstated. These SBEs apparently prefer to curtail their competitive impulses by not encroaching on rivals' market niches. To contemplate head-on competition in a rival's market niche would at best be considered unnecessarily mutually destructive of the human, physical and financial resources of both firms L and Q and, at worst, would be inviting bankruptcy of one or both high conflict firms.

Insufficient resources, inexperience in the industry (amounting even to naïvety), risk aversion, and limited perceived profits in highly fragmented market segments, are characteristics of all these SBEs. In these circumstances, the lack of direct confrontation amongst existing rivals is understandably a good survival strategy.

These SBEs' preferences for, or at least tolerance of, operating in fragmented markets are partly driven by the prospect of market expansion arising from unanticipated demand increases, some of which may be due to innovation. Firm Q (theatrical props), for example, enjoys 'rapid' market growth to the extent that it 'reacts to' rather than 'actively seeks' contracts. This has arisen from an unanticipated increase in locational filming in Scotland, generating a growth in demand for theatrical props. Given such market growth, this SBE along with its existing rivals, chooses to be content with concentrating on expanding its own segment. Confronted by a similar situation of market growth, Firm G (holiday tours) has both enjoyed expanding into its own market segment, and when it has been unable to fill orders has resorted to subcontracting. In the latter situation, 'good competitors' are invited to participate in its own market niche on specific terms. This is a questionable tactic, not without risk, because it invites subsequent 'poaching' within this niche, without bothering with the entrée of a referral. Even worse, it could lead to an invasion of the niche. However, such subcontracting arrangements are not uncommon in this and other types of markets in which SBEs are active, so the dangers of the practice may be exaggerated. The rationale for it is reciprocation. Accepting a subcontract, without subsequently invading the niche temporarily occupied, and then returning the favour with a subcontract at a later date, would confer 'good competitor' status on the rival.

Product innovation is a noted feature of inter-firm rivalry for Firms C (knitwear manufacturing), G (holiday tours) and L (wine distribution). Despite concentrating on specific geographic or customer niches, Firms G and L found it necessary to alter significantly their product mixes over a three-year period. In turn, this was reflected by similar alterations to the outputs of their main product-lines. The nature of these markets requires rapid and frequent product innovations as SBEs and their existing rivals engage in moves and counter-moves involving some element of innovation, which are aimed to protect their own particular market niches. Firm C experienced stability in its product mix, but interestingly believed that innovation was undertaken by some rivals. However, despite these innovations Firm C did not alter its product mix, yet continued to enjoy a substantial increase in output over three years. Arguably, Firm C's products were of an exceptional design quality, which enabled it to sustain and develop its market position in the face of innovation. It is also true that there is sometimes a desire for 'retro-fashions' with buyers of designer garments, and this does not give any competitive edge to the high technology producer.

Firms A (blind cleaning), D (auto repairs), and E (industrial cleaning) are in markets considered to be stagnant, or even contracting, and devoid of product innovation.[3] In these cases, SBEs are tempted to mount assaults on other established market niches, despite running the risk of thereby being labelled 'bad competitors'. These SBEs engaged in both minor and major innovations. For example, Firm E engaged in minor innovations in the supply of cleansing fluids. On a more major level, Firm A had introduced ultrasound cleaning equipment, which was a significant advance on earlier manual cleaning methods. However, in stagnant markets, neither of these innovations conferred great competitive advantage. As a result, SBEs put greater effort into increasing the switching costs of customers, which involves emphasizing service, delivery, reliability and quality.

Another factor worthy of consideration in inter-firm rivalry is fixed costs. Each of the SBEs listed in Table 5.1 has low fixed costs, both in absolute terms and in relation to other costs. This generally holds for their existing rivals given their previously noted equally balanced and similarly sized characteristics. Consequently, these SBEs are under no particularly urgent pressure either to utilize capacity fully or to flagrantly undercut the prices of competitors. Though we would not wish to overplay its significance, to some extent the low fixed costs (coupled with, and perhaps due to, specialization) account for these firms' fragmented markets, for which inter-niche confrontation is not sought.

A related property to fixed costs in explaining existing rivalry is the extent to which capital is 'lumpy'. In other words, if capacity can only be augmented in large increments, any SBE's expansion will thereby create a sudden overcapacity, possibly leading to a temptation to cut price savagely. This might be perceived as predatory pricing by rivals, leading to the danger of retaliation, or even a full-scale price war. However, none of the firms was troubled by this concern,[4] even though some contemplated expansion in the near future.

Finally, in analysing existing rivalry we need to consider exit barriers. Such barriers are generally regarded as 'low' (i.e easy or inexpensive to overcome) by SBEs in low-concentration markets. For example, the existence of specialized assets which are not easily liquidated or transferrable (i.e. asset specificity) is not prominent amongst these SBEs,[5] or even their existing rivals. By contrast these SBEs are run by owner-managers who appear to confront the rather intractable exit barrier of commitment. Because these SBEs are fairly young, they are really the embodiment of their owner-managers' aspirations. This implies a generally high (even emotional) level of commitment to operate in their chosen industry, and, a willingness – even in intensely competitive environments – to 'slog it out' with rivals, if need be over many years. Such a perceived level of commitment is very threatening to existing rivals, and if an SBE's particular market niche goes sour (or does not live-up to expectations) market instability, featuring intense competition, is a certain outcome.

Potential entrants (low concentration)

As might be expected, potential entrants into these low-concentration markets are faced with relatively minor barriers to entry. The existence of potential entrants is apparent to incumbent firms, and this therefore acts as a powerful competitive force. Generally, due to the fragmented markets in which these SBEs choose to develop specialized niches the roles of product variety, customer relationships, and/or location are very important, whereas those of scale economies, capital requirements and absolute cost advantages are relatively unimportant. Moreover, fragmented markets are dominated by goods subject to marked product differentiation which tends to promote rather than to deter entry for SBEs willing to develop new product varieties. Finally, the incumbent SBEs expressed a reluctance to deter entry through using limit pricing,[6] although some admitted it would have to be contemplated in tight competitive situations, despite their distaste for such a tactic. Generally speaking, therefore, these SBEs did expect market entry, but anticipated that entrants would carve out their own niches without undue threat or harm to pre-existing, occupied niches.

Whilst entry barriers are generally not significant, there are a few of some importance which do apply. Lack of access to (including knowledge of) distribution channels is arguably the principal deterrent to entry. In nearly all instances, the SBEs expressed confidence in the power of this deterrent to protect their particular niche. This is because owner-managers could draw on their own arduous experience of locating and then cultivating relationships with desirable suppliers and buyers. This process typically takes years (with three years being a commonly quoted figure) but cannot be neglected if the aim is to establish a sustainable market niche. Several SBEs found that locating their operations near suppliers and/or buyers served both to strengthen those relationships, and to send a visible signal of commitment to potential entrants.[7]

Substitutes (low concentration)

Substitute products produced in other industries are generally considered to be of little threat to SBEs in these low-concentration markets. Frequently such substitutes are not available. This is in large measure a reflection of these SBEs' product markets, which are often traditional or long-standing (e.g. auto repair and blind cleaning) are therefore relatively insulated from waves of new technology (e.g. holiday tours). Indeed, for many markets it is thought that customers have little propensity to substitute. Cars will continue to be driven and holidays to be taken.

Firm C (knitwear manufacturer) and Firm L (wine distributor), in particular, do acknowledge that trends can affect otherwise traditional products. Both firms seem to be enjoying a period for which their products command a relative high value/price compared to substitutes (namely wool versus acrylic and wine versus beer, respectively). Nevertheless, the owner-manager of Firm L did express concern that the customers' trend away from beer to wine, whilst beneficial in the long term, could provoke some negative consequences for the general expansion of the market. He particularly had in mind the expansion into wine distribution by big players in the powerful and profitable brewery industry. Also, the growing popularity of non-alcoholic beverages, including soft drinks and mineral water, may serve to lower the profit ceiling on wine. Even if Firm L responds to these pressures by adding, say, sparkling water to its product mix, the bottom line would be adversely affected because profit margins are much wider for wine sales, especially in the case of primary customers like hotels and restaurants.

The owner-managers of these SBEs (with the exception of Firm L) in discussing the role of substitutes produced in other industries, see themselves as being preoccupied with developing their own particular niches. Here, the intention is to insulate themselves from the competitive pressures of intra-industry rivals. The view generally expressed is that attention to providing the right quality of good or service, prompt delivery and follow-up service will ensure customer loyalty. This will not only sustain a firm's industry position but will, in effect, provide immunity from substitutes. It might well appear that this line of thinking could be myopic, if not flawed.

Buyers (low concentration)

Buyers (or customers) are a rather powerful competitive force for the SBEs in low-concentration markets. Buyer concentration tends to be high in-so-far as SBEs are reliant upon a few customers (or customer channels) for the better part of their revenues. Firm C (knitwear manufacturer) admitted that the loss of one large order dealt a severe blow to sales revenue. It also under-mined confidence, and it was said that 'suddenly planning became much more difficult'.

In several cases, the big-volume buyers are businesses themselves (rather than final customers). They are typically larger and longer established than the supplying firms. To some extent, this type of customer is preferred to the so-called 'general public' in that they are typically better informed of the SBE and its products, and will buy in bulk on a fairly steady or repeat basis. Firm A (blind cleaning), for instance, noted that less-informed customers are hesitant in making their purchases, preferring to 'shop around'. But often such customers were less understanding and appreciative of a product's 'particulars and merits'. They would also tend to be more price sensitive than bulk purchasers and more likely to switch to a rival firm.

Of course, well-informed buyers (especially large established businesses) are obvious candidates for backward integration. Generally, SBEs recognize this to be a genuine possibility; nevertheless, it is thought to be 'uncommon'. These SBEs work hard to keep such customers satisfied, and in effect raise switching costs. For example, Firm L (wine distributor) not only supplies hotels and restaurants with a wide selection of wines, but also prepares their wine menus and provides special, own-label bottles. However, the fortunes of SBEs are often tied to those of their principal buyers. If their buyers' businesses or buyers' channels falter, pricing becomes more sensitive. Then the threats of switching suppliers and even of backward integration become more potent. This situation applies acutely to Firm G (holiday tours), which is entirely dependent upon major hotels, car rental firms and travel agencies for its customers. In this case, difficulties are compounded by the cyclical sensitivity of the business.

Buyers (especially high-volume customers) tend to be very price sensitive when value added is perceived to be low. This effect is significant in the cases of Firm A (blind cleaning), Firm C (knitwear manufacturer), Firm D (auto repairs) and Firm E (industrial cleaning). Firm C in fact makes it an article of faith that prominent buyers will be price sensitive. Even though Firm G (holiday tours), Firm L (wine distributors) and Firm Q (theatrical props) consistently strive for added value, many of their customers are found to be relatively price insensitive because their purchases represent only a small fraction of their overall costs. Even so, there remained some of these firms' customers who actually viewed their purchases as an opportunity for a cost-cutting exercise. It could be, too, that the products of these customer firms are indeed more distinctive than those of Firms A, C, D and E, thereby naturally commanding higher added value.

Suppliers (low concentration)

Suppliers are almost entirely a positive competitive force for these SBEs. Suppliers' concentration is relatively low in all instances due to the fairly homogeneous nature of factor inputs provided to the SBEs. Further, suppliers' concentration is typically lower in relation to buyers' concentration. Firm C (knitwear manufacturer), Firm D (auto repairs), and Firm Q (theatrical props) indicated that most inputs are standardized and that as a result they face low switching costs in factor markets. However, Firm Q has dealt with shortages on the part of individual suppliers from time to time. Firm C observed forward integration of some suppliers, which is attributable, in part, to the standardized nature of inputs. Firm D and Firm Q, however, believe forward integration to be unlikely, or at least uncommon, since suppliers appear to lack the requisite skills, experience, and even desire to be so involved in downstream production. Forward integration of suppliers has not been evident to other SBEs in the low market concentration category. Indeed, the general prospect of forward integration is perceived to be non-threatening.

Although these SBEs in general have many suppliers to choose from, there is a tendency to stay with a select few, or even with just one in some cases. These SBEs are apparently highly informed about how suppliers differ and know precisely from experience what they value most. Moreover, suppliers themselves seem to recognize that SBEs do have several or many willing suppliers to choose from and may not hesitate to switch suppliers if doing so can measurably improve their position (e.g. in terms of cost, quality or delivery of supplies). Firm L, for instance, purchased most of its wine from just one supplier, not only because of its competitive prices, but because it offered a generous credit policy and prompt, reliable delivery. The latter characteristic was particularly effective in lowering inventory costs. The supplier clearly understands that the real value created for this SBE is optimization of cash-flow.

Given that these SBEs are relatively labour-intensive, suppliers of skilled labour serve as a potentially powerful constraining force on competitive advantage. However, with the exception of Firm G (holiday tours), these SBEs have no experience of shortages of employees to a degree that would have impeded growth. Firm G, however, finds it must offer premium rates to attract suitable prospective employees, resulting in variable costs rising by a significant 20 per cent over a three-year period. Locating the right persons has been a difficult task and is held to be responsible for curtailing Firm G's potential growth.

5.3 MEDIUM-CONCENTRATION MARKETS

Table 5.2 displays those SBEs which are considered to be competing in medium-concentration markets. In this case such markets are typically distinguished by having a few (if not just one) dominant firm(s) co-existing with a 'competitive fringe' which is composed of several, or many, much smaller firms. The competitive-fringe firms are typically not subject to direct competitive pressures by the dominant firms, provided they are content to specialize in low-volume and often specialized orders. Such orders are ignored by the large firms because of factors which are reported to be inability, disinterest, or both, but which at root must be governed by perceived lack of profitability. Indeed, the firms under study (refer to Table 5.2) occupy the competitive fringe and, not unlike their counterparts in low-

Table 5.2 Features of SBEs operating in medium-concentration markets

Firm	Product market	Geographical market	Market share (%)	Degree of product differentiation	Extent of entry/exit barriers
F	Food manufacturer	Regional	1–5	None	Medium
I	Computer software	International	<1	Little	Medium
J	Cassette tape manufacturer	UK	<1	None	High
K	Electronic instrumentation	Scotland	<1	Much	Medium
N	Bulk bag manufacturer	UK	1–5	Little	High
O	Fencing manufacturer	Scotland	1–5	None	Low
P	Printing lamination	Scotland	11–20	None	High

concentration markets, tend to be quite small in absolute size and have rather small market shares. However, all these SBEs in medium-concentration markets happen to be manufacturers and they therefore tend to possess greater amounts of capital and superior proprietary knowledge of inputs compared to their counterparts in low-concentration markets.

Existing rivals (medium concentration)

The degree of competition amongst existing rivals is fairly vigorous within the competitive fringe and indeed becomes intense (if not fatal) for those that encroach into the dominant firms' share of the market. These SBEs are clearly fringe players, given their relatively small market shares, and they are frequently located within confined geographic areas. Naturally, they first look to develop their own special niche within the fringe.

Limiting confrontation with existing (namely, fringe) rivals requires focusing the SBE's strategy on prospects for invading unoccupied and potentially defensible niches based on location, firm-specific skills and customer types. Firm O (fencing), for example, located its business in Scotland knowing that this geographic segment of the market was largely ignored by rivals, who preferred not to be confronted with the logistical problems and transport costs associated with obtaining supplies of the primary input (i.e. chestnut) from southern England. Firm I (software), Firm K (electronics) and Firm N (bulk bags) are in markets characterized by growing product differentiation. This not only reflects increasing demand for product varieties, and the desire by each SBE to get a share of it by market fragmentation, but also the diverse firm-specific skills amongst the SBEs which are brought to bear in meeting these new demands. Finally, Firm J (cassette tapes) focuses on maintaining its long-standing relationships with certain high-volume customers. This is achieved by devoting attention to service, delivery, quality and productivity. More attention is placed on increasing these existing customers' switching costs than in cultivating new customers. As a result, Firm J is able effectively to insulate itself from the predatory pressures of existing rivals.

Firm F (food manufacturer) and Firm P (lamination), however, were both ultimately sold as a result of not being able to avoid, and subsequently to overcome, direct confrontation with existing rivals. Firm F expressed concern for 'niche overlap' with rivals, which ultimately created insurmountable difficulties in effectively differentiating its product. Furthermore, the experience of operating losses led to setting on a target of high-volume production which, at least initially, proved profitable. However, this served to attract the attention of very much larger volume dominant firms, one of which ended up mounting a successful takeover of Firm F. The motivation here was no doubt twofold. Firstly, it dispatched a rival that was threatening to emerge from the fringe to become a challenger to the dominant group. Secondly, it involved the acquisition of flexible additional capacity which can be used by the acquiring firm for strategic purposes. Interestingly, Firm P (lamination) became a victim of its own success. Benefiting from the installation of advanced machinery and low overhead costs, it was capable of meeting large volume orders for its homogenous product (i.e. lamination) and did so at a very competitive price. Retaliation of a severe nature (e.g. predatory pricing) on the part of the market's dominant firm (i.e. a multinational company) was anxiously anticipated. Instead, the firm's owner-managers were tempted by a very generous bid from the multinational for their business operations as a going concern, which was too attractive an offer to be refused.

These SBEs in medium-concentration markets contend that industry growth frequently permits existing rivals to be a positive competitive force, and has always the potential to do so. The consequence of growth is often to make rivalry more relaxed. This condition is positive in that it allows new SBEs to develop their niches. It can also prove hazardous, as the experiences of Firms F and P suggest. However, expanding markets typically foster harmonious (or symbiotic), if not highly beneficial, relationships amongst so-called existing rivals. Generally, SBEs in the competitive fringe serve the interests of the dominant firms by being willing and able to fill unique (bespoke), and certainly small-volume, orders from customers who would otherwise find no firms with whom they could place such orders. These customers may of course grow to be larger, and they will eventually turn to dominant firms once the size and standardization of their purchases justifies it. Thus customers serviced by the fringe provide a breeding ground for future large-volume customers, who will be serviced by the dominant group. Also dominant firms may look to the fringe firms to meet orders which cannot be filled by themselves. Subcontracting to SBEs in the fringe may be preferable to having disappointed buyers. In any case, the fringe's productive activities do serve to widen and make more visible the market, which is obviously for the common good. Firm K (electronics) is an example of a fringe firm engaged in a mutually beneficial relationship with a dominant firm. The great bulk of its business involves designing and manufacturing test equipment (involving new printed circuit boards) for the large firms in the market. In-house production by the large firms of test equipment, which by definition is produced in small, non-standardized batches, makes little economic or technical sense to them.

It is observed that positive industry growth, coupled with sensitively governed and often constructive behaviour amongst existing rivals limits the force of competition. This is reinforced by the general observation that innovations of both the product and the process variety do not have a pervasive effect on the shaping of inter-firm competition. However, Firm I (software) and Firm N (bulk bags), do admit to developing innovations which intensified rivalry. Firm I is motivated to do this by pressure of growth against the limits of its niche. It has varied its product mix and enjoyed a 1,000 per cent increase in the output of its main product-line over three years. Moreover, it has observed a decline in variable costs of some 50 per cent. Of course, the computer software market has undergone dramatic technological changes, but the success of Firm I (software) was due to process rather than product innovation. Firm N (bulk bags) has also experienced a substantial increase in the output of its main product-line (1,200 per cent over three years). This growth was achieved with no change in Firm N's product mix, and also involved process, rather than product, innovation.

Strategic stakes and exit barriers are likely to be higher in medium- compared to low-concentration markets, principally because of the existence of dominant firms. Such firms tend to be large, as well as long-established. They can be expected to sacrifice profitability if need be, to maintain their dominance. Also, as illustrated in the case of Firm K (electronics), dominant firms do have strategic interrelationships with other firms in the market. Many of the SBEs hold specialized assets which could not be easily liquidated or transferred upon market exit. Thus asset specificity creates exit barriers. Despite these manifest barriers to exit, these SBEs, unlike their counterparts in low-concentration markets, do not appear to be run by owner-managers who are as emotionally committed to their markets. In the present cases, owner-managers see themselves more as 'being in business', rather than as personifications of their firms.

Potential entrants (medium concentration)

For most potential entrants, the only viable avenue into these medium- concentration markets is via the competitive fringe. Even then, entry barriers may be substantial. Potential entrants anticipating coming in as large-volume producers, and therefore looking directly to challenge the dominant firms, are likely to be repelled by the presence of overwhelming scale economies, absolute cost advantages, and high strategic stakes. Such barriers do also pertain to the competitive fringe but are not as obviously prohibitive. Nevertheless, these SBEs do believe that there are many signifi- cant barriers to entry, including capital requirements, technical knowledge, channel access and government restrictions (e.g. patents and packaging) creating requirements which apply more or less to the fringe.

These deterrents are particularly prominent in the markets of Firm F (food manufacturer), Firm J (cassette tapes), and Firm P (lamination). Here the products are intrinsically homogenous, forcing entrants to focus on undis- covered or ignored geographic and customer segments. Unfortunately, homogeneous product markets with competitive fringes are fundamentally unstable if the strategic emphasis is on low-cost and massive production methods.[8] Thus, new entrants and existing rivals alike strive to exploit scale economies by high-volume production, inevitably leading to the swamping of existing niches and encroachment into other occupied niches.

An interesting exception to this scenario is provided by the chestnut fencing market. The owner-manager of Firm O (fencing manufacturer) contends that entry barriers (namely, capital requirements and proprietary knowledge), as they pertain to the Scottish and Northern Ireland geographic segments, are low. The dominant firms are content with their market in the south of England as they are near the market's suppliers of chestnut. Moreover, Firm O believes only 5 per cent of the Scottish and Northern Ireland markets are being tapped. Consequently, additions to the competitive fringe would probably go unnoticed irrespective of the standardized commodity-like character of the good.

Generally, the potential entrants who are most likely to succeed are those who bring their own unique combination of resources, technical knowledge and experience to bear on the market in general and on the competitive fringe in particular. Emphasis on creating their own niche through marked product differentiation and low-volume production are conditions paramount to successful entry. Such entrants would be likely to be welcomed (at least initially) by incumbent firms as they contribute to an expanding market. Firm I (software), Firm K (electronics) and to a lesser extent Firm N (bulk bags) acknowledge and even appreciate the growth in product variety in their buoyant markets. However, they would be quick to caution potential entrants to resist challenging existing rivals directly, especially where high-volume production is concerned. Retaliation on the part of dominant and fringe firms alike could be expected, and particularly in the former case would be likely to be severe.

Substitutes (medium concentration)

The SBEs in medium-concentration markets generally seem little concerned with the threat that substitutes produced in other industries might pose.[9] In fact, Firm N (bulk bags), Firm O (fencing) and Firm P (lamination) not only recognize substitutes but are confident of their products' superior relative value/price or ability effectively to displace substitutes. Firm N (bulk bags), for example, argues that because its bulk bags are strong enough to hold coal, for instance, more convenient forms of transport (e.g. lorries) can be used rather than relying on the traditional container ships for transporting open bulk. Also, Firm P (lamination) plans to counter the growing threat of varnishing to its product (i.e. lamination) by simply adding this service to its product range. However, a substantial investment in machinery would be required.

Firm I (software) and Firm K (electronics), being in markets which are particularly dynamic and technologically driven, regard substitutes as not having a negative competitive influence. By contrast, Firm F (food manufacturer) and Firm J (cassette tapes) operate in more stable and traditional product markets and in principle should find substitutes a negative competitive force. Yet they view substitutes as fairly non-threatening, given the conservative nature of customers. In fact, Firm F believes customers are quite rigid in their purchasing habits. For a substitute to be at all potent, it would require an extraordinary marketing effort, which was considered to be inconceivable. Firm J, however, did eventually invest in advanced machinery, as a precautionary measure against advanced substitutes, despite an earlier held conviction that its cassette tapes were already produced with sufficient sound quality. Irrational as it may have seemed to its owner-manager to provide products of a technical quality that the human ear was incapable of appreciating, he was willing to flatter the consumer with an over-specification product if that was their wish.[10]

Buyers (medium concentration)

These SBEs are typically enjoying an expanding customer base, which serves to diminish reliance on any one buyer. They tend to place a premium on customer loyalty through development of personal relationships based on reliable service, prompt delivery and frequent visits. This particularly applies to Firm F (food manufacturer), Firm J (cassette tapes) Firm O (fencing), and to a lesser extent Firm N (bulk bags), which all produce nearly homogenous products. Consequently, low buyer concentration coupled with assured repeat business greatly compensate for the lack of switching costs faced by customers. Nevertheless, in several instances, customers do not take advantage of low switching costs as they appear to be quite content. Some buyers are simply unaware of existing rivals and their products.

Firm I (software) and Firm K (electronics), in particular, find buyers lacking in bargaining leverage. Switching costs of customers are quite high given the specialized nature of the firms' products. Firm K's customers have a strong need for their product (i.e. printed circuit boards) as they are crucial components of their own mass-produced products. Typically these customers lack the requisite instrumentation expertise to design test equipment, and are unwilling to invest resources in acquiring and then implementing it for just small-volume production. A contributory factor is that the typical buyer's outlay on Firm K's product is but a small proportion of overall costs. This reduces buyers' price sensitivity and raises switching costs. Switching costs are further raised because Firm K has the flexibility to provide the much needed quick turnaround so characteristic of the electronics industry. Once experienced, customers are loath to take their contracts elsewhere, for fear of a slower turnaround on orders. Finally, customer loyalty on a personal level is quite marked, given the significant and frequent social and professional interactions between SBEs and buyers. Such interactions, however engineered, also raise switching costs.

The threat of backward integration on the part of buyers is considered unimportant because of the substantial capital outlay and technical expertise required. In most cases, buyers have a further disincentive to backward integration because the products they purchase have a cost which represents a tiny fraction of their total costs.

Suppliers (medium concentration)

Suppliers are highly concentrated and tend to exert great competitive pressure on SBEs. Consider the case of Firm P (lamination). Only a few suppliers exist, and they are very aware of their power in factor markets. This arises because the machinery supplied by them is highly productive and is responsible for much of their customers' profitability. Moreover, the machinery is of considerable (if not prohibitive) cost and delivery occurs with a long and uncertain delay. It is perhaps of some surprise that such suppliers have not forward integrated.

Firm N (bulk bags) provides another illustration of the way in which suppliers can achieve a position from which they can exert considerable influence on SBEs. Forward integration on the part of suppliers to the bulk bag industry is not uncommon, and though Firm N can identify three potential suppliers it chooses to rely on just one. This supplier is local which permits Firm N to maintain a particularly low inventory through 'just in time' deliveries of basic materials for bulk bag manufacturing.[11]

Despite the fact that these SBEs in medium-concentration markets typically have only a few suppliers from which to purchase factor inputs, they generally view their switching costs as low, because of the homogeneous, commodity-like character of inputs purchased. In the cases of Firm J (cassette tapes) and Firm O (fencing), concern for the fact that product quality was driven by input quality forced them to concentrate on a very limited number of suppliers who are located some distance away in southern England. Consequently, in order to keep a tight control on transportation costs, they tend to place large orders, which require some advance notice. Otherwise, they encounter no particular bargaining pressures.

The homogenous nature of inputs supplied does admittedly permit SBEs to play off one supplier against another in terms of price, quality and delivery. Firm K (electronics), for instance, in order to satisfy effectively its customers with a fast turnaround on the production of test equipment, must seek those suppliers who can themselves respond quickly. Other things being equal, Firm K (like most other SBEs) prefers to remain loyal to particular suppliers. Such continued contracting, which creates trust and consolidates reputation, also provides a means of influencing favourably over time the terms of delivery, price and quality of inputs. Thus, blatantly playing off suppliers is a practice to be avoided if at all possible, because it destroys trust. It creates a 'sharp practice' reputation in the short run, and results in the withholding of supply benefits in the long run.

A shortage of skilled labour is typically not regarded as being responsible for impeding SBEs' growth, except for the case of Firm I (software). This is perhaps to be expected, in that these SBEs have production processes which certainly require significant and sophisticated capital inputs, but of a fairly standardized and automatically controlled variety. This limits, but does not eliminate, the contribution to be made by the skilled labour input. Firm I, however, which is involved in a very labour-intensive activity, software design, admits to a shortage of skilled labour, which has proved to be an obstacle to growth. This SBE reports difficulties both in identifying personnel with the relevant skills and in assessing existing rivals' relative labour skill advantages. Of course, computer software is sold on a very fluid market, which is prone to dramatic and frequent changes in the technical content and purpose of products.

5.4 HIGH-CONCENTRATION MARKETS

The SBEs which are assigned to high-concentration markets for this assessment of the competitive forces to which they are subjected are featured in Table 5.3. As earlier in this chapter, we provide details on product differentiation, entry/exit barriers and aspects of the markets. These markets are highly concentrated in that they contain only a few firms, each of which enjoys a large market share; and between them these firms supply almost the entire market. Such firms are also typically large in absolute size and long established. Unlike in the medium-concentration markets, a competitive fringe is not recognized in the sense of a lower layer of subordinated, passive competitors. If one does exist it apparently has no strategic bearing. Certainly the SBEs listed in Table 5.3 compete intimately with their much larger rivals. If one is in the market at all, one is in significant strategic interaction with existing rivals. Unique circumstances, considerable proprietary knowledge and first-mover advantages place these SBEs in well consolidated positions which are not to be ignored or taken lightly by rivals. Interfirm rivalry is more subtle and complex, and perhaps less potentially disruptive, than in the low- and medium-concentrated markets. With this said, we must first assess closely the impact existing rivals have on these SBEs, before broadening the assessment of competitive forces to 'extended rivals'.

Existing rivals (high concentration)

The strength of competition among existing rivals is considered 'moderate' to 'weak'. This is largely explained by marked product differentiation and acutely high market concentration, both of which tend to foster stable and

Table 5.3 Features of SBEs operating in high-concentration markets

Firm	Product market	Geographical market	Market share (%)	Degree of product differentiation	Extent of entry/exit barriers
B	Security printers blankets	International	11–20	Marked	High
H	Retail cosmetics	Regional	>50	Marked	High
M	Acrobatic aircraft construction	International	n.a.	Marked	High

predictable patterns of behaviour. Patent protection, absence of channel access and firm-specific assets are responsible for creating well-protected market segments which in some cases are nearly impregnable. Indeed, these SBEs and their few existing rivals totally control the market, and SBEs are able to command their fair share of the market despite having much larger rivals, often large multinational companies. The strategic key for these SBEs has been their ability to establish strongly defensible, and highly profitable, niches in the market.

Vigorous market growth (or at least a recognized potential for it) is also a condition of some importance in holding inter-firm rivalry in check in these highly concentrated markets. Markets enjoying increasing demand allow firms to devote their resources and attention to just keeping up with this growth rather than looking to increase market share at the expense of rivals. The latter type of beggar-thy-neighbour conduct can obviously be a catalyst for volatile and possibly destructive competition. In the case of Firm H (cosmetics), however, the market's growth has been unbalanced in its favour. Existing rivals resisted making a direct challenge believing it would jeopardize their own market segments. In particular, they did not expand their product-line by adding products similar to those of Firm H. They feared such a move would compromise their own traditional product-line's distinctiveness and thereby alienate their customer base. They enjoyed growth, but less than their share of the market action, a trade-off they were forced to accept as the consequence of being unwilling to run the risk of product innovation.

As might be expected, exit barriers are quite relevant to the intensity of rivalry, and the willingness of SBEs to stay in business under this pressure. The production of aerobatic aircraft (Firm M) and security printers blankets (Firm B) obviously both require special production facilities and machinery which is not easily liquidated, least of all without loss. Also, the expertise and experience of these SBEs' owner-managers may not be directly transferable to other economic activities. In light of the other aspects of existing rivals noted, it is difficult to ascertain with any confidence the negative impact of exit barriers. It certainly is likely that they prolong the extent to which SBEs may be locked into the industry in unprofitable situations.

Potential entrants (high concentration)

Given the high concentration of these markets and the apparent absence of a competitive fringe, the barriers to entry are possibly insurmountable to potential entrants. Product differentiation, capital requirements, absolute cost advantages, access to distribution channels, and government policy are more or less decisive in preventing entry into these SBEs' markets.

Only special or atypical circumstances are likely to permit market penetration. Consider these three SBEs themselves. Firstly, Firm B (security blankets) is essentially a phoenix operation, the result of a management buyout. Despite being a much reduced version of its former self, this SBE is able to excel in the marketplace because of a deliberate restriction of product-lines. It is thus sustained by absolute cost advantages (based on patents) and secure distribution channels. Secondly, Firm H (cosmetics) is a unique case in that it is a franchise operation. It therefore benefits from the economies of a fully integrated franchisor.[12] Thirdly, Firm M (acrobatic aircraft) owes its very existence to a substantial government grant. Government recognized an unsatisfied demand for acrobatic aeroplanes and believed many jobs would in due course be generated as Firm M extended its operations after financial inception. This rather optimistic view, which emphasized the admitted importance of a large infusion of finance capital, nevertheless suffered from inattention to the specifics of the case. In particular, there is a long period of production for aircraft. Therefore the payback period is long (i.e. there is a long period over which the desired return on investment is realized). But it is in the short run that the SBE is made or broken, and distant returns do not help an SBE with immediate cash-flow problems.

Substitutes (high concentration)

Substitutes do exist and are recognized, but are deemed to be of inferior quality and function. Firm B (security blankets) and Firm H (cosmetics) pride themselves on relying on natural or traditional materials. In this way, they have consistently maintained a superior value added/price *vis-à-vis* man-made materials. Given a negligible propensity to substitute on the part of customers, substitutes really do not place a ceiling on their industries' profits.

Firm M (acrobatic aircraft) shares the view that substitutes are a fairly benign competitive force. Second-hand, ex-military and trainer aircraft are considered the only possible substitute. However, they constitute a very dismal price-performance alternative, being much bigger and made of metal (rather than wood), thus making the plane less manoeuvrable, and prone to expensive breakdown.

Buyers (high concentration)

On the whole, buyers serve as a positive competitive force for these SBEs. Customers are highly informed and rather sophisticated. They are able to articulate their needs and wants and are often conservative in their tastes. Once they find the product(s) that meet(s) their demand, they are unlikely to switch suppliers. To some extent the buyers' disposition and behaviour are moulded by the SBEs' concern to ensure customers are informed of their products and their distinctive attributes. To illustrate with Firm H (cosmetics), descriptions of its products' ingredients and intended uses are displayed under each product in retail displays. Moreover, the firm has magnified its products' distinctiveness by exploiting its first-mover advantage in only using natural ingredients. It presents itself as adopting a popular, 'politically correct' stance. Thus a pro-environment concern is reflected in packaging which can be recycled, and an anti-vivisection concern is reflected in a policy of shunning the animal testing of products. As a result, customers maintain a strong affinity with Firm H and its products. On a marketing level this translates into increased switching costs and decreases price sensitivity. Strong, reliable customer relationships tend to generate more timely and substantive feedback from buyers, which can obviously assist SBEs in improving product offerings.

Suppliers (high concentration)

Suppliers are an extraordinary influential (if not decisive) competitive force for these SBEs. Supplier concentration is extremely high, to the extent that SBEs are reliant upon one supplier for the majority of their inputs. Firm M (acrobatic aircraft), in fact, is entirely dependent on just one supplier. Ultimately, delays in delivery combined with an inability either to locate other suppliers or to backward integrate proved fatal for this SBE.

At the other extreme, Firm H (cosmetics) has a nearly ideal situation so far as suppliers are concerned. As a franchise operation it enjoys the supplier benefits of a vertically integrated firm. It has the prerogative of choice over suppliers, for a large number of eager suppliers exist for some 30 per cent of its input purchases.

Only in the case of Firm B (security blankets) was forward integration of suppliers observed. It proved short-lived and of no real consequence. As discussed earlier, the many entry barriers (at least collectively) are nearly insurmountable.

5.5 CONCLUSION

The comparative analysis of the seventeen sample SBEs' competitive forces is richly revealing of their relative strengths and weaknesses and therefore provides a tale worth telling in explaining their market positioning.[13] Indeed, we would argue that existing rivals and potential entrants are the most compelling competitive forces confronting these SBEs. In particular, the firms 'take what is given' in their markets by locating and then developing market niches which are otherwise being ignored or overlooked. The intention is to participate in, or even contribute to, the markets' growth without countenancing direct confrontation with either existing rivals or potential entrants. This attitude or disposition is a reflection of not only the SBEs' smallness and immaturity, but also of the markets' tolerance for fragmentation.[14]

Consideration of rivals in the extended sense – that is, substitutes, buyers and suppliers – enables us to gain further insight into SBEs' relative strengths and weaknesses. A more intelligent appreciation of the firms' strategic behaviour is therefore made possible. For example, in low-concentration markets SBEs find that the competitive pressures exerted by existing and potential rivals are quite formidable and pervasive. Yet suppliers act as a very positive competitive force, and thus help alleviate those pressures. Interestingly, the reverse situation can apply to those SBEs in high-concentration markets.

6 Competitive and defensive strategies

6.1 INTRODUCTION

The comparative analysis of the five competitive forces to which the sample of SBEs is subjected, and their underlying causes, in the previous chapter, provides insight into the environment in which SBEs function. Furthermore, the approach suggests, and usually precisely indentifies, relative strengths and weaknesses within their markets. Within this context SBEs attempt to cope with the collective pressures of the forces of competition by adopting appropriate competitive strategies. Effective competitive strategies are responsible for the proper positioning of SBEs within segments of their markets in such a fashion that they can both defend themselves against the five competitive forces deployed against them, and also influence the forces of competition in their own favour. As a result, what Porter (1985) calls 'competitive advantage' – that is, above-average performance (see Appendix to this chapter) – is achieved.

The purpose of this chapter is to undertake a comparative analysis of the SBEs' competitive strategies in order to determine the extent to which competitive advantage is (or is not) achieved. In so doing, we utilize the 'value chain' analysis of Porter (1985). This analytical tool, suitably modified for the small-firms context, offers a systematic diagnosis of those SBEs' activities which involve a search for sources of competitive advantage.

Given that significant uncertainty, and apparent apprehension about it, are both characteristics of life in the SBE, particularly in the early stages of its life cycle, we also probe the extent to which industry scenarios and defensive strategies are deployed, and to what effect. These additional considerations are natural extensions or ramifications of the Porter approach. Before reading our assessment of the SBEs and their strategies, the reader may find it useful to review Porter's competitive-advantage framework, as expounded in Chapter 1. The Appendix to chapter 6 might also usefully be referred to.

Market concentration levels – that is, low, medium, and high – are used to group the seventeen SBEs of the Profiles sample into three sub-samples, for the purposes of assessing their competitive and defensive strategies.[1] This is consistent with the groupings used in our analysis of the five competitive forces to which the SBEs are subject in the previous chapter. The reader will recall that we think of those SBEs in low-concentration markets as monopolistic competitors within highly fragmented markets; those in medium-concentration markets as being fringe competitors within dominant firm/competitive fringe structures; and those in high-concentration markets as being oligopolistic competitors, subject to marked inter-firm dependencies. The latter offer opportunities for small rivals to challenge larger oligopolists.

6.2 LOW-CONCENTRATION MARKETS

Table 6.1 is a summary schema, displaying those SBEs which fall into the low-market concentration category. Also shown is the net impact which 'extended rivals' have on the competitive advantage of these SBEs. At this point the reader may find it useful to refer back briefly to Figure 1.1 of Chapter 1, which displays in diagrammatic form the five forces of extended rivalry to which the SBE is subject. Conventionally, one certainly identifies intra-industry competition as important, so existing rivals appear in the schema. To them are added potential entrants, substitutes, buyers and suppliers: these being the extended rivals. Each category of rival is given a column heading in Table 6.1. This is then cross-tabulated with the SBE, as identified by its code and product market. Entries within the table are based on our evaluation of the evidence from semi-structured interviews with owner-managers. Interviews followed the format given in Section II of the Appendix to this book. Much of that evidence has already been presented in a within-site fashion in the Profiles of Part II of the book. Readers wanting amplification of the reasons for assigning influences as (net) positive, neutral or negative on competitive advantage might in the first instance refer back to the relevant Profile for further enlightenment. In addition, much extra evidence justifying why entries in Table 6.1 were assigned as printed can be found in this current chapter itself.[2] Cross-site (i.e. column-wise in the table) inspection of these data for low-concentration markets reveals existing rivals, potential entrants and buyers as net negative influences on competitive advantage, and substitutes and suppliers as net positive influences on competitive advantage.

Competitive strategy (low concentration)

Table 6.1 highlights the collective consequences of the five forces of competition on competitive strategy. We would argue that the largely negative influence of existing rivals, potential entrants and buyers (or customers) on those SBEs arises from the fact that they operate in highly fragmented markets. Though similar in size, these SBEs experience atomistic competition, given the small size of the market share held (i.e. minuscule) and the fact that existing rivals are numerous. Because of their proclaimed and mutual admonishment of direct confrontation, these SBEs and their existing

Table 6.1 Extended rivalry for SBEs in low-concentration markets

| Firm | Product market | Extended rivals | | | | |
		Existing rivals	Potential entrants	Substitutes	Buyers	Suppliers
A	Blind cleaning	–	–	+	–	+
C	Knitwear manufacturing	–	–	+	–	+
D	Auto repairing	–	–	+	–	+
E	Industrial cleaning	–	–	+	–	+
G	Holiday tours	0	–	+	–	0
L	Wine distribution	–	–	0	–	+
Q	Theatrical props	0	–	+	0	+

Notes:
+ Net *positive* influence on competitive advantage
– Net *negative* influence on competitive advantage
0 Net *neutral* influence on competitive advantage

rivals must accept being confined to very small niches. As a consequence, inter-firm rivalry is generally quite intense: certainly this is the way these SBEs perceive the situation. Moreover, these SBEs and their competitors typically lack the requisite scale economies, degree of product differentiation and absolute cost advantages, and so on, to challenge each other directly with the intention of increasing market share. Only in the cases of Firm G (holiday tours) and Firm Q (theatrical props) is the impact of existing rivals considered other than negative, being neutral in these cases. This neutrality is attributable to expanding market demand, which means that all competing firms can relish the prospect of growth, with little fear of their niches overlapping or being taken over.

The obvious lack of significant entry barriers leaves incumbents vulnerable to the looming threat of potential entrants. Entry to these fragmented markets can only splinter them further, at best, and drive incumbent firms out, at worse. Not surprisingly, every SBE considers potential entrants a negative competitive force.

To some extent the generally negative impact of buyers is also a reflection of the negative influences of existing and potential rivals. Firms confined to limited market niches are almost by definition liable to be reliant upon a few specific customers. This is very much the case for these SBEs. Indeed, these firms' main buyers tend to be responsible for the lion's share of sales revenue, and this concentration of buyers puts considerable bargaining leverage in their hands, to the detriment of SBEs' competitive advantage.

Competitive pressures exerted by substitutes and suppliers are generally positive in impact on these SBEs. Apparently they mitigate the negative influences of the other three competitive forces, to judge by performance in terms of growth or profitability.[3] Ironically, however, the fact that they are considered to have a positive influence may be related to, or even explained by, those negative forces. For example, the traditional and long-standing nature of products of SBEs like Firm E (auto repairs) and Firm D (knit-wear) is important in explaining the perceived inferior relative value–price ratio of substitutes (should they even exist). Typically such products require fairly standardized or homogeneous inputs, which provide these SBEs with considerable bargaining leverage over suppliers.

It is quite plain that a focus strategy applies to the SBEs in low-concentration markets. All of these firms target certain limited customer, geographic and/or product segments and follow a differentiation variant of the focus strategy.[4] In particular, the SBEs are primarily interested in catering to specified customer types and are fastidious in their product quality, delivery, service and personal relationships.

Within the context of SBEs' value chains, inbound logistics include activities which may or may not be a source of competitive advantage. To the extent that they are, suppliers are found to be a positive competitive force, but as existing rivals apparently benefit equally from their influence, this essentially nullifies any potential differentiation effect from inbound logistics.

Operations, that is, activities associated with transforming inputs into outputs (or simply 'putting the product together'), are a substantial source of differentiation, to a greater of lesser degree. Competitive advantage for these SBEs derives fundamentally from their capacity to produce products which exactly match the specifications desired by their individual buyers. To illustrate, Firm L does not just sell wine but provides own-label bottles and personalized wine menus for its main customers, which include restaurants and hotels. For further illustration, consider the products of Firm G (holiday tours), Firm Q (theatrical props) and Firm C (fashion knitwear). These SBEs sell products which are tailor-made, and it is this characteristic which is primarily responsible for generating their value.

Outbound logistics – that is, activities which occur between the time the product is produced and subsequently received by the buyer – though important in general, are not significant as a source of differentiation. Because buyers have substantial bargaining leverage, they simply require these SBEs to provide the products requested, to a desired specification on demand. This is also expected to imply prompt and reliable delivery. An exception to this may be Firm Q (theatrical props), in that film producers, for example, can experience unpredictable and sudden needs for particular props. In this situation, an almost immediate delivery response is a key additional ingredient to Firm Q's outbound logistics activity, and creates a potent source of competitive advantage.

In most cases, the activities of marketing and sales are probably secondary to those of operations in effecting differentiation. Essentially, these SBEs have a penchant for engaging in the time-consuming activity of cultivating personal relationships with buyers. Few, if any, dedicate assets to, or incur costs for, such activities as promotion, advertising and channel development. The value of these more formal and tangible activities which may be directed at differentiation with a view to achieving competitive advantage, is often doubted by owner-managers. Their impact is not believed to be easily recognized or measured. Also, given that such activities are tangible, and hence visible, they may unwittingly alert rival firms to competitive strategies. This in turn may provoke an antagonistic reaction. One therefore finds more discreet methods are employed. Firm G (holiday tours), for example, finds substantial value in establishing the use of hotels and travel agencies as channels to customers. Such channels can be used as sources of differentiation in that this SBE's referrals through them convey immediately the credibility of the enterprise to the buyers. This form of marketing and sales activity is on a par with 'operations' (namely, conducting the tour) in determining competitive advantage. Service activities performed by these SBEs could easily be confused with those of marketing and sales. Recall that the principal marketing and sales activity is the nurturing of personal relations with buyers. Often this takes place in the context of after-sales visits, which are a service activity.

Firm A (blind cleaning) is perhaps the least successful in pursuing a desired focus on differentiation strategy. Despite recognizing that customers need to be educated on the product's uniqueness, this firm was apparently unable to initiate those sales and marketing activities which involve a dedication of assets and costs to the goal of generating differentiation. It tried advertising but with little effect. As the owner-manager recognized, emphasis on the firm's outbound logistics activity, through channel development, may be the means of convincing buyers of the product's distinctiveness. In pursuit of this, Firm A was contemplating the strategy of seeking endorsements from health and safety officials as a means of highlighting the product's distinctive features, that is, promoting differentiation. Alternatively, the firm was at least contemplating a focus on low cost. Unfortunately, it apparently did not have significant control of cost-drivers at its disposal, so this strategy did not seem efficacious.

Defensive strategy (low concentration)

In large part, these SBEs do not consciously deploy defensive tactics. They are so consumed with the desire to develop their own niches in the market, that they may deliberately screen out of consideration possible direct challenges by competitors. This pattern of behaviour is particularly evident when market growth is rapid and the firms are mainly engaged in reacting to, rather than contributing to, the growing demand.

Regarding the possibility of erecting or raising barriers to entry, several firms considered the tactic to be implausible. Firm E (industrial cleaning), for instance, simply regarded such action as beyond its control or influence. Firm D (auto repairs) was not prepared to undertake the substantial capital outlays which were thought to be needed to effectively block channel access, and hence to make defensive advantage effective. Generally, these firms preferred to create barriers to entry in a more personal and discreet manner. Specifically, they sought to increase the switching costs of their buyers through steadfast attention to maintaining customer satisfaction. According to Firm A (blind cleaning), limits might be set on the creation of barriers to entry, particularly if it seemed to involve a reduction in customer orientation, as this could be construed as unethical.[5]

Most of the firms would prefer to encourage 'good' competitors whenever possible. Mutual respect and goodwill amongst rivals foster industry stability and good reputation. In cultivating mutual respect and goodwill these SBEs try to resist being involved in retaliation of an inflammatory nature. In particular, they tend to avoid undercutting rivals' prices or bettering their rivals' product guarantees. Such retaliatory measures, in the view of Firm C (knitwear manufacturer), would be inordinately costly and time-consuming. A Pyrrhic victory, at best, would be the expected outcome. At worse, the industry structure could be destroyed. As a weaker alternative, the firms subscribe to the more acceptable (if not entirely ethical) tactic of matching, rather than bettering, competitors' prices and guarantees. At the same time as they concentrate on enhancing their products' quality, they are also trying to set proper examples for their industries in terms of high trading standards. If mutually successful in achieving such agreed standards, a 'fraternity' amongst competitors develops, according to Firm C (knitwear manufacturer).

Setting a proper example and acting in a 'fraternal' fashion might well be regarded (perhaps naïvely) as providing sufficient grounds for lowering the inducement for attack by rival firms. There certainly is little, if any, attempt by these SBEs to manage overtly their competitors' assumptions. Perceived inability, ignorance or a preference for maintaining a low profile are the major factors behind the shunning of this tactic. In addition, these SBEs do not usually appear to be prepared to reduce profit targets as a means of lowering the inducement for attack. But then only firm L (wine distribution) has actually experienced a direct challenge from competitors. In this case, it did accommodate to this new competitive pressure by reducing its profit target.

The extent to which these firms are willing to engage in deterring competitors is very limited indeed. While Firm A (blind cleaning) indicates it would deter by competitive pricing and Firm C (knitwear manufacturer) tries to deter by informing potential competitors of difficulties in the industry, deterrence is essentially absent. Firm L (wine distribution), for instance, insists it must simply 'ride out' (i.e. accept temporarily lower profit expectations) rival firms' market penetration, believing their strategies to be short-term orientated. At the other extreme, Firm G (holiday tours) enjoys such a rapidly expanding market that an involvement in deterrence is thought to be quite unnecessary. In either cases, these SBEs would just get on with keeping their customer base satisfied, without worrying about directly resisting competitors. If buyers were lost to rivals, new buyers would be sought to fill the void.

Nevertheless, most of these SBEs attempt to stay abreast of possible changes in the industry structure and/or competitors' behaviour. Attending trade shows is not only good for public relations and cultivating customers but is also a harmless and inexpensive way of 'checking out' the competition. Suppliers and buyers can also be significant sources of information regarding the activities of competitors. Given that buyers are a particularly strong competitive force and possess significant bargaining leverage, they are necessarily highly informed about competitors as they go about their business of aggressively seeking optimal product purchase plans. Frequently this information can be tapped by the SBE. Finally, firms are alerted to the intentions and capabilities of rival firms by studying their advertising. Usually this is more of the informational than persuasive variety, and hence provides useful clues as to the conduct and resources of rivals.

6.3 MEDIUM-CONCENTRATION MARKETS

Table 6.2 provides a schema of SBEs in medium-concentration industries, and displays the net impact of the competitive forces to which they are subject. As before, extended rivals are identified at each column head, and their consequences for SBEs in medium-concentration markets noted, on the three-point scale of positive, negative or neutral. It will be observed that typically potential entrants and suppliers have a neutral influence on competitive advantage, with the occasional instance of the negative. As compared to the SBEs in low-concentration markets, these SBEs have less pressure from potential entrants but less positive influence from suppliers. Substitutes remain a generally positive influence, but buyers are now generally

Table 6.2 Extended rivalry for SBEs in medium-concentration markets

Firm	Product market	Existing rivals	Potential entrants	Substitutes	Buyers	Suppliers
			Extended rivals			
F	Food manufacturing	−	0	+	0	0
I	Software manufacturing	−	0	+	+	0
J	Cassette tapes	−	0	0	0	0
K	Electronics	0	0	+	+	0
N	Bulk bag manufacturing	−	0	+	+	0
O	Fencing manufacturing	+	−	+	+	0
P	Printing lamination	−	0	+	+	−

Notes:
+ Net *positive* influence on competitive advantage
− Net *negative* influence on competitive advantage
0 Net *neutral* influence on competitive advantage

a positive influence for these SBEs, compared to a negative influence for the SBEs in low-concentration markets. For both cases, existing rivals (i.e. incumbent) are typically a negative influence on competitive advantage.

Competitive strategy (medium concentration)

A collective consideration of the SBEs' competitive forces, as stylized in Table 6.2, is quite helpful in determining and/or illuminating their competitive strategies. Recall that the SBEs in medium-concentration industries are typically confined to the competitive fringe of oligopolies. The dominant oligopolists (or cartel, if they work together) command considerable market power, which is largely attributable to scale economies and significant absolute cost advantages. As a result, SBEs attempt to confine their growth and development to well-defined niches within the competitive fringe, usually without thought of challenging the dominant group. Firm P (lamination), for example, did not work within these constraints, and ultimately the result was that his operations were sold to a dominant firm, after an offer which could not be refused. While rivalry with dominant firms is thought to be self-destructive and is therefore avoided, competing with other fringe SBEs takes place in a fashion which is similar to that found among SBEs in low-concentration markets. That is to say, competition is fairly non-confrontational unless an SBE wanders from its own dedicated niche into that of a rival. Given the many rivals operating in the competitive fringe, these SBEs largely consider rivalry to be a negative competitive force (albeit of an impersonal or indirect nature). The exception is Firm O (fencing manufacturing), which enjoys a large geographic market which is intentionally ignored by dominant firms and fringe competitors alike, largely because of the peripherality of the markets. Also somewhat unusual is the case of Firm K (electronics), for which the net impact of existing rivals is deemed to be neutral. Despite the recognized competitive pressures exerted by the many fringe rivals, resulting in splintered market shares, this SBE maintains a symbiotic relationship with a firm in the dominant group, meeting subcontracted small-batch orders for test equipment. In fact, its primary buyer is this dominant firm.

In some contrast to the case of low-concentration markets, potential entrants must be careful to be selective in their industry positioning. Clearly, a firm directly seeking entry into the dominant firms' segment of the market will be met with overwhelming resistance. More likely, a potential entrant will initially look to fill market gaps in the competitive fringe. In so doing, it will not wish to antagonize unnecessarily the existing rivals, given the significant deterrents in their hands, involving features like scale economies, absolute cost advantages, distribution channels, and so on. While these deterrent features are available to dominant firms and fringe firms alike, their potency is much diminished in the latter case. As a consequence, there is recognized scope for admitting additional members into the competitive fringe within medium-concentration markets. Potential entrants must simply be circumspect in their approach, and the evidence is that they are fairly deliberate in their circumspection. Hence, with the exception of Firm O (fencing manufacturing), the impact of potential entrants on these SBEs is regarded as 'neutral': neither particularly negative nor positive.

The view we proffer of a stable market dichotomy with, on the one hand, a competitive fringe and, on the other, a coordinated group of dominant firms,[6] is reinforced by our general observation that there is typically an absence of substitutes from other industries. If they do exist, they tend to be inferior. In part, the adoption by incumbents of a relatively advanced technology, a notable barrier to entry, provides one explanation of this stable market structure. Firm I (design and manufacture of computer software) and Firm K (design and manufacture of electronic test equipment) provide exemplars of SBEs working within this kind of market structure. Such firms may not explicitly recognize, therefore, the role of substitutes as a positive competitive force, simply because they are perceived to be highly unlikely to impinge upon them.

Given the possibly small, even nearly insignificant positive effect of substitutes, and the sharply demarcated configuration of existing rivals which makes the prospect of entry necessarily a fine calculation, it is perhaps unsurprising that on the whole it is buyers who serve as the main positive competitive force. The proliferation of specialized products, and the attendant expansion of the customer base, combine, more or less, to make buyers an object of favour with SBEs, so far as their influence on competition is concerned. Buyers of the products of Firm F (food manufacturing) and Firm J (cassette tape manufacturing) are perhaps closest to being exceptions to this, in that the products they purchase are rather homogeneous and buyer loyalty is low (i.e. switching is not unusual because switching costs are low).

The influence of suppliers as a competitive force is much more complex. Generally suppliers are a less positive competitive force for these SBEs in medium concentration markets, compared to those in low-concentration markets. These SBEs are all manufacturers and their products have rather high value-added. They often have few available suppliers, especially in instances like the provision of sophisticated productive inputs, like plant and equipment. Firm P (printing lamination), for instance, was dependent on a sole supplier of a very costly machine which was fundamentally important to its commercial success. However, in the other cases, there were a number of favourable factors which more or less nullified the potentially negative influences of suppliers. These included congenial (if not loyal) relationships with suppliers, the absence of threats of forward integration, and often low switching costs. As a result, suppliers are treated as neutral in their overall impact on these SBEs in medium-concentration markets, with the exception of Firm P (printing lamination).

Since the SBEs considered in this section are limited to the competitive fringe, they naturally do not compete broadly across the market, and therefore pursue some type of focus strategy. These SBEs target various forms of niche: by customer type; geographical location; and product market segment, for example, either singly or in combination.

Firm F (food manufacturing), Firm I (computer software) and Firm K (electronic test equipment) focus on differentiation. Of the three, Firm K appears to best exploit differentiation through its value activities and thereby creates competitive advantage. In particular, it skilfully links its value chain with that of its buyers. It does so because its main product, printed circuit boards (PCBs), is produced in small bespoke batches for larger firms in the industry to use as test equipment. Hence, it is particularly the operational activities of the SBE and its buyers which must be mutually understood by SBE and buyer alike. Further, they must be closely integrated, as the product which is passed from one to the other is truly tailor-made. Obviously related drivers of differentiation within the SBE's operations include: flexibility of scale and market position; proprietary learning; and location, in both geographical and characteristics space.[7]

Two further significant sources of differentiation which originate in value activities are outbound logistics and service to buyers. Given the necessarily close relationship between the firm and its buyers, it is to be expected that the SBE is capable of responding quickly to contractual obligations. This significance is heightened if the product has high technical content and is fundamental to the buyers' own very success. Furthermore, after-sale involvement with buyers is crucial to SBEs like Firm K. It ensures that Firm K supplies printed circuit boards of sufficient quality and desired specification to satisfy buyers. The owner-manager ensures that they are also amenable to high-volume production methods, with some potential for sharing scale economies.

Inbound logistics and sales and marketing also make their contributions as value activities which contribute to that aspect of the SBE's competitive advantage which is attributable to differentiation. Buyers frequently require a short period of time between placing an order and having it fulfilled (i.e. a quick turnaround) so Firm K must insist on a timely delivery of inputs. Within marketing and sales, strong personal relationships with buyers (i.e. full and free channel access) allied to the perceived need (which is constantly met) for educating the buyers on the technical aspects of product development, contribute in an almost inevitable way to the creation of value.

Finally, it is worth noting that Firm K (electronic test equipment) does have insight into the configuration of its buyers' value chains, because its owner-manager has a full grasp of buyers' purchasing criteria. Having succeeded in acquiring several contracts which provide ready access to valuable internal knowledge of the buyers and their needs, the owner-manager is provided with a distinct edge in winning future contracts. In a sense, the buyers' switching costs are raised. Firm I (software manufacturing) is much less successful in creating that form of uniqueness which is particularly valued by its buyers. Despite an avowed commitment to staying ahead of its rivals by offering buyers new, technologically advanced products, Firm I tends to adapt existing (off-the-shelf) technology. Though technology is deemed to be a vital driver of differentiation, this SBE would arguably generate more value through differentiation by creating its own technology, especially given the robustness of the computer software industry, in terms of the buoyancy of new product demand. This firm, however, resists investment in research and development, being put off by what appear to be prohibitive costs. Hence, rather than placing emphasis on operations for effecting differentiation, Firm K concentrates on marketing and sales activities like product promotion and aggressive personal selling. However, in so doing, it tends to emphasize high-volume sales and is willing to tolerate the narrowing of profit margins. With its reliance on marketing and sales, Firm K appears to be jeopardizing its quest for competitive advantage because it is, in effect, confounding a low-cost approach with that of differentiation – that is, it provides a classical example of being 'stuck in the middle'.

Firm F (food manufacturing) also seems to be running the risk of being stuck in the middle. Its reported strategy is similar to that of Firm I (software manufacturing). It aims to emphasize high volume, even at the expense of slim margins in order to pursue gains from scale economies, and is also, rather faintheartedly, committed to developing product differentiation. Despite an avowed preference for highlighting its commitment to product variety and quality, Firm F has no activities within it of this sort which could reconfigure the value chain by creating new sources of differentiation. By contrast, cost-drivers like capacity utilization, location, learning, and policies as they relate to suppliers and buyers (e.g. credit), are evidently important to the goal of minimizing costs. Indeed, it might occasionally be pursued at the expense of differentiation.[8]

Firm J (cassette tape manufacturing), Firm O (fencing manufacturing) and Firm P (lamination) focus on low cost as a means of achieving competitive advantage. All three firms produce weakly differentiated products and greatly benefit from exploiting timing as a principal cost-driver, in a sense to be explained. These firms have enjoyed first-mover advantages as they relate to market entry and/or preferential treatment by suppliers. Firm O (fencing manufacturing), for example, recognized a tendency for its competitors to ignore what were perceived to be the peripheral markets of Scotland and Northern Ireland, concentrating rather on the locationally convenient market of England. Firm P (printing lamination) was successful in establishing itself because of a supplier's unusually favourable terms for leasing or purchasing advanced machinery. After observing Firm P's remarkable success, this supplier drastically altered its terms of future sales. Cost-drivers of this sort, which are obviously governed by timing, apply to the value chain activities of inbound logistics and operations. SBEs also benefit from learning as a cost-driver, as it applies to these same activities.

For instance, Firm J (cassette tape manufacturing) has reconfigured its operations in such a way that new combinations of labour and machines have improved efficiency, based on a new (and enlarged) desired scale of operations. Finally, possibly the most significant source of competitive advantage for Firms J, O and P is to be found in their limited support activities, with special reference to infrastructure. These firms' infrastructures (which include overheads) are distinctly minimal in comparison to those of existing rivals, allowing them to maintain and sustain a low-cost position.

Firm N (bulk bag manufacturing) is unique in comparison to other SBEs considered here under the heading of medium concentration, in that its focus strategy blends both low-cost and differentiation elements without apparently leading to its falling foul of the 'stuck in the middle' syndrome.[9] Perhaps this SBE's most durable and telling sources of competitive advantage are location and experience. Firm N is geographically well-situated in that it is close to both its primary suppliers and buyers. Because this firm's owner-manager has previous knowledge of existing rivals (acquired as an employee) he has a good understanding of how his own firm's value chain matches up with those of his rivals. Thus it its not a quirk that Firm N's value chain abundantly displays activities which feature both cost and differentiation drivers. Indeed, several drivers of both kinds are found in every one of its primary value activities. Only a lack of scale economies seems to curtail their competitive advantage.

Defensive strategy (medium concentration)

In some contrast to SBEs in low-concentration markets, those in medium-concentration markets are less myopic and more diligent so far as the formulation of defensive strategy (and tactics) are concerned. They tend to avoid the traps of being overfocused on their customers, and seek understanding of the behaviour of rivals, be they existing or potential, dominant or fringe. This well-balanced approach to strategy is a function, in some measure, of accumulated market experience, reasonable financial resources, and a fair degree of proprietary know-how.

In terms of increasing barriers to entry, these SBEs do attempt to raise their buyers' switching cost through nurturing personal relationships. They are adept at maintaining flexibility to meet the often changing needs of buyers. The intention is to build up customer loyalty, which is in keeping with behaviour observed for SBEs in low-concentration markets. However, in addition, SBEs in the medium-concentration markets appear more likely to respond to new product gaps, and are more active in seeking to invest in productivity-enhancing capital goods with a view not only to promoting growth but also to fortifying their market positions. Firm J (cassette tape manufacturing) and Firm P (printing lamination), in particular, undertook investment in new machinery for these very purposes. These firms well understand that growth (though desired) may well provoke a response, especially from the markets' dominant firms.

These SBEs are less concerned with encouraging 'good' competitors and more inclined to signal intentions to defend their niches primarily through expansion and consolidation. Firm growth and development is viewed partly as a means of accumulating retaliatory resources. Consolidation is basically achieved by assuming blocking positions. For instance, Firm O (chestnut fencing manufacturing) plans to build a manufacturing facility in Northern Ireland, where its largest customer is located, as a means of staving off potential entry.

Reducing profit targets, matching guarantees, and managing rivals' assumptions are tactics not to be overlooked by these SBEs as methods of lowering the inducement for rivals to attack. Consider by way of illustration the case of Firm P (printing lamination). With the acquisition of highly productive machinery, it has been successful in encroaching on the market share of the market's dominant firm. Whilst the other fringe competitors are perhaps comforted by the way in which Firm P has exposed the dominant firm's apparent vulnerability, they must now perceive a new element of threat to their own market positions *vis-à-vis* that of the emerging Firm P. Elsewhere, Firm J (cassette tape manufacturing) is confident of no new competition, given prices that have for long been unattractively low to potential entrants' perceptions. Indeed, these prices are so unattractive that rivals who need to finance the necessary (and expensive) capital inputs (i.e. computerized machinery) are unlikely to survive, let alone to achieve moderate profitability. The prospect of slim profits also serves as a deterrent to new rivals in the cases of Firm F (food manufacturing) and Firm N (bulk bag manufacturing). Capital costs are also significant as a barrier to entry in these firms' markets. Industry scenarios are more likely to be considered by the SBEs in medium-concentration markets, as they are astute about, and apparently quite sensitive to, the conduct of their rivals and to other industry elements. They are therefore able to formulate views as to what they feel the future might portend. In interviews, owner-managers use a vocabulary of repositioning, diversification, 'sitting tight', and so on, suggesting the utilization of scenarios, at least on an informal basis. Firm I (software manufacturing) and Firm P (lamination) used industry scenarios with some alacrity, and were perhaps encouraged to do so by their notably dynamic markets, for which niches could rapidly experience encroachment, absorbtion or simply obsolence.

Indeed, these SBEs are quite active, even aggressive, in extracting market intelligence. On the basis of this, they are adept at changing conditions to enhance their abilities to respond to attack and to deploy overall defensive strategies. Suppliers, buyers, the media, trade shows, courses and conferences are cited in various combinations as important sources of market intelligence. Only Firm J (cassette tape manufacturing) could be regarded as being somewhat passive in its defensive efforts. This is perhaps attributed to its being more mature and therefore secure in its market. Thus its main market niche is well defined and resilient, as evidenced by loyal customers, who have for a long period of time provided repeat business. Moreover, this SBE is more than content to cater to the market's small-volume demands, which continue to be buoyant. As a result, it has a track record of not threatening rivals, thereby making for a stable existence. At the other extreme, Firm I (software manufacturing) is particularly aggressive and calculating in its methods of acquiring market information. In addition to using many of the aforementioned sources of information, this SBE engages in what it called 'reverse engineering'. By this technique it would break down rivals' products to better understand the technical basis of those firms' product capabilities, and would then proceed to develop products of its own of a superior nature. Firm I essentially subscribes to the philosophy that offensive actions provide the best defensive strategy.

6.4 HIGH-CONCENTRATION MARKETS

Table 6.3 depicts the three firms which reside in high-concentration markets. Positive, negative and neutral influences on competitive advantage for each one of the extended rivals are identified. In this way the table provides a summary picture of the overall nature of competitive forces to which these SBEs are subject. Potential entrants, substitutes and buyers are unambiguously a positive influence on competitive advantage. This was only true of substitutes for low market concentration, and for substitutes and buyers for high market concentration. Suppliers are less clearly a positive influence in the current context, but rivals are not a negative influence. In many ways, the situation seems more auspicious for SBEs in high-concentration markets. That impression can be misleading, as competition is intense, and any deviation of an extended rival exercising a positive influence on competitive advantage can have devastating consequences for an SBE.

Table 6.3 Extended rivalry for SBEs in high-concentration markets

Firm	Product market	Existing rivals	Potential entrants	Substitutes	Buyers	Suppliers
			Extended rivals			
B	Security blankets	0	+	+	+	0
H	Cosmetics	0	+	+	+	+
M	Acrobatic aircraft	+	+	+	+	−

Notes:
+ Net *positive* influence on competitive advantage
− Net *negative* influence on competitive advantage
0 Net *neutral* influence on competitive advantage

Competitive strategy (high concentration)

A brief inspection of Table 6.3 suggests that these SBEs in high-concentration markets must be adopting the proper competitive strategies, thus enjoying considerable competitive advantage in their markets. For almost the entire array of forces creating extended rivalry, their influences on competitive advantage are regarded as positive. Collectively, it would appear that each SBE is in commanding control of its environment. However, a closer examination of the evidence reveals that certain individual competitive forces are rather more potent than others and perhaps also more deterministic (as distinct from random) in their impact. Thus, for example, potential entrants have a powerful and non-random impact on competitive advantage, even in the presence of other neutralizing or indeed negative forces. Recall that these SBEs, because of unusual or atypical circumstances, compete in very specialized and limited markets where only a few rivals (e.g. multinational companies) exist. Thus the potential impact of SBEs contemplating market entry is significant, almost irrespective of what, for example, existing rivals are doing or how suppliers are behaving.

Despite the nearly universal positive impact of the other competitive forces, Firm B (security blankets) and Firm H (cosmetics) compete intimately with very powerful and long-established multinationals. Firm B in a previous incarnation tried unsuccessfully to match its rivals in offering a broad product-line. In its present (i.e. phoenix) form it focuses on a limited number of products which are protected by patents. Nevertheless, it recognizes attempts by competitors to overcome this barrier, legally and otherwise.

Firm H (cosmetics) competes quite closely with its well-established rivals, and to do so it has reconfigured the market for cosmetics by successfully emphasizing the natural and wholesome quality of its products. Its competitors have been slow to react, knowing that imitation may well undermine their own long-held commitments to products which emphasize the more intangible or elusive traits of romance and glamour, all of which are suggested by expensive advertising, promotion and packaging. However, given Firm H's enormous success, eventually rivals are likely to develop new matching product lines. They might possibly do this within distinctive separate companies, to avoid compromising the market identity of their own traditional products.

So, despite maintaining fortified market positions, rivals are not content to accept what they regard as the threatening presences of Firms B and H. Thus existing rivals are deemed neutral as a competitive force in both cases. But, clearly, these neutral positions can swiftly alter and with dramatic consequences. Competitive strategy, and indeed competitive advantage, hinge decisively on the competitive force exerted by existing rivals.

Similarly, Firm M (acrobatic aircraft) is favourably influenced by all but one competitive force. But, unlike in the cases of Firms B and H, that one competitive force (i.e. suppliers) did succeed in making Firm M defunct. This SBE's founding was as a result of a government grant given to fill what was perceived to be a considerable void in the small aircraft market in the niche of aerobatic aeroplanes. Given a significant recognized demand, no serious substitutes and no rival producers, it appeared that the firm could only succeed. However, only one supplier of an essential input could be identified and it proved devastatingly unreliable in the end. The highly favourable nature of the other competitive forces were ultimately without consequence.

Given these SBEs' relative lack of resources, they are restricted in their geographical and/or product scope. They are not considered to compete broadly across their various markets, despite being taken seriously as a competitive force by market-wide rivals. Hence, these SBEs follow a focus strategy. In doing so, their natural tendency is obviously to emphasize both differentiation and low cost.

Turning to a consideration of these SBEs' value chains, Firm H (cosmetics) is perhaps a prime example of a firm able to thrive as a result of generating value from activities throughout its value chain. It does so because ·in large part it benefits from the proven sustained competitive advantage of its franchisor. Firm H's value chain is naturally very much moulded by that of the franchisor.

In considering marketing and sales activities, for example, Firm H does not deviate from prescribed and proven practices and policies of the franchisor. It is not so much that the franchisor's activities are replicated by, but rather are shared with, the firm. Both differentiation and low-cost value emanate from activities which are grounded on a particular ethos. This espouses concern for the environment and for the fate of developing countries. To illustrate, the products not only consist entirely of natural ingredients, but are not animal-tested. Also, the franchisor emphasizes its concern for endangered species by donating a share of its earnings to various wildlife funds. In keeping with its pro-environmental stance, where excess and waste are to be disparaged, Firm H adheres to modest packaging, subdued advertising and a product refill policy. These activities are not only consonant with differentiation but also with low cost.

In further generating differentiation and low-cost value, a 'trade not aid' policy with developing countries is pursued. This not only enhances a benevolent, outward-looking image which translates into greater differentiation, but also engenders lower costs. Interestingly, whilst differentiation value is garnered from cultivating a positive reputation so far as developing countries and the environment are concerned, within the context of marketing and sales activities, procurement activities are simultaneously identified as an important cost-driver. Of course, the linkage between marketing and sales and procurement activities could be recognized as itself driving costs.

Timing and location proved to be decisive differentiation drivers for Firm

H itself. Firm H emerged in the wake of the franchisor's rapid early success and the absence of any franchisee in a particular large city. Locating on the city's high street was regarded as not only obviously important to the SBE from general considerations of competitive advantage, but also as strategically important in conferring first-mover advantages. Within a few years, the owner-manager of Firm H opened a second franchised shop on the high street.

Those value activities of Firm B (security blankets) which are largely responsible for competitive advantage are operations and marketing and sales. Scale economies are an important cost-driver for SBEs like Firm B which are producing standardized products. The achieving of competitive advantage from exploiting scale economies is very much contingent on possessing the right technology. Learning is a similarly important cost-driver, as Firm B has significantly reconfigured its operations with proper job scheduling. The discretionary policy of placing workers on salary rather than hourly wages is yet another identified cost-driver. Proprietary knowledge, as reflected in patent-protected products, coupled with a top management which is personally responsible for marketing and sales (ie. conducting customer visits) serve as a valuable linkage in effecting differentiation value. As a result, customers are more appreciative of such products and their merits.

Defensive strategy (high concentration)

With the exception of Firm M (acrobatic aircraft), the other SBEs, Firm B (security blankets) and Firm H (cosmetics) treat defensive strategy rather seriously, given the close and personal inter-firm rivalry to which they are subjected. Defensive strategy considerations are particularly pertinent to these SBEs in that existing rivals, though few in number, are quite formidable in terms of size, market experience, and commitment. Firm M (acrobatic aircraft) never evolved to the point where defensive strategy would be relevant. In fact, its owner-manager admitted to welcoming rivals as a means of increasing customer awareness of the market. Unfortunately, because of the specialist supply difficulties, this SBE did not survive long enough to bring its first acrobatic aeroplane to market, though it had constructed and flown a demonstration model.

Promptly filling product gaps whenever they occur is viewed as a means of increasing entry barriers. In so doing, Firm B (security blankets) and H (cosmetics) both explained that it was by cultivating buyer relations that they were able to be timely in anticipating market changes that generated new product gaps. Naturally, being sensitive to changing customer needs and trading on a personal basis enhance loyalty, as well as inhibiting competitor challenges. On balance, the owner-managers of both firms expressed some confidence in the efficacy of existing barriers to entry (e.g. proprietary knowledge and first-mover advantages). Hence they did not place undue emphasis upon (or suggest a sense of urgency about) filling product gaps, nor did they suggest any sense of urgency in identifying them. Rather, they were confident that should the need arise to fill product gaps, they would be able to do so.

In spite of what has been described as rather intense inter-firm competition, Firms B and H attempt to adhere to what are regarded as proper standards of trading within their industries. Retaliation (e.g. matching guarantees, undercutting prices, etc.), for instance, is generally regarded as a tactic which falls short of these standards and they would prefer to avoid it if at all possible. Having to resort to retaliation is thought to be an admission of vulnerability about the firm and/or its products. However, Firm B (security blankets) has found itself in the uncomfortable dilemma of having to cope with a multinational rival which has both engaged in product imitation irrespective of the Firm B's patent protection, as well as price matching. Firm B has responded by seeking legal counsel and communicating via letter its concerns to this particular rival. This has dimmed the enthusiasm of the multinational, which has now abandoned its predatory behaviour.

Maintaining a high profile and refusing to reduce profit targets (which might otherwise provoke a price war) are considered salient factors in lowering the inducement of rivals to attack. To illustrate, Firm H (cosmetics) has located its franchise operation on the high street of a major city which sends an immediate and clear signal of market commitment to potential and actual rivals as well as establishing a credible high profile. Similarly, Firm B's (security blankets) provision of patented products to high-profile customers (i.e. central banks) is compelling evidence of its market.

In addition to projecting strong images and commitment, deterrence can be augmented by the use of industry scenarios. This might not be done formally or explicitly, but it is a widely used device, albeit informally and without being labelled as such. Certainly, the SBEs are adept at anticipating and planning for various scenarios which are likely to unfold in the future. They are motivated to do so by the intimate inter-firm competition and apparently high strategic stakes amongst all rivals. Much has been hitherto suggested in this regard for both Firms B and H.

Firms B and H both utilize various sources of information in order to sustain their defensive strategies. Suppliers, customers and trade shows are noted sources or channels for identifying new and popular products, as well as for providing insight into competitors.

6.5 CONCLUSION

Much terrain has been surveyed in this Part so far. Hence, it is perhaps useful to attempt to encapsulate the key points in this conclusion. We shall also reflect somewhat on some of the more salient aspects of the analysis.

The seventeen firms we considered are small in relation to the markets in which they operate. We have revealed that this has encouraged them to adopt a focus strategy. Lack of resources and market uncertainty predominately account for their implementation of a focus strategy by serving particular geographic, customer and/or product niches. Market uncertainty impinges heavily on many of the SBEs given their youth and immaturity. Of course, limited resources also restrict access to information, especially so far as marketing and sales activities are concerned. Moreover, newly emerging SBEs naturally have organizational structures which are informal and non-hierarchial. Indeed, these SBEs are largely operated by only one, or a few, authoritarian figures (i.e. owner-managers) who are primarily, and perhaps solely, responsible for the collecting and processing of market information.

Our comparative analysis strongly implies that two of the five extended rivals (i.e. existing and potential) are particularly influential as competitive forces in shaping SBEs' competitive strategies and indeed in determining the extent of their competitive advantage. It is transparently evident, however, that a collective consideration of all five competitive forces included under the 'extended rivalry' heading is necessary for a complete analysis. Substitutes, buyers and suppliers must also be included to provide not only a broader scope for, but a richer insight into, the effectiveness of these SBEs' strategic behaviour. Certainly, without including an assessment of extended rivalry, it would have been impossible effectively to utilize value-chain analysis in identifying sources of differentiation and low-cost value within these SBEs' activities.

The relatively (if not absolutely) limited size and often juvenile nature of the SBEs considered did not lead us to neglect to examine the measures which were undertaken to implement defensive strategies. Generally, our finding is that defensive strategy is treated fairly informally and is not apparently given proactive, systematic or detailed attention. Rather, these SBEs are more typically preoccupied with identifying (or creating) and then developing their own market niches, perhaps naïvely assuming (or hoping) they will be ignored by other firms. This is especially so of SBEs in low-concentration markets who are in an early stage of their life cycle and command only modest resources.

APPENDIX: STATISTICS ON THE PERFORMANCE OF SBEs

Ways of evaluating the performance of small firms are in their infancy. Typically SBEs are not in an equilibrium state and may be growing very fast which makes performance evaluation difficult. It is really only when an SBE has exited from business that a sensible retrospective calculation can be made of internal rate of return on an annualized basis. This is the sort of calculation that venture capital investors make with their investee firms. However, though such firms are still small, they are bigger than the 'micro firms', with employment typically of fewer than ten persons, which are the concern of this study. We have reported in Reid and Anderson (1992) on a complementary sample of SBEs with similar characteristics and noted there that venture capital involvement was non-existent. Venture capitalists set hurdle rates of return (annualized IRR) of at least 25 per cent and often as high as 45 per cent. Their complete non-involvement with micro firms suggests prospects of 'poor' (in their sense) returns, certainly below 25 per cent. Of course, other factors come into play, especially high riskiness, but also the high transactional costs both of due diligence in investigating SBEs as potential investees and of providing advice to the owner-manager on a regular and proactive basis.

Within the small business community it is thought that rates of return for the SBE are very low, perhaps as low, in real terms, as 3 or 4 per cent. Very often, this would imply a return which was less than the cost of money, which may make small business ownership seem irrational. However, a distinction should be made between long-standing SBEs and newly formed ones. The latter are much closer to the 'entrepreneurial event' as Shapero (1984) calls it. Risk is higher, and presumably expected returns are higher. This might explain at least the temporary willingness of the owner-manager to be highly geared, with a lot of debt to service, in the early stage of the life-cycle of the SBE.

Table 6.4 gives some insight into performance of the Profiles sample of SBEs, and this may be considered alongside the more general and multi-dimensional analysis of competitive advantage in the body of the text. As before, SBEs are grouped by levels of market concentration, and data are presented on assets, age, profitability, growth and survival.

Apart from the age (in months) and survival variable (In, for 'in business'), all the figures given should be treated with considerable scepticism. Asset and profitability figures are self-reported by owner-managers and appear to us to be mildly to grossly inaccurate. Asset figures were asked for in the reinterview and in the initial interview, both for the same year (1985), and figures could diverge considerably. The figures we requested were book value net of depreciation. We also requested in the reinterview a figure for net profitability, defined as net profit (net of taxes and directors' fees) divided by the book value of the assets. This is given as π per cent in the table. We were also able to independently compute profitability, which again led to marked discrepencies. For example, Firm C's reported profitability was 54 per cent, whereas our independently computed profitability was 29 per cent. Growth rates are computed from the real asset figures (all expressed in 1985 prices). The g per cent of the table is computed on an annual basis.

It is clear from the table that typically SBEs experience very high growth rates early in the life-cycle. We know from work reported in the companion volume by Reid (1993, ch. 11) that there is a negative correlation of age with growth rates for SBEs: small SBEs grow faster than large SBEs. Negative growth rates (Firms M and F) are associated with going out of business. High growth rates are not necessarily associated with high profit-

Table 6.4 Summary statistics on performance

SBE	Product	Assets			Age	Profit-ability (π%)	Growth rate (g%)	In?
		Start	1985	1988				
Low market concentration								
A	Blind cleaning	16	16	n.a.	16	n.a.	0	Y
C	Knitwear manufacturing	2	7	n.a.	17	54	176	Y
D	Auto repairs	5	9	5	6	83	160	Y
E	Industrial cleaning	11	30	49	9	2	230	Y
G	Holiday tours	4	15	15	15	33	220	Y
L	Wine distribution	8	27	46	13	100	219	Y
Q	Theatrical props	1	7	n.a.	7	n.a.	1,028	N
Medium market concentration								
F	Food manufacturing	151	130	n.a.	40	n.a.	−4	N
I	Computer software	6	100	1,571	17	24	1,105	Y
J	Cassette tapes	6	100	159	125	20	150	Y
K	Electronic instruments	3	20	62	12	135	566	Y
N	Bulk bags	5	50	341	15	2	720	Y
O	Fencing manufacturing	17	50	41	22	15	106	Y
P	Printing lamination	1	180	n.a.	29	n.a.	7,406	Y
High market concentration								
B	Security printers blankets	81	105	157	32	41	11	Y
H	Cosmetics retailing	17	65	1,327	5	n.a.	678	Y
M	Acrobatic aircraft	37	35	n.a.	9	n.a.	−7	N

Notes:
Age is in months from financial inception.
Profitability ($\pi\%$) is as reported by the owner-manager in 1988 for the year 1985.
Growth rate ($g\%$) is annual growth rate of real assets.
In? Y for 'in business' in 1988, N for 'out of business' in 1988.
Assets (figures are all in 000s at 1985 prices).
Start is starting assets.
1985 and *1988* are assets in 1985 and 1988 (n.a. means 'not available').

ability. Indeed, with larger numbers of firms it is possible to detect a growth/profitability trade-off, as noted in Reid (1993, ch. 11). That is, if the goal is rapid niche invasion, growth may occur at the expense of profitability. This may be an entirely rational strategy. Indeed, it may be equivalent to *long-run* profit maximization, as once the niche is invaded, it can at a later date be exclusively harvested. But to achieve this position, some sacrifice of short-run profits may be necessary.

Concerning profitability, the figures again vary widely, and in some cases are not available. For example, for Firms F and M, this was because these SBEs went out of business. Firm Q had technically not quite gone out of business, though we have recorded it as such, but was going out of business. For Firms H and P we suspect profitability was so high the owner-managers did not wish to report figures, which is of course their right. Our general feeling is that the SBEs in low market concentration environments tended to overstate profitability, especially by a neglect of owner's remuneration, though we are sure this is true, to some unknown degree, for nearly all the SBEs. The Profiles (see Part II) make remarks on discrepancies in reporting profitability and assets which give some flavour of the problems we face here.

The conclusion we draw from conventional performance data is that they are very unreliable for our purposes. It seems probably that most of our SBEs enjoyed profitability levels much above those of similarly sized more mature firms, even allowing for some exaggeration in reporting. The best yardstick for performance is probably the case of Firm J (cassette tapes), which we have selected for this purpose because it it considerably older (ten years) than most of the other SBEs in the Profiles sample, and hence arguably closer to an equilibrium state. It enjoyed a 20 per cent profitability, which would typically keep it clear of the rate of borrowing, but would be below what venture capitalists would require for involvement. By the yardstick of 20 per cent, most of our SBEs enjoyed superior profitability. Some that did not, went out of business. Others that did not (Firms E and N, for example), we know to be rather successful firms over the period analysed, so suspect some bias or error in reporting.

Performance evaluation for our SBEs obviously has to be more subjective. High growth rates and niche invasion are clearly important, as are the establishing of channels and identifying the 'real customers' early in the SBE's life cycle. This is all to say that performance is a complex multidimensional attribute, as reflected in the analysis of the body of the text.

7 Financial considerations of competitive advantage

7.1 INTRODUCTION

This chapter takes a close look at the degree to which the SBE achieves competitive advantage by addressing its financial considerations, thereby adding another useful dimension to business strategy. The SBEs under examination are typically in their infancy (i.e. the early stage of development) and groping around in an unfamiliar and complex business environment to establish themselves in fragmented markets. Thus the attaining of immediate competitive advantage (in the sense of above-average industry performance) may be regarded as optimistic, if not downright unrealistic. More pragmatic, especially for the nascent SBE, is the setting of an initial objective of sheer survival, to be followed in due course, by a consideration of the means for achieving competitive advantage. Therefore, as our analysis emphasizes, it is useful to do more than simply to show how changes in the SBE's assets, sales, employees, for example, reflect competitive advantage. The previous two chapters have looked into niche invasion, channel access, innovation, and so on. One should also be considering the financial stresses, and subsequent adjustments, that must be withstood in the early days of the SBE's existence before prospects of competitive advantage are quite in sight.

We start therefore, by stepping back and considering the 'entrepreneurial event' (Shapero 1984) of firm formation within our sample. Sources of advice, the nature of funding and/or government assistance, and so on, are critical aspects of successfully launching an SBE and will thus require our attention. Next, we proceed to an assessment of the SBE's early development. This is a vitally important formative period in the life of the SBE. Controlling cash-flow and balancing debt against equity to sustain viability and promote growth, are aspects of financial monitoring and risk management which are particularly crucial to an emerging SBE. These issues having been broached, we proceed to a more grounded appraisal of the SBE's quest for competitive advantage. This extension of the competitive-strategy/competitive-advantage framework to financial considerations provides a further novel element in our modified framework for the analysis of SBEs, especially in fragmented markets.

7.2 INCEPTION

The birth of an SBE typically takes place within an environment of inordinate uncertainty. Almost invariably, entrepreneurs attempt to perform myriad business activities with limited resources in terms of time, premises, plant, knowledge and funding. Prerequisites to the successful completion of these tasks are the locating and utilizing of appropriate information sources.[1] Often these sources are of a local, and indeed personal, nature. However, these sources are part of an overall information network[2] which is not readily appreciated or understood by the owner-manager, at least initially. Furthermore, comprehension of how information is processed and disseminated may be as important to successful small-firm inception as the information itself. Hence, the astute owner-manager must not only be able to identify the relevant information sources beyond the immediate or local level, but must also know how to access it. Accessibility is paramount, but only once knowledge of the network and its channels is obtained.[3]

As suggested, there is considerable complexity and variation in the types of information which are relevant to the stage of inception. Matters of funding, tax liability, legal status, premises, production technique, government assistance, and so on, must all be carefully addressed prior to getting a firm up-and-running. Quite probably, and indeed naturally, family and friends may be initially approached. They help the prospective owner-manager to hatch ideas and provide a source of encouragement. Of course, they also provide an obvious prospective pool of employees and partners in the new venture. Equally obviously, one need not find the necessary mix of backgrounds and ability within the immediate family, and the perspective offered by the family may be lacking in objectivity. It is not surprising, therefore, that when asked who they contacted for advice on how to get their businesses started, the owner-managers of only six of the seventeen firms cited family and friends (see Table 7.1). Perhaps they lacked any real expertise or at least gave that perception to prospective owner-managers. Nevertheless, in four of the six cases in which family and friends were consulted, they were regarded as the most important source of advice. This is consistent with the not uncommon situation in which it is a family tradition to own and run an independent business.

A bank manager and an accountant might well be approached for advice given their assured expertise in financial matters, especially so if they already have a client relationship with the prospective owner-manager. Arguably, obtaining sufficient funding is of the utmost concern for the SBE. Indeed, most new SBEs do not have adequate financial resources or knowledge. If they did, they would not necessarily start as small enterprises. The main sample from which our seventeen Profiles were drawn supports this view in that forty-five out of fifty-two firms (87 per cent) seeking advice indicated they had consulted either their bank manager or accountant (or both) in the start-up stage. For our Profiles, as Table 7.1 shows, six SBEs

Table 7.1 Importance of sources of advice at inception of SBE

Source of advice	Level of importance*					Total
	1	2	3	4	5	
Family and friends	4	1	1	0	0	6
Bank manager	1	2	2	1	0	6
Accountant	0	3	2	1	1	7
Enterprise trust	4	4	2	0	0	10
Scottish Development Agency+	1	2	4	4	0	11
Local government	1	1	0	1	0	3
Other**	2	0	0	0	0	2

Notes:
* '1' is most important, '2' is second most important, etc. Entries in table are raw numbers
   from the Profiles sample nominating most important, second most important sources, etc.
+ The SDA has since been reorganized into a new institution called Scottish Enterprise.
** 'Other' includes suppliers, existing rivals, customers and lawyers.

sought advice from their bank manager whilst seven SBEs did so with their accountant. Not revealed in the table is the fact that eight consulted at least one of these two sources.

During the early 1980s, in the aftermath of a national (indeed international) economic recession, when nearly all of the seventeen Profiles sample SBEs were founded, there were many publicly sponsored schemes (e.g. Loan Guarantee, Enterprise Allowance and Business Expansion). These were coupled with a variety of highly visible and effective advisory services and agencies (e.g. enterprise trusts), which were then either being initiated or expanded. As a result, entrepreneurs in some respects were less reliant than one might expect on bank managers and accountants for advice on how to launch their SBEs. Of course, it might be argued that new SBEs are typically ignorant of, or underestimate, the value of financial advice. Thus, bank managers and accountants (in particular) have little incentive to invest in the marketing of an expertise which they feel they are unlikely to sell to the small business community.

Banks have traditionally played a significant role in assisting the birth of SBEs. Again referring to the main sample from which the seventeen Profiles were taken, thirty-four out of fifty-two (65 per cent) owner-managers who sought advice noted consultation with their bank manager; and no other advisory source received more citations. In ten instances, the bank manager was regarded as the most important source of advice. As indicated earlier, a bank's significance is not particularly surprising given that small firms are invariably reliant upon some external funding and will initially look to their banks to meet this need.[4] Indeed, most SBEs do not confront those problems of undercapitalization, which banks are typically well placed to solve, given projects that satisfy a quality threshold. Having said that, one of the primary attractions of banks is their provision of the overdraft (i.e. revolving credit) facility, which is commonly used by small businesses for meeting the ever-present short-term requirements of working capital needs and/or cash-flow difficulties. The overdraft's attraction rests in its convenience and ready availability, as well as its cheapness. Owner-managers perceive it to be the least costly type of finance in that interest charges only apply to outstanding borrowings, which at any time may be less than the overall amount made available by the bank. Often the understanding or agreement between owner-manager and banker is that such borrowing shall not be applied to funding long-term capital projects.

The results from the main sample show that banks are by far the most significant source of finance at inception (with family and friends a distant second).[5] In fact, out of the thirty-three firms that started with the aid of external finance, twenty-eight (85 per cent) relied on bank funding of some kind. Amongst our Profiles, only four firms – namely, G (holiday tours), F (food manufacturing), N (bulk bag manufacturing) and M (acrobatic aircraft) – utilized outside funding and each of them noted bank borrowings along with other external sources. Only in the case of Firm F (food manu-facturing) did the acquisition of borrowed funds entail some difficulty. This was attributed to the 'conservative' attitude of lenders to novel business propositions. It should be added that of the twelve firms which declared sole reliance on owner-managers' financial injections at start-up, eight did not face obstacles to outside finance. These observations are reflected in the main sample where forty out of seventy-three (55 per cent) were wholly self-financed at birth.[6] Of those forty firms, twenty-five (63 per cent) preferred to be self-financed.

Despite the not uncommon criticism levelled against banks for their reluctance to lend to new small firms in particular, the evidence indicates that owner-managers may be reluctant to approach banks, and have a strong preference for financial independence (at least initially). Being free of financial risk of any sort (including the payment of interest on loans) may limit growth or competitive advantage prospects, but these are offset by complete avoidance of costs associated with borrowing. Also avoided is the possibility of outside interference in the management of the SBE's oper-ations which outside financial involvement is perceived to entail. Further, the typical SBE is inclined to take a 'go slow' approach especially in its early phase of development, where uncertainty is notably prevalent, thereby avoiding the noted (and dangerous) tendency to hubris.[7] This approach has further merit in that it could foster a stronger, more secure, position in the market over time. Hence, the SBE could be better placed not only to determine directions of growth but also to attract outside funding (often on more favourable terms). Another disincentive to borrowing is the common requirement for the borrowing firm to provide collateral or security. New SBEs are commonly expected to secure their loan, not only with the assets of the firm, but also with the personal assets (e.g. the home) of the owner-managers and or their guarantors. In cases where the owner-manager is the most important asset holder within the business, he may well be expected to secure a loan by taking out a life insurance policy on himself. These assets tend to be firm-specific and are not easily liquidated. Typically cash and heritable securities are of very modest proportions indeed. Four of the SBEs considered in this book relied on external borrowings at inception: Firm G (holiday tours), Firm F (food manufacturing), Firm N (bulk bag manu-facturing) and Firm M (acrobatic aircraft). They were required to secure their loans with at least the assets of their operations.

The accountant is important to the emergent SBE because of his exper-tise in preparing financial documents and determining tax implications. He is notably useful to such a firm in the preparation of a business plan. A carefully prepared and convincing business plan is the main prerequisite to raising external funding. The business plan is the instrument by which potential financiers are persuaded of the firm's potential for success. The accountant's particular contributions to the business plan include pro-forma balance sheets, projected profit-and-loss statements, cash-flow forecasts, and so on. The accountant is also valuable in ascertaining the ramifications of various tax regimes. These can shape or even determine the most tax-efficient type of business (e.g. sole trader or limited company), that is, the one the prospective owner-manager(s) should best undertake. In addition, his advice on the kind and timing of capital outlays is crucial. Using an accountant can greatly ameliorate the risk of displaying financial naïvety or even ineptitude when presenting a business plan to potential investors. Often there is an inverse relationship between the financial acumen of owner-managers and the immaturity of their firms. Hence, young SBEs should be particularly reliant on accountants, especially at inception.

Table 7.1 shows that seven firms cited their accountant as a source of advice in forming their business. The main sample from which the seventeen firms were taken revealed that thirty-two out of the fifty-two firms (62 per cent) which sought advice at inception noted the use of their accountant, with twenty-two of those firms (69 per cent) regarding it as the most important source of advice. Indeed, the accountant compared most favour-ably with other sources of advice.

Arguably, the enterprise trust is considered the most significant source of advice amongst the seventeen firms who are the subjects of our Profiles.[8] As indicated in Table 7.1, ten out of the thirteen (77 per cent) firms seeking advice mentioned an enterprise trust. And eight of those ten considered it to be at least second in importance. In the main sample, the enterprise trust was also highly regarded and compared favourably with the bank manager and accountant in significance.

The importance of enterprise trusts is not surprising given their unique institutional form, and the close alignment of their *raison d'être* (based on the Business in the Community ethos) with the general purpose of Scottish Enterprise. Their success as an institutional form is reflected in their rapid growth in numbers over the past decade. They are essentially products of local initiatives resulting from a joint partnership between business, government and community. The objective of this partnership is the fostering of an enterprise culture, primarily through the encouragement and support of new SBEs. Involvement of the private sector is noteworthy in this new development. In addition to providing funding support, private sector participants ensure that experienced managers or specialists (e.g. consultants and bankers) are seconded from industry to the enterprise trusts for a sufficient period of time (say, three years) that their involvement can have a significant impact. The advice they offer is essentially free, independent and non-political. In addition, enterprise trusts can readily find suitable (and often low-cost) premises. They help to attract financing for viable ventures more effectively than the prospective owner-managers themselves, given the trusts' high calibre and well-connected staff. It is worth emphasizing that in addition to being accessible (i.e. locally situated) to nascent SBEs, enterprise trusts are the link or conduit to other important sources of support and information (e.g. the then Scottish Development Agency, or under the current regime, the local enterprise company or Scottish Enterprise).

The Scottish Development Agency (SDA), despite being ranked fourth in terms of importance as a source of advice by the SBEs in the main sample, appears from looking at Table 7.1 to be more significant than at first sight. Like enterprise trusts, the SDA, and its successor Scottish Enterprise, are devoted to encouraging an enterprise culture through the provision of various services (e.g. advice, training, premises, etc.) to new and emerging businesses. Unlike enterprise trusts, the SDA was entirely a public entity, and Scottish Enterprise is only partially so. They are, at least relatively speaking, large bureaucratic organizations operated in some measure by public servants, though now with a larger private sector input. Moreover, they are not locally placed, and even with the new local enterprise companies are higher up the communication network and thus removed from the territory of most SBEs. Despite being a significant source of advice for both the main sample and sub-sample under consideration, many SBE's expressed some dissatisfaction with the way in which the SDA seemed more selective in giving assistance, with special treatment accorded to so-called high fliers. This 'picking winners' doctrine has now become defunct, and indeed in Reid and Jacobsen (1988, ch. 6) we advanced some of the earliest arguments against it.

Local government authorities might well be regarded as useful sources of information for the SBE, especially given their commitments to cooperative efforts with enterprise trusts. However, in both the main sample and in the sub-sample as indicated in Table 7.1, local government was rarely cited as a useful source of advice. However, there were exceptions: Firm M (acrobatic aircraft) and Firm Q (theatrical props manufacture), in particular, considered their local authorities as very important sources of advice. This may well be attributed to the fact that the firms were furnished with a substantial investment grant and an interest-free loan, respectively, from their local governments.

Indeed, to a non-trivial extent, SBEs are the beneficiaries of special finance schemes (e.g. tax credits, investment grants) at inception, which may be determinants of their early survival and development. Typically, the sources of advice hitherto discussed are instrumental, more or less, in the SBE's acquisition of finance through such schemes. Out of the seventeen firms in our study only seven mentioned at least one source of financial assistance. In just three cases (Firms L, N, and O) the assistance was regarded as necessary to their inception.

7.3 DEVELOPMENT

The early years of the SBE are particularly telling with respect not only to its survival but also to its quest for competitive advantage. Because the SBE typically begins operations with meagre financial resources, as described above, the owner-manager's imperative is to grow, and perhaps quickly. This requires the injection of additional funding, the life-blood of any enterprise. Three sources of such funding exist: (1) retained earnings, (2) external equity capital and (3) external borrowings. Usually, some combination of the three is utilized and it is this which determines the capital structure of a firm. The proportions in which these types of finance are used can be regarded as the result of an equilibrium calculation between risk and return as jointly determined by the deliberations of owner mangers and creditors. The desired or 'target' capital structure will in some measure reflect value maximization by the SBE. It will be influenced by the degree of risk aversion of those injecting resources. Though reliance on more debt enhances the owner-manager's expectations of the rate of return, it simultaneously increases the riskiness of the firm. Owner-managers who prefer to undertake no borrowings thereby avoid one category of financial risk. Naturally business risk is attached to all SBEs' operations which are aimed at generating future returns on equity. This is inherent and cannot be ignored. Further, the greater is the debt taken on by the SBE, the greater, by an increasing magnitude, is the business risk borne by the owner-manager.

The proportion which borrowing (including loans, and trade credit) used by an SBE to finance its operations bears to owner-manager's personal financial injections is referred to as financial leverage or 'gearing' (i.e. debt ÷ equity). For example, if an owner-manager put £20,000 into his SBE and borrowed £30,000, his gearing would be $3/2 = 1.5$. Owner-managers who are interested in maintaining control of their SBE, but who lack the ability or desire to inject additional funds into it, will either look to increase their debt holdings, or settle for less than the expected (or even the potential) growth rate. Creditors, on the other hand, are concerned about the amount of equity committed by the owner-managers in securing the loan. Banks in particular, are keen to see debt collateralized. They may only issue debt finance in special circumstances if the gearing ratio looks likely to exceed one. It is common for banks (as well as other major lenders) to make credit available if sufficient collateral, based on liquidation or market value, is contractually guaranteed. Often these terms of contract require the personal property (namely, securities and home) of the borrowing owner-managers to be part of this guarantee, given that the firm-specific nature of assets of the firm may limit their marketability. To some extent, the risk undertaken by banks, for instance, is often mitigated or diluted by the participation of other creditors, especially so far as inventory financing is concerned. Generous credit terms are often provided by suppliers with the stock serving as collateral. Also, flexible leasing/rental arrangements in terms of vehicles, equipment, machinery and premises are factors which can inflate gearing ratios.

In a very real and important sense, the management of cash-flow is paramount to the SBE, especially in its early, developmental years. The relation between debt and equity is nevertheless significant, especially if the health of the SBE is being examined over a period of time. Problems can be better diagnosed in the light of growth opportunities which may be presented at discrete junctures in time. At such points perhaps substantial and rapid injections of debt finance are required. SBEs anticipating such events in the future may meanwhile underperform, in the sense of limiting the scale of their indebtedness, thereby restricting their exposure to financial risk. It should be borne in mind that establishing a good record on which to borrow in the future may be jeopardized if the SBE is burdened with a large amount of debt to service, especially in its early years.

In the initial interviews owner-managers were asked about their gearing ratios. In practice, the gearing ratio is the level of borrowing divided by the owner-manager's personal financial injection into his SBE. Debt is typically in the form of a business loan or overdraft facility from a UK clearing bank, and equity is typically inside equity (i.e. no outside equity was involved). Owner-managers were asked what they expected to happen to their gearing ratios over a three-year future time horizon. In turn, three years later at the reinterview, without being reminded of what was said earlier, the owner-manager was asked what had actually happened to the gearing ratio in the preceding three years. The outcome of this investigation is given in Table 7.2 (see p. 172) for the Profiles sample. Of the fifty-one entries for expected gearing changes, seventeen (33.3 per cent) were for a fall in gearing, seven (14 per cent) were for a rise in gearing, eighteen (35 per cent) were for gearing staying the same, and nine (18 per cent) were for 'don't know'. Thus only a small minority expected a rise in gearing at any time over a three-year time horizon. Turning now to the actual gearing changes, one finds of all the entries in the table that sixteen entries (31 per cent) were 'don't knows' or 'not available'. Of the remaining thirty-five, eleven (22 per cent) were for a fall in gearing, eleven (22 per cent) were for a rise in gearing, and thirteen (25 per cent) were for no change in gearing. In other words, expected gearing had a bias towards falling, whereas actual gearing had no bias, though the typical gearing pattern (expected and actual) was to stay the same.

There is a possible sample selection bias both here and in the parent sample in that SBEs which sustained much higher than expected gearing ratios are more likely to have gone out of business, given that, other things being equal, higher gearing implies greater exposure to risk, and therefore greater probability of failure (Reid 1993, ch. 9). Comparing percentages in the raw data for the parent sample (Table 7.3, see p. 172), it is apparent that SBEs were typically optimistic about their ability to lower gearing one year ahead. There is evidence that expectations caught up with outcomes in the second and third years ahead. There also seems to be a general tendency to over-estimate the extent to which a change in gearing is possible. Thus 'Stay the same' is actually a more likely occurrence in each year than expected. Returning now to gearing expectations and outcomes for the Profiles sample, we look again at the data summarized in Table 7.2.

The third column of Table 7.2 may be thought to reflect the particularly risk-averse nature of our sample of SBEs in that nine of them started operations with a gearing ratio of zero, though various screening and signalling arguments could also be invoked here to explain this set of obser-vations.[9] By 1988 four of these same SBEs had either maintained, or returned to, a gearing ratio of zero. Of course, as might be expected, the successful launching of a business enterprise may require a substantial sum of funding from external sources. Owner-managers are often obsessed with not granting external equity stakes to outsiders. They clearly get a psychic return or derive utility from fully controlling their enterprises, which explains why they are often unwilling to relinquish control, even in part. External sources of debt finance are therefore sought for the requisite funding in preference to equity. Obviously, given the quite high gearing ratios of Firms C, G, Q, F, O and M, lenders had enormous confidence that these SBEs had good prospects. It should also be said that the financial risk was spread among multiple lenders in each case, and that, furthermore, assets outside the firms were often used in conjunction with the SBEs' assets to secure the borrowings. As a result, the gearing ratios cited for these SBEs at inception are somewhat exaggerated. It should be added too that, by and large, these SBEs did experience a decrease in their gearing ratios by 1985 and expected further declines in the following three years. A combination of increased equity (via ploughed-back earnings) and retirement of debt were the principal reasons cited for this expected decline in gearing. With the figures reported in 1988 we find some additional evidence to support the view that these SBEs are concerned to reduce reliance on borrowing in relation to net worth.

Typically these SBEs have utilized external borrowings from inception. Their reasons for raising new debt finance are depicted in Table 7.4 (see p. 173). Five uses to which debt finance were put are identified: new or expanded

172   *Profiles in Small Business*

Table 7.2 Expected and actual gearing ratios for Profiles sample

Firm	Start year	Actual gearings			Expected changes			Actual changes		
		Start	1985	1988	1986	1987	1988	1986	1987	1988
Low market concentration										
A	1984	0	0.33	n.a.	<	>	=	n.a.	n.a.	n.a.
C	1983	3.5	0.3	n.a.	>	?	?	<	>	?
D	1984	0	0	1.33	=	=	>	<	<	>
E	1984	1.0	0.5	2.86	=	=	=	=	=	>
G	1984	3.0	0.75	1.6	<	=	>	<	=	>
L	1984	0	0	0.5	>	?	?	>	<	>
Q	1985	2.5	2.5	n.a.	<	<	<	n.a.	n.a.	n.a.
Medium market concentration										
F	1982	4.0	3.0	n.a.	<	<	<	n.a.	n.a.	n.a.
I	1983	0	0	2.7	>	=	?	>	>	>
J	1975	0	0	0	=	?	?	=	=	=
K	1984	0	0.08	0	=	?	?	=	=	=
N	1984	0	0.5	0	<	=	=	<	<	<
O	1983	10.0	1.0	0.33	<	<	<	<	>	=
P	1983	0	0.33	n.a.	=	<	<	n.a.	n.a.	n.a.
High market concentration										
B	1982	0.5	0	0	=	=	=	=	=	=
H	1984	0	0	0	>	=	=	<	<	>
M	1984	2.5	2.5	n.a.	<	<	<	n.a.	n.a.	n.a.

Notes:
< Fall (i.e. less than previously).
> Rise (i.e. more than previously).
= Stay the same.
? Don't know.
n.a. Not available.
Gearing is defined as: (debt ÷ equity). In practice this means borrowing divided by owner manager's personal financial injection.

Table 7.3 Expected and actual gearing ratio for parent sample

	Fall	Rise	Stay the same	
Year 1	45%	30%	24%	Expected
	28%	26%	46%	Actual
Year 2	45%	19%	34%	Expected
	44%	16%	40%	Actual
Year 3	44%	20%	33%	Expected
	41%	15%	44%	Actual

Note:
Each entry is the per cent of SBEs in the parent population nominating the category fall, rise or stay the same for gearing.

premises; purchase of plant and equipment; increase of inventories or stocks; hiring of additional employees; cash-flow problems. Of these five, probably only the first two are sensible uses from a business strategy standpoint. Interestingly, none of the SBEs in high-concentration markets had raised new debt finance for any purpose. Perhaps most significantly, the owner-manager of each SBE that raised new debt finance claimed that part of the reason for borrowing funds was to resolve cash-flow problems. From a business strategy standpoint this is not a proper use of debt finance. This might convey a picture of poor financial management for the Profiles sample, with SBEs allowing themselves to be 'saddled' with inappropriate levels of debt.[10]

This impression is rather justified if one examines Table 7.5 (see p. 174). It identifies six factors which contribute to cash-flow problems. Each group of SBEs by market concentration contains businesses which have had cash-flow problems. Five of the seventeen SBEs had not experienced cash-flow problems. For those that did, a ranking system for the importance of various causes of cash-flow problems is used, with 1 as most important, down to 6 as least important. One expects, and finds confirmed, that not all problems may be relevant to any one SBE. An important general feature that Table 7.5 reveals is that the SBEs for which we have constructed Profiles did not observe tight control procedures with suppliers and customers. Delinquent debtors are a frequently nominated and important category of problem. This had consequences which were magnified somewhat by what owner-managers reported as inadequate overdraft facilities with banks. Inadequate credit terms with buyers will also have made it difficult to rehabilitated delinquent debtors. It could be added that the evidence indicates that typically these SBEs did not properly ascertain their working-capital needs.

Table 7.4 Uses to which new debt finance was put (inception to 1985): low, medium and high market concentration

Uses	Low							Medium							High			Total
	A	C	D*	E	G	L	Q	F	I*	J*	K	N	O	P	B*	H*	M*	
(1) New premises	–	X	–	–	X	–	–	X	–	–	X	X	–	–	–	–	–	5
(2) Purchase of plant	–	–	–	X	–	–	–	–	–	–	X	X	–	X	–	–	–	4
(3) Increase in stocks	–	–	–	X	–	X	–	–	–	–	X	X	–	–	–	–	4
(4) New hiring	–	–	–	X	–	–	–	–	–	–	X	X	–	–	–	–	–	3
(5) Cash-flow	X	X	–	X	X	–	X	–	–	–	–	–	X	X	–	–	–	7

Notes:
A–M SBEs in Profiles sample.
X   Debt finance was put to this use.
–   Debt finance was not put to this use.
*   This SBE did not use debt finance at all.
Use to which debt finance was put: (1) new or expanded premises; (2) purchase of plant and equipment; (3) increase in inventories or stocks; (4) hiring of additional employees; (5) cash-flow problems.

Firm C (knitwear manufacturing) might deserve a less harsh judgement in that its cash-flow problems were primarily attributed to 'overinvestment', as in the cases of Firms B, J and P. As indicated in Table 7.4, both Firm C and Firm G (holiday tours) financed 'new/expanded premises' with borrowings, presumably with prospects of growth in mind.[11] After all, such investments are often made in a 'lumpy', rather than incremental, fashion.

Table 7.6 offers some insight into the impact of debt finance and cash-flow problems on growth and development for the SBEs which are the subjects of our Profiles. It is useful to consider it in conjunction with Tables 7.2 and 7.5. Of those starting operations with gearing ratios greater than one, only Firm G (holiday tours) with a ratio of 3.0 in 1984 (at inception) and 1.6 in 1988, showed any meaningful competitive improvement as measured by changes in sales and employees. In fact, the owner-managers of Firm F (food manufacturing) and Firm M (acrobatic aircraft) had ceased operations by 1988. At some point between 1982 and 1985, Firm F had actually increased its gearing ratio to as high a level as 8.0. Firm C (knit-wear manufacturing) and Firm Q (theatrical props) are suspected to be operating at the margin of solvency at best.

By contrast, Firms D, E, L and I started cautiously (see Table 7.2). They had very modest resources, which in part was attributable to their having made no or little use of debt finance. However, by 1988 each of these SBEs had acquired some, if not considerable, debt as reflected in the figures under the 1988 'Actual gearing' column in Table 7.2. It is perhaps not surprising to see that the expectations for gearing changes over the period

Table 7.5 Rankings of factors causing cash-flow problems: low, medium and high market concentration

Causes of cash-flow problems	Low							Medium							High			Total
	A	C	D*	E	G	L*	Q	F	I	J	K*	N*	O	P	B	H*	M	
(1) Insufficient overdraft	–	–	–	4	1	–	–	1	–	–	–	–	3	2	–	–	–	5
(2) Delinquent debtors	1	2	–	1	2	–	–	–	1	2	–	–	2	–	–	–	–	7
(3) Overinvestment	2	1	–	3	–	–	–	–	–	1	–	–	–	1	1	–	–	6
(4) Suppliers' credit	–	–	–	5	–	–	1	–	–	–	–	–	1	–	–	–	–	3
(5) Delinquent suppliers	–	–	–	6	–	–	–	–	–	–	–	–	–	–	–	–	1	2
(6) Buyers' credit	–	–	–	2	–	–	–	–	–	3	–	–	–	–	–	–	–	2

Notes:
* SBE reported no cash-flow problem.
– SBE did not report this as causing a cash-flow problem.
1, 2, 3, 4, 5, 6 in the table denote importance of this identified cause of cash-flow problems, with 1 denoting most important, 2 denoting next most important, etc.
Problems contributing to cash-flow difficulties: (1) insufficient overdraft facility;
    (2) delinquent debtors; (3) overinvestment; (4) inadequate credit terms with suppliers;
    (5) delinquent suppliers; (6) inadequate credit terms with buyers.
Total: denotes total number of SBEs nominating each problem.

Table 7.6 Sales, asset and employment growth

Firm	Product market	Start year	Sales (£000s)		Assets (£000s)*			Employees**	
			1985	1988	Start	1985	1988	1985	1988
Low market concentration									
A	Blind cleaning	1984	18	n.a.	16	16	n.a.	2	n.a.
C	Knitwear manufacturing	1983	22	n.a.	1.5	7	n.a.	5	5
D	Auto repair	1984	n.a.	40	5	9	6	2	2
E	Industrial cleaning	1984	150	400	10	30	54.6	6	10
G	Holiday tours	1984	7	500	4	15	15	0	6
L	Wine distribution	1984	72	360	8	27	52	1	4
Q	Theatrical props	1985	35	n.a.	0+	7	n.a.	4	n.a.
Medium market concentration									
F	Food manufacturing	1982	650	n.a.	130	130	n.a.	47	n.a.
I	Computer software	1983	250	3,500	5	100	1,780	15	90
J	Cassette tape manufacturing	1975	200	150	2	100	180	4	4
K	Electronics	1984	25	750	2.5	20	70	5	39
N	Bulk bag manufacturing	1984	200	1,600	5	50	385	27	57
O	Fencing manufacturing	1983	96	160	15	50	46	3	6
P	Lamination	1983	240	n.a.	0+	180	n.a.	5	n.a.
High market concentration									
B	Security blankets manufacturing	1982	600	927	70	105	177	11	16
H	Cosmetics	1984	245	1,060	16	65	1,500	8	14
M	Acrobatic aircraft	1984	0	n.a.	35	35	n.a.	1	n.a.

Notes:
* Assets refer to book value and are nominal prices.
** Full-time employees.
0+ Only a small sum (< £100).
n.a. Not available.
Sales and assets are in nominal prices: 1988 figures may be deflated to 1985 values using the divisor 1.13.

1986–8 are rather mixed and do not match up very well with the actual changes for this period. This may be attributed to a risk-averse disposition on the part of owner-managers, juxtaposed with the SBE's environment. The SBE's existence is fraught with both threats and/or opportunities requiring external debt, and the consequence is additional financial risk. Firm D (auto repair) and Firm I (computer software), to illustrate, relied on no borrowings between the time of start up and 1985, as indicated by the zero gearing ratios in columns four and five of Table 7.2. In addition, these SBEs are amongst those shown in Table 7.4 to have shunned debt finance. Moreover, as indicated in Table 7.5, cash-flow problems were negligible. These conditions are perhaps reinforced by the rather vigorous growth in total assets for these SBEs during the period from inception to 1985, as seen in Table 7.6. However, between 1985 and 1988 Firms D (auto repairs) and I (computer software) turned to debt finance in a dramatic fashion, perhaps hoping to use it as a spur to further growth. Table 7.2 shows the 1988 gearing ratios standing at 1.33 and 2.7 for these firms, respectively. Interestingly, as revealed in Table 7.6, Firm I was projected into the 'super-growth' category, while Firm D contracted. Such is the nature of financial risk; a more leveraged position *pari passu* increases the expected returns. Whether or not they are always realized, remains to be seen. Certainly both firms should look to reduce their reliance on external debt at some future point, with Firm D's capital structure obviously requiring urgent attention. Further, Firm D was subject to a number of limitational factors absent from Firm I's case (e.g. local market, high buyer concentration, low innovation etc.).

Firms J, K, N, P and H are arguably the most successful SBEs of our Profiles, judged in terms of combined financial risk and growth, from the time of inception to 1988, as we observe from Tables 7.2, 7.4 and 7.6. In each case these SBEs operated with little or no debt in their early years and by 1988 managed to eliminate their financial risk as reflected in zero gearing ratios. Yet they were able to achieve some rather startling positive growth rates. Moreover, given the expected and actual changes in gearing there appears to have been a consistent preference for internally generated funds as the principal means of promoting growth and development. Certainly Table 7.4 indicates that Firms K, N and P did develop some reliance on debt finance, but it was primarily used to assist retained earnings in effecting growth rather than, say, to overcome inefficiencies in cash-flow management. Of course, some firms (i.e. J, P, and B) did admit to facing cash-flow problems, as shown in Table 7.5. It could be said that Firm P (printing lamination) is the exception in this group given that no sales, assets and employees are reported for 1988 and that it utilized debt finance in overcoming cash-flow problems and so on. However, the firm did experience very rapid and substantial success, as indicated by the statistics in Table 7.6. This SBE moved from nominal or very meagre assets in 1983, its first year of operations, to assets of £180,000 five years later, leveraged by very little debt. Indeed, with a gearing ratio of zero at inception and moving to 0.33 in 1985, Firm P amassed some £120,000 in equity within three years. Of course, the reader will recall its success was in large part attributed to an unusually inexpensive leasing arrangement with a supplier of highly sophisticated and productive machinery. Ultimately low overheads, and tightly controlled labour and capital outlays, combined with dramatic surges in sales volume proved too much of a threat to the dominant multinational rival, who purchased Firm P's operations for a very substantial sum in a way that was not to be refused.

7.4 CONCLUSION

The analysis in this chapter is somewhat tentative, in that a new extended framework for competitive-strategy analysis is implied and explored, but not fully advertised. The crucial elements in the emerging framework are clear, however: a close attention to leverage and an attempt to keep it low, though not necessarily zero; a prudent use of debt finance for proper purposes of growth and development (e.g. purchase of new plant) rather than for 'putting out fires' (e.g. solving cash-flow crises); a tight control on cash-flow, monitoring customers (buyers) particularly closely and refusing them extended debtor status. There are other components too, but these are the main ones. Added to the existing dimensions of competitive strategy discussed in Chapters 5 and 6, they powerfully augment the SBE's capacity to achieve competitive advantage.

However, it would not do to suggest a reorientation of competitive strategy, even less a replacement for it in the shape of financial ratios analysis. The rich framework of earlier chapters is still vital – we merely argue for its extension. As Eugene Brigham puts it, in a book which is one of the world's standards of financial management, 'the financial analyst ... of a small firm ... must "look beyond the ratios" and analyse the viability of the firm's products, customers, management, and market' (Brigham 1992: 70).

Part IV
Conclusion

8 A grounded view of small business

8.1 INTRODUCTION

It should be apparent as the argument has unfolded in this book that theory and evidence go hand in hand, according to the methodology we have deployed throughout. In Chapter 1, a set of models from industrial organization (monopolistic competition, dominant firm with a fringe of competitors, conjectural oligopoly), and a detailed framework of analysis from business strategy (competitive strategy and competitive advantage), suitably modified for small firms, were presented as the tools of analysis for the work before us. In the course of six chapters these tools have been put to work in a detailed way on our Profiles sample.

In using these models or tools in this fashion, we had in mind four primary purposes. Firstly, they provided a way of organizing a complex body of evidence exhaustively and coherently. No categories were excluded, and because analytical tools governed the way material was organized, sense was more readily made from the data than would have been the case if the organization of material had been merely tidy (e.g. organizing SBEs by sector). Secondly, they have brought insight and understanding into the functioning of small business enterprises (SBEs), both at the individual level and in a comparative sense. One understands better, now that the tools have been put to work, why competitive strategies are more important than defensive strategies for these young firms, and why profitability is higher for SBEs engaged in oligopolistic competition for significant and protected market shares, compared to those subject to monopolistic competition in highly fragmented markets, for example. Thirdly, our tools of analysis assist in the formulation of predictions; for example, that highly geared firms, other things being equal, are especially exposed to risk and therefore more vulnerable to poor performance and/or failure, than lower-geared rivals. Finally, they help us to make prescriptive statements of significance both for the individual SBE, and for the small business counsellor or economic policy advisor. For example, to improve the chance of obtaining external funding, the most useful single action the owner-manager should undertake is to get advice on how to present a professional business plan, preferably from an accountant. In short, the methods of applying the chosen tools of analysis to the body of data have brought advantages of organization, explanation, prediction and prescription to our work.

A feature of the way in which we have proceeded is that in the substantive part of this work – essentially Chapters 2 to 7 – almost no analytical statement is unaccompanied by example. Our view, therefore, of the use of theory is that it must be grounded: one is strictly required to say that here is an example, or even better, here are many examples, of SBEs to which the theory one is exposing can be related and applied. It will not do to say, 'Let's imagine a firm of the following sort, and explore the implications thereof in a mathematical sense' – that is certainly poor economics, and probably even worse mathematics. No plea for the intellectual division of labour will mollify this view, because the overwhelming evidence is that much new theory is untested, and even worse, untestable. It is not just that one type of person does the theory and another type deals with the evidence. It is that typically 'never the twain shall meet'. The discipline of groundedness fights against this dichotomy.

8.2 GROUNDED THEORY

The roots of grounded theory lie in fieldwork methodology (Glaser and Strauss 1967). The interpretation we have adopted of this term has been considerably modified and extended from its original conception in subject areas like social anthropology and social psychology. Its form, as applied to industrial economics, has been expounded and exposed by Reid (1987a; 1987b, ch. 3). Its use is there identified with the case study method, to which it is especially well suited, but its range can certainly be extended to econometric methods. To illustrate the latter point, we may refer to the case of the kinked demand curve analysis. Many of the Profiles discussed in Chapters 2, 3 and 4 provided evidence for kinked demand curves, of one form or another. For example, Profile G (holiday tours) in Chapter 2 presents a particular variant in which small price changes lead to inelastic response because of switching costs, but demand is elastic for 10 per cent price increases and inelastic for 10 per cent decreases. Sweezy, in his original analysis of the kinked demand curve, said that he believed 'the real world is very much more like the model which I have analysed than the usual models' (Sweezy 1937: 157). Here he is making an appeal to grounded theory and Reid (1981: 29) has argued that Sweezy's informal contacts with the business community would have provided him with some concrete basis for his kinked demand curve theory. Wied-Nebbeling (1975), Nowotny and Walther (1978) made the theory better grounded, with improved, less-informal empirical methods. Maskin and Tirole (1988) and Bhaskar (1988) made the theory more rigorous, by expressing it in modern game-theoretic terms. The subsequent collaboration by Bhaskar, Machin and Reid (1991), which is fully treated in Reid (1993, ch. 10), illustrates the way in which a grounded theory approach can work in industrial economics, and shows the method in action on the same parent sample from which the Profiles sample was drawn.

Here the concern was with modelling observed pricing asymmetries over the trade cycle. Existing evidence indicated that 7 per cent of SBEs would match price increases in a recession (compared to 19 per cent in normal conditions and 46 per cent in boom conditions); whereas 46 per cent would match price decreases in a recession (compared to 24 per cent in normal conditions and 19 per cent in boom conditions). Existing theory by Bhaskar (1988), based on a quick-response game displaying perfect equilibrium, did not embrace business cycle effects. A generalization was developed, which hinged on considering capacity constraints on output at high levels of demand. This extension was also well grounded, in that it was known that 70 per cent of SBEs could identify a capacity or maximum possible output. This extended model was successfully tested on the data, and confirmed the ubiquity of interdependence of pricing decisions of SBEs, as well as asymmetries in their pricing over the business cycle. This approach is at some distance from the highly qualitative one first adopted in the grounded theory literature, and actually does square up well with many requirements of positive economics. Kirk and Miller would also claim that 'Qualitative research has always retained the proper ideals of hypothesis-testing research: sound reasoning and the risking of theory' (Kirk and Miller 1985: 17). The new pricing model was far better grounded than most theoretical work in industrial economics. Furthermore, it was developed in a way which was known to be capable of empirical implementation. As well as displaying predictive properties, the model also had useful explanatory properties, allied to the attractive characteristic that it ran in terms of profit-maximizing behaviour.

Our Profiles are in a sense prior to econometric methods, or indeed to serious formulation of new mathematical theories. Certainly, the collaboration mentioned above could not have progressed in the way it did, had it not been for earlier drafts of the Profiles being available as material for grounding new theoretical developments; and the influence on the econometric testing procedure adopted is readily apparent. As Flaherty (1984), herself a good theorist in industrial organization, has observed from her own fieldwork on the international semiconductor industry, such work can help theorists to focus on those assumptions which are well grounded. This may save them from a struggle with a great variety of possible assumptions, few of which may have operational significance.

Even without this sort of justification, the prosecution of a grounded study like the one detailed in this book has, we believe, merits in and of itself. Learning to analyse an SBE in the fashion displayed enables one to develop an extensive knowledge base and a capacity for what physicians would call 'good clinical judgement'. One develops an intuitive ability to appraise an SBE rapidly, and this can be invaluable both in running a business oneself and in acting as a small firms' counsellor. To support this intuition, many of the tables used to make analytical points in Chapters 5, 6 and 7 can be used as recording devices or score cards for appraising business. This is true, for example, of Tables 5.1 to 5.3, which provide a scoring device for market structure, and of Tables 6.1 to 6.3, which provide a scoring device for competitive advantage. Small firms' counsellors faced with the problem of screening clients may find it useful to run through these score cards as a first cut at their client list.

8.3 FILLING CATEGORIES

If the grounding of theory is important one has to address the problem of how one validates the categories to be used in further analysis. It is these categories (e.g. barriers to entry, bargaining power of customers) that are the building blocks of theory. The complete Porter schema is a coherent theory of business strategy. Its first two categories are *competitive forces* (i.e. extended rivalry) and *competitive strategy* (i.e. three main categories of cost leadership, differentiation and focus). Its third and last category is *defensive strategy*, which involves an examination of entry barriers, retaliation, deterrence, and so on. We noted (see section 6.2) that for SBEs in low-concentration markets 'defensive strategy' was not a category that could always be filled, in the sense of grounded theory. Raising entry barriers was though to be implausible, entry deterrence was limited, and most SBEs sought to discover, and then to co-exist with, so-called good competitors. Most of the strategies of defence suggested in the business strategy literature were thought to be assuredly destructive of the sense of fraternity which is common amongst competing SBEs.

By contrast, in the medium-concentration markets there is some evidence that defensive strategy is more important (see section 6.3). Accommodating strategy, like encouraging 'good' competitors, was relatively less important than in the low market concentration cases. Expansion, consolidation, encroachment, repositioning, are some of the more active defensive strategies used.

In the case of SBEs in highly concentrated markets, defensive strategy was taken seriously, and rather than being conceived of as passively defensive, or even as encroaching, it was thought of as pre-emptive in nature. It was as though the owner-manager thought, 'How can I keep one step ahead of my (extended) rivals, and anticipate what they might do to harm me, and then take steps to block their actions before the plans ever get off the ground'. Product gaps would be promptly filled whenever they appeared, to raise entry barriers; and intensive use would be made of scenario analysis. The defensive emphasis would be preventative rather than retaliatory. The quality of the latter approach was thought to fall short of standards of proper trading, and in any case was thought to give an undesirable signal of vulnerability.

What we have done here is to explore the extent to which the category 'defensive strategy' was filled for the Profile SBEs. This was certainly the case for SBEs in medium- and high-concentration markets. However, in the low market concentration case that was not so. In Reid (1993) five other SBEs are profiled, and they all operated in what were categorized as 'fragmented markets'. Such markets have low seller concentration and no stable industry leadership, making them correspond closely with our low market concentration cases, where industry leadership is stable. Typically this role is assumed by a price leader or dominant group of firms, from whom SBEs took their lead. Reid concludes for the complementary sample of SBEs in fragmented markets that 'defensive strategies were less rich and pursued with less conviction, if at all' (Reid 1993: 133–4). As with the Profiles of this volume, it was found that emphasis was put on finding and working with 'good' competitors, avoiding negative actions like retaliatory moves, and using more subtle methods, like trade intelligence, for defence. It is clearly in this area that it is most difficult to apply the full competitive-advantage/ competitive-strategy approach. This inability to fill the defensive strategy category in the commonly observed low market concentration case is a criticism of the existing framework, and should lead to an improved form of business strategy analysis for the small firms' case.

8.4 COMPARATIVE ANALYSIS

In industrial economics the method of industrial econometrics has been with us for a long time – almost as long as macro-econometrics. One of its most popular forms is cross-section analysis, involving estimated equations across firms (or sectors) at a single point in time. Schmalensee (1989: 1000) has argued that this method is a search for empirical regularities which are robust and which can stimulate further theoretical work. This in turn might lead to hypothesis-testing on other bodies of data. In many ways the comparative (or cross-site) analysis of Part III can be justified in this way. Our cross-site analysis corresponds to the econometrician's cross-section analysis – and shares some of its virtues and vices. The cross-site, or comparative, approach has some advantage over the cross-section approach. One typically has many more control variables at one's disposal for a Profile than does the econometrician with his equation. Of course, in cross-site analysis extensive qualitative evidence can also be brought to bear in adducing causes for observed inter-firm differences.

We believe that the cross-site or comparative analysis of Chapters 5, 6 and 7 is something of a new departure in small firms analysis, because it is conducted within a tight analytical framework and is applied to data that have been gathered in a heavily instrumented fashion. One might contrast the approach we have adopted with other recent examples that use some case study methods, such as Samson (1990) and Pratten (1991). In these works there has been no organizing principle for cross-site analysis, so the analysis is very informal, though thought provoking. The reader is rather left to draw his own comparative conclusions from cases that are dealt with seriatim, but then never put through the analytical filter of thorough cross-site analysis.

Our conclusion on the exclusion of the category of defensive strategy from the fragmented markets case in section 8.3 above would not have been possible without the highly structured methodology used. In a sense it allowed a cross-tabulation (if that word could now be used in an extended sense) of market structure (e.g. monopolistic competition) with dimensions of defensive strategy (e.g. blocking channel access).

8.5 CONCLUSION

We hope we have convinced the reader of this volume that there is some value in a grounded approach to industrial economics. A carefully conceived fieldwork methodology, followed by a deliberately analytical approach to the Profiles, has, we hope, warded off many of the stock criticisms one gets of work of this sort. At its simplest, we wanted to augment the empirical support for the scientific analysis in Reid's *Small Business Enterprise* (1993). It is hoped this book will fulfil that purpose if the reader wishes to use it in that way. We have been very careful to keep the instrumentation and terminology identical between the volumes, so hopefully accessing this book after the other will really be like 'returning to the laboratory' in a scientific sense.

Furthermore, we believe this book also stands on its own as an attempt to do something new and fresh with cross-site and within-site analysis of cases of small business enterprises. It is our hope that this work will foster a closer relationship between industrial organization and business strategy and, more broadly, between economics and management.

Appendix

Appendix
Summary of instrumentation

I. ADMINISTERED QUESTIONNAIRE

1. **General**
   SIC code
   Starting date
   Employee details
   Legal form of business
   Turnover
   Product groups and products
   Principal market
   Market share
   Major and minor competitors
   Extent of product differentiation
   Customer characteristics

2. **Pricing**

   Price/volume decision
   Price-level determination
   Competitor interdependence in pricing
   Pricing over the business cycle

3. **Costs**

   Division into fixed and variable costs
   Marginal cost
   Capacity constraint
   Total cost schedule

4. **Sales and competition**

   Market research methods

Price elasticity: controlled by magnitude of price change, competitors'
reactions, and phase of business cycle
Extent of elbow room in pricing
Pricing strategy by market segment
Price discrimination and bulk discounting
Price controls
Transaction v. list price
Forms of advertising
Advertising over the business cycle
Forms of competition, including dominant form

5. **Finance**

Start-up advice
Initial and current assets
Start-up finance: availability, types, security
Trajectory of gearing ratio over next three years
Usefulness of special financial schemes (e.g. EAS)
Cash-flow difficulties
External finance
Expected growth

II. SEMI-STRUCTURED INTERVIEW

1. **Competitive forces**

1.1 *Rivalry*

Probe on:
Industry concentration and balance
Industry growth
Fixed costs relative to value added
Intermittent overcapacity
Extent of product differentiation
Diversity of competitors
Level of strategic stakes
Entry and exit barriers

1.2 *Customers*

1.2.1 Bargaining leverage of customers

Probe on:
Customers' concentration

Seller dependence
Relative buyer volume
Customers' switching costs
Ability to backward integrate
Extent of customers' information

1.2.2 Price sensitivity of customers

Probe on:
Significance of costs in relation to total costs of customers
Extent of differentiation of products purchased
Profitability
Bearing of your product on customers' product quality
Motivation of customer

1.3 *Suppliers*

Probe on:
Extent of suppliers' concentration
Suppliers' in relation to customers' concentration
Availability of substitutes
Significance of suppliers' product as a customer's input
Extent of differentiation of supplier group's products
Switching costs of customers as compared with suppliers
Ability to forward integrate

1.4 *Potential entrants*

Probe on:
Economies of scale
Product differentiation
Capital requirements
Switching costs
Access to distribution channels
Absolute cost advantage including:
    Product know-how or design characteristics
    Favourable access to inputs
    Favourable location
    Government subsidies
    Learning or experience curve
Government policy (regulation, pollution control, etc.)
Expected retaliation
Entry deterring price

1.5 *Substitutes*

Probe on:
Products that perform the same function as industry's
Relative value/price of substitutes
Substitutes produced by high-profit industries
Collective industry response to substitutes
Customers' propensity to substitute

2. Competitive strategy

2.1 *Cost Leadership*

Probe on:
Value chain and assignment of costs and assets
Cost drivers and their interaction
Competitors' value chain
Relative costs of competitors and their sources
Strategies to lower relative costs including:
> Control of cost-drivers
> Reconfiguration of value chain
> Reconfiguration of downstream value

Trade-off between differentiation and cost reduction
Sustainability of cost-reduction strategy

2.2 *Differentiation*

Probe on:
Identification of real customer
Identification of customer's value chain
Customer's purchasing criteria
Existing and potential sources of uniqueness in firm's value chain
Identification of existing and potential sources of differentiation
Value activities that create the most valuable differentiation for
    customers (relative to costs of differentiation)
Sustainability of differentiation strategy
Cost reduction in activities that do not affect differentiation

2.3 *Focus*

Probe on:
Whether strategy is towards cost or differentiation focus or both
Strategically relevant segments including:

Product variety
Customer type
Channel (i.e. immediate buyer)
Customer location
Significance of chosen segment(s) for competitive advance
Interrelations among segments
Sustainability of focus against:
Broadly targeted competitors
Imitators
Segment substitution

3. **Defensive strategy**

3.1 *Increasing barriers to entry*

Probe on:
Filling product gaps
Blocking channel access
Raising customers' switching costs
Raising costs of product trial
Defensively increasing scale economies
Defensively increasing capital requirements
Foreclosing alternative technologies
Tying up suppliers
Raising costs of competitors' inputs
Defensively pursuing interrelationships with other firms
Encouraging government or agency policies that raise barriers
Forming coalitions to raise barriers
Forming coalitions to co-opt challengers

3.2 *Increasing retaliation which challengers can expect*

Probe on:
Signalling commitment to defend
Signalling erection of barriers
Establishing blocking positions
Matching guarantees
Raising own penalty of exit or of loss of market share
Accumulating retaliatory sources
Encouraging 'good' competitors
Setting examples
Establishing defensive coalitions

3.3 *Lowering the Inducement for Attack*

Probe on:
Reducing profit targets
Managing competitors' assumptions

3.4 *Deterrence*

Probe on:
Choosing defensive tactics to block likely attacks
Managing the firm's image as a tough defender
Setting realistic profit expectations
Using industry scenarios to examine deterrence possibilities
Knowledge of specific sources of barriers
Anticipation of likely challengers (especially dissatisfied competitors)
Forecasting likely avenues of attack

3.5 *Responding to attack*

Probe on:
Putting priority on early response
Investing in early discovery of moves by:
    Contact with suppliers
    Contact with advertising media
    Monitoring of attendance at trade shows
    Contact with most adventurous customers in industry
    Monitoring of technical conference, college courses, etc.
Basing response on reasons for attack
Deflecting challengers
Taking challengers seriously
Viewing response as a way to gain position
Disrupting test or introductory markets
Leapfrogging with new product or process
Litigation (e.g. patent, anti-trust suits)

III. REINTERVIEW QUESTIONNAIRE

Part 1

Identity of firms and owner-manager
Whether still trading, and if not what became of firm and owner-manager

Part 2

Characteristics of SBEs interviewed earlier

Retrospective questions on data too sensitive to request in 1985: net profit; profitability

Innovation and competitiveness

Size in 1988 of SBE examined in 1985: turnover; employment; assets

Output changes: scale; returns to scale; output mix; main product-line

Skill shortages: extent of; effect on growth; how filled (e.g. training, paying premium rates)

Financial structure: gearing in 1988; trajectory of gearing 1986, 1987 and 1988

Perception of enterprise culture

Notes

1 THE SMALL BUSINESS ENTERPRISE

1 A certain minimum background in economics is useful, such as one would get from reading, say, the introductory text by Parkin and King (1992, Part 5). More advanced material than this is only pursued in notes, which have been partly specially devised for more specialized or expert readers.

2 This refers to a net increase.

3 Theories of the firm that do this are, respectively, Kihlstrom and Laffont (1979), Lucas (1978) and Oi (1983).

4 Treatment of these more advanced topics of moral hazard and adverse selection are in particularly clear form in Gravelle and Rees (1992, ch. 22). See also Reid (1987b, ch. 9).

5 The formal analysis of hierarchy and control loss is a technical issue. See, for example, Reid (1987, ch. 9) for a compressed account.

6 See, for example, Burgess (1984) for a general introduction to the fieldwork method, and Burgess (1982) for some practical guidance on methods.

7 The Ardrossan, Saltcoats and Stevenston Enterprise Trust (ASSET), launched in 1982.

8 By instrumentation we mean the technical devising of methods for gathering data, e.g. the designing of a questionnaire or a semi-structured interview agenda. The questionnaire or agenda are also known as 'instruments'. Key influences here are Nowotny and Walther (1978) and Wied-Nebbeling (1975).

9 Notably the trilogy, Porter (1980, 1985, 1990).

10 See the companion volume Reid (1993, ch. 11) for models and estimates.

11 See ibid., ch. 9.

12 A full account of the database and methods employed is in Reid (1993, ch. 2).

13 This puts the typical SBE of this book into the category of what has recently been described as a 'micro-firm'. This is the firm that employs less than ten people, and such firms account for roughly 90 per cent of all businesses in the United Kingdom. See the recent report by the Small Business Research Centre (1992).

14 'Form of firm' is a categorical variable, which was coded as follows: sole proprietorship = 1; partnership = 2; private company = 3.

15 See, for example, Hay and Morris (1991, ch. 8) for a fuller account of this index of industrial concentration, and several others.

16 Reid (1977) develops this method in formal terms, and derives a number of comparative statics results. Donsimoni (1985) takes the analysis further by showing that the most efficient firms will end up in the dominant group or cartel. This outcome is stable.

17 See Hay and Morris (1991, ch. 4) for a modern textbook account of this model, taking account of recent developments in the analysis of differentiated product

markets. The article by Corchón (1991) particularly studies welfare and efficiency properties of this model in a mathematical fashion. It is shown rigorously that if the typical customer derives utility from variety, then the optimum position of the monopolistic competitor is at a point at which unit costs are still falling.

18 See Hay and Morris (1991, ch. 3) for a comprehensive discussion of oligopoly models. Of specific relevance to this book is the model developed by Bhaskar (1988). A crucial extension of that model is discussed in Reid (1993, ch. 10).

19 For an elementary introduction to address models, see Eaton and Eaton (1988, ch. 13). A more advanced treatment is available in the survey article by Archibald, Eaton and Lipsey (1986).

20 In this section and the subsequent section (1.7) we draw freely on the writings of Porter (1980, 1985, 1990). Other examples of this approach in the current context are provided by Jacobsen, Reid and Anderson (1992, 1993). Our earliest attempt to use this framework in a small firms context, and so far as we know the first place in which it was so deployed, was in Reid and Jacobsen (1988).

21 See Porter (1980: 4).

2 LOW MARKET CONCENTRATION

1 See Krouse (1990, chs 4, 5) for an extensive modern discussion of this class of market model.

2 For a clear statement of the 'within-site' and 'cross-site' (or comparative) methods, as applied to fieldwork data, see Miles and Huberman (1984).

3 Now transformed into Scottish Enterprise, combining training and enterprise functions, and devolving much activity to the regions in the shape of local enterprise companies. This process of devaluation had started under the Scottish Develoment Agency and was well developed at the time of our study.

4 See De Meza and Webb (1988) for further analytical details.

5 In the analysis of Leland and Pyle (1977), the value of the SBE is increasing in the equity stake of the entrepreneur.

6 See Krouse (1990, ch. 10) on a variety of entry-deterring strategies, including those that set price (temporarily) artificially low. In the case of Firm C, the price set was intended to be 'non-revealing' of this SBE's cost structure. Particular attention was paid to keeping the wages to out-workers, a principal 'cost-driver', a secret from rivals.

7 This is an effect which is typically associated with large, corporate enterprises. It was most notably analysed by Penrose (1959), using rather informal methods. Slater (1980) provides a more rigorous treatment, like Penrose suggesting a growth–profitability trade-off caused by managerial diseconomies. There is some confirmation for this hypothesis in the companion volume, Reid (1993, ch. 11).

8 This elbow-room in pricing can be attributed to switching costs or, more generally, to transactions costs. See Reid (1981, ch. 4) for a theoretical analysis of this phenomenon.

9 Strategic overinvestment can be used as an entry deterring strategy. Under certain circumstances this overinvestment can lead to a limit-pricing outcome, in which the pre-entry price is less than the monopoly price consonant with unanticipated entry. See Krouse (1990, ch. 10).

10 Firm D is particularly well suited to price discrimination practices, because (a) it can identify customers with markedly different price elasticities of demand, with elasticity usually being lower, the wealthier the purchaser, and (b) it can effectively rule out resale of its services, as each vehicle is damaged in a different way, and therefore every repair has a bespoke character. See the discussion by Varian

(1989) in Schmalensee and Willig (1989, ch. 10). It is to be noticed that a fundamental prediction of price and discrimination theory is confirmed. The wealthy customer (the Volvo dealer) has the less elastic demand and happily pays the higher price; the poorer customer (small dealer on low profit margins) has the more elastic demand and grudgingly pays the lower price – indeed he is almost 'not worth the trouble' to the discriminatory monopolist. The analogy is not complete, because Firm D is only a brand monopolist, but the model has clear leverage on reality.

11 Setting up several independent businesses is an alternative to diversifying product range and enjoying the risk-spreading, return-preserving benefits identified by Ungern-Sternberg (1990). It has the same effect, and possibly some legal advantages when downside outcomes take the entrepreneur into bankruptcy.

12 In this case we have an SBE which is already thinking of how to maintain focus before letting product proliferation run it into problems of 'span of control' (i.e. diseconomies of scope).

13 See Reid (1981) for a full discussion of theory and evidence on this point. Further analysis of this point is made in Chapter 8 below and in the companion volume Reid (1993, ch. 10).

14 This type of cut-throat or predatory behaviour can be understood by an analysis of the firm's ability to sustain a price set 'at cost' (and presumably at an overall loss) for a sufficient length of time to put off 'extended rivals'. It is usual to invoke a 'long purse' type of argument to explain the outcome. That is, the firm with the best asset position (the 'longest purse') would be the one to benefit from this strategy. Here, Firm L probably does not have the longest purse and will suffer from the action inflicted on the market. However, it is clearly in much better shape to absorb this treatment than many rivals (e.g. it is well established, with low overheads and reliable delivery). It may be that less efficient rivals will be shaken out of the market early, leaving both Firm L and the brewing company imitating the action with more market territory in the long run. The long-purse argument does not require that predation should fully work itself through to ruin for the prey. The prey (say, less-efficient SBEs than Firm L, e.g. younger, less well-established firms) would leave the market early if they knew they were bound to lose anyway. Thus Firm L's intuition that it could ride out the predation phase may have been well-founded. The original long-purse argument was due to Telser (1966), and was an early use of the 'perfect equilibrium' concept. It has since been extensively analysed in the literature. See Krouse (1990, ch. 12) for a modern treatment, and also Tirole (1988, ch. 9).

15 Whilst it is the economist's typical pattern, for the parent sample, the following unit cost case, right up to capacity, was the most frequently observed form of short-run cost curve. See the treatment in the companion volume, Reid (1993, ch. 4).

16 That is, again, the kinked demand curve case.

17 This appears inconsistent with the kinked demand curve case, but probably arises from the considerable inelastic portion of the demand curve (the 'elbow room') before the asymmetric outcomes of the kink come into play.

18 That is, for a 10 per cent increase in price, there would be a roughly 10 per cent decrease in demand.

3 MEDIUM MARKET CONCENTRATION

1 This is a popular model in industrial organization, and has been extensively analysed by one of the authors, Reid (1977, 1980). The model has a long history, as noted in Reid (1977) and is variously known as the partial monopoly model,

the dominant-firm price leadership model, and the k-firm cartel with competitive fringe model. The most important contemporary theoretical paper was Saving (1970), and the paper by Landes and Posner (1981) has been influential in the regulatory literature of industrial organization. Krouse (1990, ch. 12) provides a good modern survey. The key result is that the degree of monopoly power of the dominant group depends upon the industry elasticity of demand, the degree of market concentration, and the elasticity of supply of fringe competitors.

2　That is, a multi-price or price discrimination policy was adopted.

3　For example, under new food labelling requirements, packaging had to include detailed descriptions of the products.

4　This is not always so. A preoccupation of enterprise policy has been the lowering of compliance costs. See the case studies by Ian Orton in Peacock (1984, chs 3, 5, 6).

5　That is, the extra cost of supplying each additional unit fell as more was supplied. This was the most common pattern of costs for the parent sample.

6　For example, it had helped them to identify the increasing popularity of whole-meal bread.

7　This SBE provides an example of one of the categories of the analysis of entre-preneurship by Holmes and Schmitz (1990). Selling-on a going concern is a rational strategy.

8　A kind of inter-temporal price discrimination, involving charging high prices to the early keen customers with high reservation prices, and then reducing price progressively to 'skim off' customers with lower reservation prices.

9　The 'time to market' is the period which elapses between getting a good idea, and effectively selling that idea in the shape of a new product.

10　That is, the person who had the power and resources to conclude a contract for sale.

11　Learning effects are associated with the level of cumulative output. The effect was first associated with airframe production, as in the classical study by Alchian (1963), but was shown by Rapping (1965) and others to occur in many pro-duction settings. Arrow (1962) was the first to formally model what he called 'learning by doing' and it has since been embodied in oligopoly models. Firm I seems to be aware of the danger of pre-emption of a market opportunity if too much is invested in pre-entry learning. Getting into the market early and then depending on the beneficial effects of learning by doing to offset the lack of pre-entry learning can be a rational strategy if first-mover advantages are appreci-able. The work of Glazer (1985) suggests that in successful markets first-mover advantages are tangible, but across all markets they are not. For less successful markets, early entrants suffer, and later entrants learn from their mistakes. Formal analyses of learning and performance are in Spence (1981) and Fudenberg and Tirole (1983).

12　For the parent sample, a select group of 'super-growth' firms (< 10 per cent of sample) was identified, of which Firm I is one.

13　Here, the reader should refer to the earlier remarks made on predatory pricing in note 14 of Chapter 2.

14　These give access to customer contacts.

4　HIGH MARKET CONCENTRATION

1　The relevant algebra for oligopolistic competition when products are differenti-ated and conjectures are non-trivial is given in the article by Cubbin (1983). An advanced textbook treatment is contained in Krouse (1990, ch. 3).

2　The way of doing so was first discussed in an advanced paper by Iwata (1974).

More recent attempts include Appelbaum (1982) and Slade (1986).

3 These data have been used to good effect to show that for SBEs in the parent sample, price conjectures can be linked in an important way to market outcomes. The relevant theory and econometric estimates are reported upon in the companion volume (Reid 1993, ch. 10).

4 Between 1985 and 1986, a roughly 37 per cent increase in output of the main product line had been associated with a less than proportionate (roughly 25 per cent) increase in average variable cost. This seems to indicate dynamic decreasing returns to scale, which is somewhat implausible. It is likely that this effect is partly of a pecuniary character (e.g. arising from increasing factor prices) and partly due to changes in the technology (e.g. quality-enhancing changes with consequences for the quality of output which are not captured by treating the output of 1985 as physically identical to that of 1988).

5 The ratio of gross profits less taxes to the book value of assets.

6 It is difficult to see how this squares with disposal of very expensive and highly specialized machinery in a thinly traded market. We have assumed this is a misperception, though it may be that what was being said was that entry barriers were higher than exit barriers.

7 The respondent frequently described the kind of aircraft he intended to build as 'acrobatic' rather than 'aerobatic'. We have sometimes adopted this usage.

8 That is, just three aircraft were the break-even requirement on volume production.

5 COMPETITIVE FORCES

1 Survival in itself, over a three-year period, is explored in detail in the companion volume by Reid (1993, ch. 9). It is found that, for the parent population, the best two predictors of survival for an SBE are the product range and the gearing ratio. Other things being equal, a 10 per cent increase in the product-groups would raise the probability of survival by 3.4 per cent; and a 10 per cent reduction in the gearing ratio would raise the probability of survival by 1.9 per cent.

2 Data on all of these characteristics were obtained by interviews in the field with the owner-manager, the first four characteristics being directly reported by respondents to an administered questionnaire in 1985. The fifth characteristic (entry/exit barriers) has been evaluated by us from evidence gathered using a semi-structured interview with owner-managers later in 1985. These remarks are also true for Tables 5.2 and 5.3.

3 As Porter would point out, however, there are still rational strategic alternatives in declining markets. Owner-managers must develop an 'end-game' strategy. This will certainly involve obvious options like divestment or harvesting, but also, he would argue, leadership and niche strategies. In the leadership case, the aim is to be profitable in an above-average fashion by being the best and/or last survivor. Maintaining profitability in the face of decline might require aggressive tactics to ensure more rapid retiral of other SBEs from the market or a variety of other strategies like reducing rivals' exit barriers, or raising market stakes (e.g. with new products). In the niche strategy, the aim is to identify a segment of the declining market that offers high returns, whilst other market segments decline rapidly. The alert SBE will divest from the declining segments, and pre-emptively invade the stable segment. Firms A, D and E had adopted the strategy of raising the stakes by innovation.

4 Including the manufacturing Firms C (knitwear manufacturing) and Q (theatrical props).

5 Williamson would see asset specificity as all-pervasive, and would distinguish between site, physical, human asset, dedicated-asset and brand-name-capital specificity. In terms of this extended definition, only human-asset specificity, which arises from learning by doing, is relevant to the case discussed in the text. See Williamson (1989) in Schmalensee and Willig (1989, ch. 3).

6 In its classical form, limit pricing refers to the price an incumbent firm can set to blockade or impede a potential entrant from entering a market and trying to operate in the industry despite scale disadvantages as compared to the incumbent. Technically, the limit price is that price on the demand curve which is associated with the least output that promises the entrant no profitable production plan. This limit price may blockade, effectively impede or ineffectively impede entry. If entry is not blockaded, the incumbent needs to weigh up the costs and benefits of entry prevention. It may be rational to permit some level of entry, and empirical evidence on dynamic limit pricing by once dominant large firms in the United States by Masson and Shaanan (1982) suggests this strategy is used in practice. In the other cases of our SBEs, it is as likely that they themselves will be the targets for limit pricing as that they use the strategy against others, especially in medium-concentration markets when SBEs are in the competitive fringe. A modern treatment of limit pricing is contained in Gilbert (1989). Here it is shown that not only are structural barriers to entry important (e.g. scale economies) but also the ability of the incumbent to affect the potential entrant's conjectures about the consequences of entry.

7 Commitment in this sense is important and all-pervasive in the low market concentration cases. The recent analysis of commitment by Ghemawat (1992) has been of influence in writing this chapter.

8 This is not to deny the validity of the static-stability analysis of Donsimoni (1985). We are suggesting it may break down if dynamic strategic goals of invasion and encroachment emerge.

9 Indeed, a few respondents were at a loss even to identify them, and resorted to trying to discuss alternative products *within* their industries.

10 However, as high audio quality was always 'bundled' with high physical quality of the cassettes (e.g. durability), the consumers' preferences may not have been so irrational, given an obvious preference for high physical quality.

11 Just-in-time delivery is associated particularly with inter-firm relations in Japanese manufacturing. As producers in the United Kingdom have become more aware of inventory costs, especially so far as holding stocks of bulky materials are concerned, they have started to imitate Japanese methods.

12 See Dnes (1992) for a modern discussion of franchisor–franchisee relations.

13 An alternative, more compressed analysis, is contained in Jacobsen, Reid and Anderson (1993), where competitive forces are immediately linked with competitive strategy. Here, we defer the latter topic to Chapter 6.

14 This remark is particularly applicable to the low- and medium-concentration markets.

6 COMPETITIVE AND DEFENSIVE STRATEGIES

1 The original rationale for using this grouping was that an earlier paper (Jacobsen, Reid and Anderson 1992) found that the performance link, in terms of above-average performance, with structural characteristics like market concentration, was weak and therefore only a starting-point for a full explanation. Thus more complex structural characteristics plus, more importantly, non-structural characteristics like the strategies deployed by SBEs, are superimposed upon these standard market concentration groupings. A further benefit of grouping by

market concentration is that, in this case at least, each group can be associated with a unique market structure, as explained in the text.

2 Indeed, the reader may wish to use a blank version of Table 6.1 as a kind of score card for evaluating influences on competitive advantage. For those with the benefit of the companion volume, a suitable starting-point for practice of this art might be the seven cases considered by Reid (1993, Part III).

3 Individual Profiles in Part II of this volume give these figures. A summary of the growth figures, in terms of sales, assets and employees, is given in Table 7.6 below. Age, asset and profitability figures are also given in the Appendix to this chapter in Table 6.4 below. Of course, performance is much more multi-dimensional than these few statistics would reveal, and a consultation of the whole Profile analysis for each SBE is necessary for a complete evaluation. Limitations of a narrower view of performance evaluation are explored in the Appendix to this chapter.

4 Though some might deny this. For example, the owner-manager of Firm A (blind cleaning) claimed in an interview that his interest was in a low-cost focus strategy (see section 2.2 above). However, he clearly thought his service was significantly differentiated from his rivals, and had been the only one in his market segment to invest in modern ultrasound equipment. He was particularly successful at customer relations ('Give me that job, and I will take it off your hands'), and in every way seemed to be following a differentiation focus. Further, it seems that a cost focus would have been beyond his reach, given his small scale of operation. One concludes therefore that what he meant was that he always kept costs at a minimum, which is of course not the same as adopting a low-cost focus, and indeed is not inconsistent with a differentiation focus. We return to this point at the end of this sub-section.

5 Owner managers made frequent references to unethical competition, and their views on 'acceptable standards of trading' governed their conduct, in some measure. For example, it set severe limits on what might be contemplated in terms of defensive strategy. These issues, as they apply to the full parent sample, are treated with some detail in the companion volume (Reid 1993, ch. 12).

6 Here, existing rivals already prove a powerful competitive force.

7 Characteristics space (i.e. the space of differentiated goods' characteristics) is defined by analogy with physical space, in modern industrial economies. The conditions under which spatial models can be linked to product differentiation models are explored in Krouse (1990: 156–7).

8 It will be recalled from the Profile in Chapter 3 that Firm F was ultimately sold to an existing rival. Being 'stuck in the middle' creates a vulnerability to take-over. Note that we are not saying that Firm F was badly run; indeed, the Profile indicates to the contrary. Rather, we are saying that at that point in this SBE's business history, the strategy adopted was not the best available. We should also note that a trade sale can be a legitimate goal of entrepreneurship.

9 Of course, whether this delicately balanced strategy can continue to be sustained is open to question. The low profitability self-reported by the owner-manager (2 per cent in Table 6.4) is, if accurate, a possible indicator of future problems.

7 FINANCIAL CONSIDERATIONS OF COMPETITIVE ADVANTAGE

1 This is a general need of small firms, which transcends cultures. For an analysis inspired by the Chinese context, but relevant to many others, see Zhiyou (1990).

2 A diagram of such a network is provided in Reid and Jacobsen (1988: 71).

3 'Channels' are the actual individuals within organizations who can provide the desired information.

4 For firms of this size, it seems that the involvement of outside equity, in the most obvious form of venture-capital backing, is almost unknown. None of the firms in the main sample had venture-capital involvement. For a complementary sample of-similarly sized firms from the same universe of firms, but of generally greater age (fifteen and a half years), and at a later date, Reid and Anderson (1992) have also found no venture-capital involvement. Indeed, awareness of the venture-capital market, and knowledge of its functioning were both slight. The same was also true of private investors (so-called 'business angels').

5 In the complementary sample of Reid and Anderson (1992), of those two-thirds of owner-managers who avoided lack of finance by using external finance (purely, or mixed with internal), there was an almost exclusive preference for loan finance ($^{40}/_{43}$ = 93 per cent; with 95 per cent confidence interval 83–99 per cent). This was typically of the overdraft, business loan, etc., form.

6 In the complementary sample of Reid and Anderson (1992) the typical route taken to avoid lack of funding, nominated by over half of the SBEs ($^{37}/_{64}$ = 58 per cent $\pm$ 12 per cent) was by a mix of internal and external finance. The preference was for the former, as indicated by the proportion that used exclusively their own (internal finance), such as savings and ploughed-back profit, it being about one-third of those who consciously avoided lack of funding ($^{12}/_{64}$ = 33 per cent; with 95 per cent confidence interval 20–47 per cent). In terms of qualitative evidence, the preference for using internal finance was very often motivated by its perceived lower cost in relation to the alternative of a bank loan, or fear of loss of control if the alternative was outside equity participation.

7 In *The Wealth of Nations* Adam Smith noted; 'The chance of gain is by every man more or less over-valued, and the chance of loss is by most men under-valued' (Smith 1776: 125).

8 The enterprise trust is the most local form of business advisory unit under the current framework of Scottish Enterprise, considered as an enterprise-stimulating institution. There are currently over forty of them in Scotland. Reid and Jacobsen (1988, ch. 5) provide a detailed analysis. A preference for enterprise trusts might be expected for our sample, given that our sampling frame was partly based on their client lists. It is possible, of course, that whilst consulted, they may not have been perceived as important.

9 For example, according to Leland and Pyle (1977), a higher entrepreneurial share should signal a higher value for the SBE.

10 This might be true for the Profiles sample but for the larger parent sample, the most frequently nominated use of debt finance (37 per cent) was purchase of plant and equipment, which seems a rational and appropriate pattern of use.

11 Here again, questions about financial management are raised, because Firms C and G also partly used borrowings to cope with cash-flow problems.

References

Alchian, A.A. (1963) 'Reliability of progress curves in aircraft production', *Econometrica* 31, 679–93.

Appelbaum, E. (1982) 'The estimation of the degree of oligopoly power', *Journal of Econometrics* 19: 287–99.

Archibald, C., B.C. Eaton and R.G. Lipsey (1986) 'Address models of value theory', in J.E. Stiglitz and G.F. Mathewson (eds) *New Developments in the Analysis of Market Structure*, London: Macmillan.

Arrow, K.J. (1962) 'The economic implications of learning by doing', *Review of Economic Studies* 29: 155–73.

Bhaskar, V. (1988) 'The kinked demand curve: a game theoretic approach', *International Journal of Industrial Organization* 6: 373–84.

——, S. Machin and G. Reid (1991) 'Testing a model of the kinked demand curve', *Journal of Industrial Economics* 6: 373–84.

Birch, D. (1979) 'The job generation process', working paper, MIT program on Neighbourhood and Regional Change, Cambridge, Mass.

—— (1981) 'Who creates jobs?' *The Public Interest* 65 (Fall): 3–14.

Brigham, E.F. (1992) *Fundamentals of Financial Management*, 6th edn, Fort Worth, Texas: Dryden Press.

Burgess, R.G. (ed.) (1982) *Field Research: A Source Book and Field Manual*, London: George Allen & Unwin.

—— (1984) *In the Field: An Introduction to Field Research*, London: George Allen & Unwin.

Coase, R.H. (1992) 'The institutional structures of production', *American Economic Review* 82: 713–19.

Corchón, L.C. (1991) 'Monopolistic competition: equilibrium and optimality', *International Journal of Industrial Organization* 9: 441–52.

Cubbin, J. (1983) 'Apparent collusion and conjectural variations in differentiated oligopoly', *International Journal of Industrial Organization* 1: 155–63.

Daly, M. and A. McCann (1992) 'How many small firms', *Employment Gazette* 100 (2): 47–51.

De Meza, D. and D.C. Webb (1988) 'Credit market efficiency and tax policy in the presence of screening costs', *Journal of Public Economics* 36: 1–22.

Dnes, A.W. (1992) *Franchising: A Case-Study Approach*, Aldershot: Avebury.

Donsimoni, M-P. (1985) 'Stable heterogeneous cartels', *International Journal of Industrial Organization* 3: 451–68.

Eaton, B.C. and D.F. Eaton (1988) *Microeconomics*, New York: Freeman.

Flaherty, M.T. (1984) 'Field research on the link between technological innovation and growth: evidence from the international semiconductor industry', *American Economic Review (Papers and Proceedings)* 74: 67–72.

Fudenberg, D. and J. Tirole (1983) 'Learning by doing and market performance', *Bell Journal of Economics* 14: 522–30.

Ghemawat, P. (1992) *Commitment*, Cambridge, Mass.: MIT Press.

Gilbert, R.J. (1989) 'Mobility barriers', in R. Schmalensee and R.D. Willig (eds) *Handbook of Industrial Organization*, Amsterdam, North Holland, vol. I, ch. 8, pp. 475–535.

Glaser, B.G. and A.L. Strauss (1967) *The Discovery of Grounded Theory: Strategies for Qualitative Research*, New York: Aldine.

Glazer, A. (1985) 'The advantages of being first', *American Economic Review* 75: 473–80.

Gravelle H. and R. Rees (1992) *Microeconomics*, 2nd edn., Harlow, Essex: Longman.

Hay, D.A. and D.J. Morris (1991) *Industrial Economics and Organization*, 2nd edn., Oxford: Oxford University Press.

Holmes, T.J. and J.A. Schmitz (1990) 'A theory of entrepreneurship and its application to the study of business transfers', *Journal of Political Economy* 98: 265–94.

Iwata, G. (1974) 'Measurement of conjectural variations in oligopoly', *Econometrica* 42: 947–66.

Jacobsen, L.R., G.C. Reid and M.E. Anderson (1992) 'Industrial concentration and competitive advantage in the new firm', *Atlantic Economic Society (Best Papers Proceedings)* 2: 143–7.

—— (1993) 'Extended rivalry and competitive advantage in the new small firm', in A. van Witteloostuijn (ed.) *Studies in Industrial Organization*, Amsterdam: Kluwer.

Kihlstrom, R.E. and J.J. Laffont (1979) 'A general equilibrium entrepreneurial theory of firm formation based on risk aversion', *Journal of Political Economy* 87: 719–48.

Kirk, J. and M.L. Miller (1985) *Reliability and Validity in Qualitative Research*, London: Sage.

Krouse, C.G. (1990) *Theory of Industrial Economics*, Oxford: Basil Blackwell.

Landes, W. and R. Posner (1981) 'Market power in antitrust cases', *Harvard Law Review* 94: 937–96.

Leland, H. and D. Pyle (1977) 'Information asymmetries, financial structure and financial intermediation', *Journal of Finance* 32: 371–88.

Lucas, R.E. (1978) 'On the size distribution of business firms', *Bell Journal of Economics* 9: 508–23.

Maskin, E. and J. Tirole (1988) 'A theory of dynamic oligopoly: price competition, kinked demand curves and Edgeworth cycles', *Econometrica* 56: 571–99.

Masson, R.T. and J. Shaanan (1982) 'Stochastic-dynamic limiting pricing: and empirical test', *Review of Economics and Statistics* 64: 413–22.

Miles, M.B. and A.M. Huberman (1984) *Qualitative Data Analysis*, London: Sage.

Nowotny, E. and H. Walther (1978) 'Die Wettbewerbintensitat in Osterreich: Ergebnisse der Befragungen und Interviews', in E. Nowotny, A. Guger, H. Suppanz, and H. Walther *Studien zur Wettbewerbintensitat in der Osterreichischen Wirtschaft*, Vienna: Orac Verlag, pp. 87–263.

Oi, W.Y. (1983) 'Heterogeneous firms and the organization of production', *Economic Inquiry* 21: 147–71.

Parkin, M. and D. King (1992) *Economics*, London: Addison-Wesley.

Peacock, A.T. (ed.) (1984) *The Regulation Game: How British and West German Companies Bargain with Government*, Oxford: Blackwell.

Penrose, E.T. (1959) *The Theory of the Growth of the Firm*, Oxford: Blackwell.

Porter, M. (1980) *Competitive Strategy*, New York: Free Press.

—— (1985) *Competitive Advantage*, New York: Free Press.

—— (1990) *The Competitive Advantage of Nations*, New York: Free Press.

Pratten, C. (1991) *The Competitiveness of Small Firms*, Cambridge: Cambridge University Press.

Rapping, L. (1965) 'Learning and World War II production functions', *Review of Economics and Statistics* 47: 81–6.

Reekie, W.D., D.E. Allen and J.N. Crook (1991) *The Economics of Modern Business*, 2nd edn., Oxford: Blackwell.

Reid, G.C. (1977) 'Comparative statics of the partial monopoly model', *Scottish Journal of Political Economy* 24: 153–62.

―― (1980) 'The dominant firm with convex technology', *Managerial and Decision Economics* 1: 112–16.

―― (1981) *The Kinked Demand Curve Analysis of Oligopoly: Theory and Evidence*, Edinburgh: Edinburgh University Press.

―― (1987a) 'Applying field research techniques to the business enterprise', *International Journal of Social Economics* 14: 3–25.

―― (1987b) *Theories of Industrial Organization*, Oxford: Blackwell.

―― (1993) *Small Business Enterprise*, London: Routledge.

Reid, G.C. and M.E. Anderson (1992) 'A new small firms database: sample design, instrumentation, and summary statistics', Discussion Paper (No. 9207), Centre for Research into Industry, Enterprise, Finance and the Firm (CRIEFF), Department of Economics, University of St Andrews.

Reid, G.C. and L.R. Jacobsen (1988) *The Small Entrepreneurial Firm*, Aberdeen: Aberdeen University Press.

Samson, K.J. (1990) *Scientists as Entrepreneurs: Organizational Performance in Scientist-started New Ventures*, Dordrecht: Kluwer.

Saving, T. (1970) 'Concentration ratios and the degree of monopoly', *International Economic Review* 11: 855–67.

Schmalensee, R. (1989) 'Inter-industry studies of structure and performance', in R. Schmalensee and R.D. Willig (eds) *Handbook of Industrial Organization*, Amsterdam: North Holland, vol. 2, pp. 951–1009.

Schmalensee, R. and R.D. Willig (eds) *Handbook of Industrial Organization*, Amsterdam: North Holland.

Shapero, A. (1984) 'The entrepreneurial event', in C.A. Kent (ed.) *The Environment for Entrepreneurship*, Lexington, Mass.: D.C. Heath.

Slade, M.E. (1986) 'Conjectures, firm characteristics, and market structure', *International Journal of Industrial Organization* 4: 347–69.

Slater, M. (1980) 'The managerial limitation to the growth of firms', *Economic Journal* 90: 520–8.

Small Business Research Centre (1992) *The State of British Enterprise: Growth, Innovation and Competitive Advantage in Small- and Medium-sized Firms*, Cambridge: SBRC, University of Cambridge.

Smith, A. (1776) *The Wealth of Nations*, Glasgow edn, edited by R.H. Campbell and A. Skinner, Oxford: Oxford University Press, 1976.

Spence, A.M. (1981) 'The learning curve and competition', *Bell Journal of Economics* 12: 49–70.

Stiglitz, J. and F. Mathewson (eds) (1986) *New Developments in the Analysis of Market Structure*, London: Macmillan.

Sweezy, P. (1937) 'Demand under conditions of oligopoly', *Journal of Political Economy* 47, 568–73.

Telser, L. (1966) 'Cut-throat competition and the long purse', *Journal of Law and Economics* 9: 457–66.

Tirole, J. (1988) *The Theory of Industrial Organization*, Cambridge, Mass.: MIT Press.

Ungern-Sternberg, T. von (1990) 'The flexibility to switch between different products', *Economica* 57: 355–69.

Varian, H.R. (1989) 'Price discrimination', in R. Schmalensee and R.D. Willig (eds)

Handbook of Industrial Organization, Amsterdam: North Holland, vol. 1, pp. 597–654.

Wied-Nebbeling, S. (1975) *Industrielle Preissetzung*, Tübingen: Mohr.

Williamson, O.E. (1989) 'Transaction cost economics', in R.Schmalensee and R.D. Willig (eds) *Handbook of Industrial Organization*, Amsterdam: North Holland, vol. 1, pp. 135–82.

Zhiyou, Z. (1990) 'Information needs of small and medium enterprises', in K. Ganzhorn and S. Faustofferi (eds) *Bridging the Information Gap – For Small and Medium Enterprises*, Berlin: Springer-Verlag, pp. 23–34.

Index